Origins of a Story

Center Point
Large Print

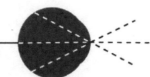

**This Large Print Book carries the
Seal of Approval of N.A.V.H.**

Origins of a Story

202 True Inspirations Behind the World's Greatest Literature

JAKE GROGAN

CENTER POINT LARGE PRINT
THORNDIKE, MAINE

This Center Point Large Print edition
is published in the year 2018 by arrangement with
Cider Mill Press c/o Simon and Schuster.

The text of this Large Print edition is unabridged.
In other aspects, this book may vary
from the original edition.
Printed in the United States of America
on permanent paper.
Set in 16-point Times New Roman type.

ISBN: 978-1-68324-810-1

Library of Congress Cataloging-in-Publication Data

Names: Grogan, Jake author.
Title: Origins of a story : 202 true inspirations behind
   the world's greatest literature/ Jake Grogan.
Description: Large print edition. | Thorndike, Maine :
   Center Point Large Print, 2018.
Identifiers: LCCN 2018009044 I ISBN 9781683248101
   (hardcover : alk. paper)
Subjects: LCSH: Fiction—Authorship. | Creation (Literary, artistic, etc.) |
   Large type books.
Classification: LCC PN145 .G76 2018 I DOC 809.3—dc23
LC record available at https://lccn.loc.gov/2018009044

To my mom and dad

CONTENTS

INTRODUCTION

Directly before leaving home for Fordham University, I was offered advice that never left me. It went something like, "Make a list of the people who inspire you, then go learn everything you can about who inspired them." Unoriginal, I suppose, but it's influenced the way I think about and consume books ever since. Whenever I read, I find my mind wandering back to the story's beginnings—even long after I put the book down. What kernel of thought inspired Harper Lee to write *To Kill a Mockingbird*? What about Tolkien and *The Fellowship of the Ring*? Long before I thought to write this book, I would research these little questions as a way to enhance my reading experience. After a friend suggested I try to compile them all in one place, I set to work with a more organized structure.

I began by breaking the concept of origin into two key questions: how and why. *How* did the author come up with something? *Why* did the author write about it? Amazingly, my findings were largely similar—the *how* usually centered on an author's experience, both in life and as a reader (as much as the two can be separate things), while the *why* almost always grew directly out of the how. Was it a perfect science? Of course not—the important context differed from book to book. No matter, though; nobody said that a fun read couldn't be disproportioned.

The roots of these famous works run deep and in many directions. That the concept of Mary Shelley's *Frankenstein* came from a dream is incredible; that the dream came as the result of one of the deadliest volcanic eruptions in civilized history is unbelievable. And I had no idea that *Green Eggs and Ham* was the result of a bet that challenged Dr. Seuss to write a book containing fifty words or less. Or that *Portnoy's Complaint* was originally written as a satirical monologue meant to accompany a slideshow during the production of *Oh! Calcutta!* Hell, Margaret Mitchell wrote *Gone with the Wind* because her husband got sick of carrying books to and from the library for his ailing wife! These aren't bits of context—these are stories.

Any work of art, whether it be literature, art or anything in between, is an aggregation of influences and inspirations. If context within a story is crucial, then just as crucial is the context beyond the page. To consider both is to see a clearer, fuller picture of the books you love. That is, after all, the point of this book.

Perhaps these tales of inspiration will inspire

you to tap into your inner artist and create something magical. Perhaps they will change how you consume art, as you consider what went into every pen stroke and key strike. Perhaps you'll learn something new about your favorite work of literature. Whatever their effect, never forget that behind every story is a story worth reading about.

MATILDA

Roald Dahl

1988

Roald Dahl would sit in his garden hut writing far into the night, his mother's old armchair the seat from which his genius flowed. His necessities were few: six pencils, an electric sharpener and an old sleeping bag that he could put his legs into to stay warm. "I remember waking up at night and going to the bathroom and seeing the glow of the light in the little hut while it was still dark outside," said Lucy Dahl, his daughter, in an interview with NPR. "I don't know what time it was but that was during the days when he was adapting screenplays and the deadlines would kill him. He didn't like working on deadlines. But he did it because he had to."

He may not have loved having to write for money, but it was that dedication and work ethic that allowed him to produce such works as *James and the Giant Peach* and *Charlie and the Chocolate Factory*. "Most of them were pretty bad," Roald Dahl said in a 1972 BBC4 interview about telling stories to his daughters, "but now and again you'd tell one and see a little spark of interest. And if they said the next night, 'Tell us some more about that one,' you knew you had something."

Of course, Dahl no longer had young daughters to help him gauge whether a story was worth pursuing when he wrote *Matilda* in the mid- to late 1980s. Lucy believes that his inspiration for his last long children's novel was born more out of fear than anything else, saying, "*Matilda* was one of the most difficult books for him to write. I think that there was a deep genuine fear within his heart that books were going to go away and he wanted to write about it."

Dahl approached the task of writing children's books as anything but; he would slave over his writing until he had produced a final product, which was often essentially rewritten in his editing phase. In a December 1986 letter to Lucy, Dahl wrote, "The reason I haven't written you for a long time is that I have been giving every moment to getting a new children's book finished. And now at last I have finished it, and I know jolly well that I am going to have to spend the next three months rewriting the second half. The first half is great, about a small girl who can move things with her eyes and about a terrible headmistress who lifts small children up by their hair and hangs them out of upstairs windows by one ear. But I've got now to think of a really decent second half. The present one will have to be scrapped. Three months' work gone out the window, but that's the way it is. I must have rewritten *Charlie* [*and the Chocolate Factory*] five or six times all through and no one knows."

Rewriting the second half of *Matilda*, while certainly ambitious, was a night in the hut compared to the overhaul he conducted after realizing that Matilda Wormwood should not be a wicked child. In an audio excerpt from 1988, Dahl says, "I got it wrong. I spent six, or eight, or nine months writing it, and when I'd finished, it wasn't right. It just wasn't right. And I hadn't backed up and I hadn't kept changing, because your character, the main character, the little girl, keeps changing all the time. I hadn't bothered to go back and rewrite that several chapters. So I started, a year ago, I started the whole book again and rewrote every word. I knew where I was wrong and I was able to get the character right."

CHARLOTTE'S WEB

E.B. White

———

1952

When asked by his editor to share the reasons behind writing *Charlotte's Web*, E.B. White wrote a letter to the publisher's marketing department that started, "I have been asked to tell how I came to write *Charlotte's Web*. Well, I like animals, and it would be odd if I failed to write about them. Animals are a weakness with me, and when I got a place in the country I was quite sure animals would appear, and they did." But White's love for animals didn't necessarily inspire his writing the book; rather, it led to his forming relationships with two animals that inspired the book's main characters.

As the owner of a functioning livestock farm in Maine, White had grown accustomed to slaughtering the animals he took care of. "A farm is a peculiar problem for a man who likes animals, because the fate of most livestock is that they are murdered by their benefactor," he wrote. While usually the case, there was one instance in which a pig fell ill and, rather than kill it, White decided to nurse it back to health. The pig succumbed to its illnesses despite White's efforts, an event he wrote about for *The Atlantic* in his "Death of a Pig," saying, "He had evidently become precious to me, not that he represented a distant nourishment in a hungry time, but that he had suffered in a suffering world." In his letter, White wrote, "Day by day I became better acquainted with my pig, and he with me, and the fact that the whole adventure pointed to an eventual piece of double-dealing on my part lent an eerie quality to the thing . . . Anyway, the theme of *Charlotte's Web* is that a pig shall be saved, and I have an idea that somewhere deep inside me there was a wish to that effect."

E.B. White happened upon Charlotte, then just a barn spider, on a cold evening in October. A gracious spectator to the marvels of any and all species, he saw that Charlotte was in the process of spinning her egg sac and proceeded to get a stepladder and an extension light so that he could have a better view of her becoming a mother. He couldn't bear to leave the egg sac alone while he travelled back to New York on business, writing, "A few days later, when it was time to return to New York, not wishing to part with my spider, I took a razor blade, cut the sac adrift from the underside of the shed roof, put spider and sac in a candy box, and carried them to town." He placed the box on his dresser for several weeks before the eggs hatched and little spiders emerged from the air holes. "They strung tiny lines from my comb to my brush, from my brush to my mirror, and from my mirror to my nail scissors," White wrote. "They were very busy and almost invisible, they were so small. We all lived together happily for a couple of weeks, and then somebody whose duty it was to dust my dresser balked, and I broke up the show."

And as for why he wrote the book itself? "I haven't told why I wrote the book, but I haven't told why I sneeze, either," White wrote. "A book is a sneeze."

OF MICE AND MEN

John Steinbeck

1937

"I was a bindle-stiff myself for quite a spell," Steinbeck told the *New York Times* in a 1937 interview. "I worked in the same country that the story is laid in." Born and raised in Salinas, California, Steinbeck came from an affluent family in an area that was economically dependent on common field hands. Long car rides through the valley with his father and two sisters exposed him to the poor living conditions that migrant workers endured, generating an interest that he later cultivated while travelling with the workers as a young adult. He felt that their story—that of the poor and voiceless in desperate pursuit of the American dream—was worth writing about. This was especially true thanks to the fact that they worked and lived in Steinbeck's precious valley. In a letter to a friend, he wrote, "I think I would like to write a story of this whole valley, of all the little towns and all the farms and the ranches in the wilder hills. I can see how I would like to do it so that it would be the valley of the world." That was Steinbeck's muse—people trying to make something of themselves by living off of his beautiful California land.

His choice of title does much to further that sentiment. *Of Mice and Men* was taken from the poem "To a Mouse" by Robert Burns, which reads, "The best laid schemes o' mice an' men / Gang aft agley." That translates to "The best laid schemes of mice and men / Often go awry."

Steinbeck also drew inspiration from the people of his past, writing characters that were loosely based on some of the workers that he travelled with. In the same interview with the *Times*, he says, "Lennie was a real person. He's in an insane asylum in California right now. I worked alongside him for many weeks. He didn't kill a girl. He killed a ranch foreman. Got sore because the boss fired his pal and stuck a pitchfork right through his stomach. I hate to tell you how many times I saw him do it. We couldn't stop him until it was too late." That kind of impactful moment was likely one of several that ultimately led Steinbeck to pursue one of his greatest works.

THE GIRL ON THE TRAIN

Paula Hawkins

———

2015

———

"My seventeen-year-old self wasn't thinking about writing a book about those people, but she felt something—a sense of connection so strong it felt like longing—which has never gone away," Paula Hawkins wrote, in the "Special Guests" section of *The Magazine*. "Later, much later, on a different commute to a different bit of London, a less romantic me thought idly about what I might do if I saw something shocking on my commute. If I witnessed, *Rear Window*–style, an act of violence from my train carriage. I wondered what I would do. Would I tell someone? Go to the police? Would they believe me? Would I believe me? If all you had was one fleeting glance, of a hand around a throat, say? What if you'd seen a moment of passion, not a moment of violence? I concluded that I probably wouldn't tell anyone, I'd probably just push the image away, convince myself I'd imagined it. It was the kernel of something, that thought. The germ of a story, one I might write about. I think I knew that then. But still, I didn't act."

It would take one of the worst economic

collapses in modern history to push Hawkins out of her comfort zone, comprised mainly of her work as a personal finance journalist for a London newspaper. The novels, romantic comedies written under the pseudonym Amy Silver, sustained her for five years. She changed course after her fourth novel failed to meet the publisher's expectations—yet another dire situation turned inspirational moment for Hawkins. The Zimbabwe native turned her attention to a story she knew she could cultivate; after all, she already had the start of it in place. All she needed was a reason to act.

"And then along came Rachel, the protagonist of *The Girl on the Train*," writes Hawkins, in the same interview as above. "Only she wasn't Rachel at first, she was someone else, nameless and unformed, wandering around in another story in my head. She was a drunk. A drunk girl, an unreliable, lost person, sinking towards rock bottom, a terrible witness, the worst person in the world to solve a mystery. It wasn't until I put this drunk girl on the train that I found her voice, and once I had, she became Rachel, she came storming out almost fully formed, with all her bitterness and longing, all her regrets and recriminations, and above her fateful love of looking, out of the window of her train, into the houses on the side of the tracks."

THE GIVER

Lois Lowry

1993

When asked in an interview to explain what inspired her to write *The Giver*, Lois Lowry quickly dismissed the belief that it was in any way a political narrative. "I'm not a political animal, really," she said. Rather, the story came from a much more personal experience—that of her father's battle with old age and memory loss. "It became more and more apparent that he was losing memories that to me were so important," Lowry said. "On the other hand, at the same time I realized that he was content because he had forgotten every sad or scary thing that had ever happened to him. He had forgotten World War II, in which he participated. He had forgotten my sister who had died young, his firstborn child." Her father's condition, specifically that he was free of the burdens brought on by painful memories, invited Lowry to consider what a world without memories might look like. "And so I began to think about writing a book about people who had found a way to manipulate human memory, so they wouldn't have to remember anything bad," she said in an interview with NPR. The next step was clear: put pen to paper. "When a writer begins to think questions like that that begin with what if, that's when a story begins to take shape. That was the beginning of *The Giver*."

A military and middle child, Lowry cites her constantly moving from place to place and having her siblings take up most of her parents' time as the reason behind her immersion in the imaginative world of literature and storytelling. Her notebook always scribbled with stories and poems, she became a freelance writer and photographer before transitioning to children's stories in the mid-1970s. Thus began her long and versatile writing career. Writes Lowry, "My books have varied in content and style. Yet it seems to me that all of them deal, essentially, with the same general theme: the importance of human connection . . . *The Giver* takes place against the background of yet another very different culture and time. Though broader in scope than my earlier books, it nonetheless speaks to the same concern: the vital need for humans to be aware of their interdependence, not only with each other, but with the world and its environment."

ORDINARY PEOPLE

Judith Guest

1976

"I started writing it as a short story," wrote Judith Guest about her novel, "and just wasn't ready to put the people down, so I thought I'd work on what happened before the story started . . . and then what happened after it . . . and before I knew it I was about two hundred pages in." Before becoming a full-time writer, Guest worked as a public school teacher and was thus around children quite a bit, likely influencing the teenage aspect of the book. She left in the middle of writing *Ordinary People*, a novel celebrated for addressing mental illness in the mid-1980s, while everybody else was writing about the Vietnam War. She writes, "A writer never knows if a topic is merely her own pet obsession or a subject whose time has finally come. In that same time period, notable books about the war in Vietnam were coming out, but they went unread because people weren't yet ready to read about Vietnam. For some reason they were ready to read about teen suicide."

Guest's novel frequently references depression—namely, the various forms it takes, and how hard it can be to re-acclimate to society after experiencing its depths. As Guest says, "I wrote it because I wanted to explore the anatomy of depression—how it works and why it happens to people; how you can go from being so down but able to handle it, to being so down that you don't ever want to handle it, and then taking a radical step with your life—trying to commit suicide—and failing at that, coming back to the world and having to 'act normal' when, in fact, you have been forever changed."

BLACK BEAUTY

Anna Sewell

1877

Using a relatively unique storytelling device, Anna Sewell wrote *Black Beauty* from an animal's point of view in order to start a conversation on animal welfare in the late 1800s. Dependent on horse-drawn carts due to an illness that restricted her mobility, Sewell had long held close bonds with her family's horses, at a time when animals were seen as tools and little else. In Victorian England, horses were used in nearly every facet of civilization—often pushed past the point of exhaustion without any regard for their well-being. That common mentality led Sewell to create her narrator, Darkie, who is supposedly inspired by a Sewell family horse named Bess. Sewell believed that giving the horses a voice and a detectable point of view might inspire people to treat the animals more humanely.

BRAVE NEW WORLD

Aldous Huxley

———

1932

In his first novel *Crome Yellow*, Aldous Huxley writes: "An impersonal generation will take the place of Nature's hideous system. In vast state incubators, rows upon rows of gravid bottles will supply the world with the population it requires. The family system will disappear; society, sapped at its very base, will have to find new foundations; and Eros, beautifully and irresponsibly free, will flit like a gay butterfly from flower to flower through a sunlit world." The book itself a work of satire, this passage describes a world eerily similar to the future depicted in *Brave New World*.

Already an established magazine contributor, poet and satirist, Huxley drew inspiration for his dystopian novel from the work of H.G. Wells.

In fact, *Brave New World* was originally meant to be a parody of books like Wells' *A Modern Utopia*—Huxley wrote in a letter to a friend that he had "been having a little fun pulling the leg of H.G. Wells," before he "got caught up in the excitement of [his] own ideas." He started and finished the book in 1931 while living in France, despite much of the book's inspiration coming from his travels abroad.

The book represents Henry Ford as a sort of deity for the World State, where individuals often reference "Our Ford" instead of "Our Lord." Huxley's decision to include Ford in the book can be traced back to time he spent travelling on a boat toward the Philippines. During his trip, he stumbled upon Henry Ford's 1922 manifesto, *My Life and Work*. While the work certainly influenced Huxley's decision to include Ford, it would be wrong to limit its effect just to that character; in fact, it's possible that the manifesto influenced the World State's very nature.

Brave New World had plenty of other clear influences. On a visit to an English chemical plant, Huxley was amazed by the "anomalous oasis of pure logic in the midst of the larger world of planless incoherence." Huxley linked that incoherence to characteristics he had observed in American youth culture—specifically while on a trip to San Francisco in the 1920s. The promiscuity, freethinking and consumerism all left a bad taste in his mouth—so bad, in fact, that the World State he builds in his novel seeks to eradicate its very existence.

CAT'S CRADLE

Kurt Vonnegut

——

1963

Kurt Vonnegut spent much of his time as a General Electric public relations specialist searching for a story that would grab the public's attention. Walking from lab to lab, talking to scientists and "asking what they were up to" led Vonnegut to Dr. Irving Langmuir, a decorated scientist and Nobel laureate who stood at the forefront of atomic theory. If Vonnegut's general interactions with G.E. personnel inspired *Cat's Cradle*, Langmuir inspired the character Dr. Felix Hoenikker. In an interview with *The Paris Review*, Vonnegut says, "Dr. Felix Hoenikker, the absentminded scientist, was a caricature of Dr. Langmuir, the star of the G.E. research laboratory. I knew him some. My brother worked with him. Langmuir was wonderfully absentminded. He wondered out loud one time whether, when turtles pulled in their heads, their spines buckled or contracted. I put that in the book. One time he left a tip under his plate after his wife served him breakfast at home. I put that in. His most important contribution, though, was the idea for what I called 'Ice-9,' a form of frozen water that was stable at room temperature. He didn't tell it directly to me. It was a legend around the laboratory—about the time H.G. Wells came to Schenectady . . . Langmuir was told to be [Wells'] host. Langmuir thought he might entertain Wells with an idea for a science-fiction story—about a form of ice that was stable at room temperature. Wells was uninterested, or at least never used the idea. And then Wells died, and then, finally, Langmuir died. I thought to myself: 'Finders, keepers—the idea is mine.' Langmuir, incidentally, was the first scientist in private industry to win a Nobel Prize." Of course, ice-nine is the substance-turned-superweapon that Hoenikker discovers in *Cat's Cradle*.

CHARLIE AND THE CHOCOLATE FACTORY

Roald Dahl

1964

To find Roald Dahl's inspiration for *Charlie and the Chocolate Factory*, look no further than this passage from the book:

> "You see, Charlie, not so very long ago there used to be thousands of people working in Mr. Willy Wonka's factory. Then one day, all of a sudden, Mr. Wonka had to ask every single one of them to leave, to go home, never to come back."
>
> "But why?" asked Charlie.
>
> "Because of spies."
>
> "Spies?"
>
> "Yes. All the other chocolate makers, you see, had begun to grow jealous of the wonderful candies that Mr. Wonka was making, and they started sending in spies to steal his secret recipes. The spies took jobs in the Wonka factory, pretending they were ordinary workers, and while they were there, each one of them found

out exactly how a certain special thing was made."

While Dahl's love of wax-wrapped treats made him interested to write this book, it wasn't a childhood tour through a chocolate factory that inspired the story. It wasn't even a singular event. It was the state of the candy-making industry during the early to mid-1900s—particularly in Europe.

It has always been difficult to patent candy recipes, and companies would often create exact replicas of their competitors' products under different names. Not only did this cripple the smaller, mom-and-pop stores in the industry, it also led to cases of espionage among the larger companies. In fact, many candy makers would hire detectives to keep an eye on their employees, in an effort to weed out any moles that had been placed there by a competitor. The candy recipes themselves were extremely confidential; only the most loyal and trusted employees with rank were allowed to know what went into each product.

Dahl hated the bottom-line mentality that was killing the tiny sweetshops he so adored as a child. At age thirteen, Dahl served as a taste-tester for Cadbury while living at his public boarding school; his age represented their key demographic. Writes Dahl in his autobiography,

"It was lovely dreaming those dreams, and I have no doubt at all that, thirty-five years later, when I was looking for a plot for my second book for children, I remembered those little cardboard boxes and the newly-invented chocolates inside them."

FAHRENHEIT 451

Ray Bradbury

1953

The 1950s were a decade marked by fear and pessimism. The Red Scare had reached a fever pitch in the U.S., the Soviets were arresting authors and banning books and both world super-powers engaged in a troubling arms race—all in the shadow of the two nuclear bombs dropped in Japan. The possibility of a dystopian American society had become real, and it affected much of the literature of the time. More specific to Bradbury, though, was an encounter he and a friend had with a police officer on Wilshire Boulevard.

As Bradbury recalls in a speech at Moorpark College, "A police car pulled up, and the police-man got out and asked, 'What are you doing?' 'We are putting one foot in front of the other,' I told him. This was the wrong answer . . . I became so upset that I took from my pocket a small packet of soda crackers. I put them in my mouth and sprayed him with crumbs. The policeman contented himself with brushing the flakes off his uniform, reprimanding me severely . . . When I got home, I wrote a short story called *The Pedestrian*, in which I carried the whole thing into the future forty years, where it is suddenly a criminal offense to walk anywhere, anytime, under any circumstances. So this is where you get your ideas and act upon them impassionedly within the hour!" Eventually Bradbury swapped out a walking ban with a literature ban, and *The Pedestrian* became *Fahrenheit 451*.

MEMOIRS OF A GEISHA

Arthur Golden

———

1997

When asked what sparked his interest in geishas as a subject, Arthur Golden responded, "I studied Japanese language and culture in college and graduate school, and afterward went to work in Tokyo, where I met a young man whose father was a famous businessman and whose mother was a geisha. He and I never discussed his parentage, which was an open secret, but it fascinated me. After returning to the U.S., I began work on a novel in which I tried to imagine this young man's childhood. Gradually I found myself more interested in the life of the mother than the son and made up my mind to write a novel about a geisha."

What followed was an eight-hundred-page draft detailing the life of a Kyoto geisha following World War II, substantiated by extensive research done on the subject. "I wrote a draft based on a lot of book-learning," says Golden, when asked about his first attempt at writing the novel. "And I thought I had a pretty good idea of what the world of a geisha was like, and I wrote a draft. Then a chance came along to meet a geisha, which, of course, I couldn't turn down. And she was so helpful to me that I realized I'd gotten everything wrong, and I ended up throwing out that entire first draft and doing the whole thing over again."

Golden developed a short-lived friendship with the Geisha, named Mineko, and drew heavily from their interactions as he worked on his new manuscript—especially when creating on his protagonist, Sayuri. "I had imagined that geisha probably sprinkled their conversations with high-handed references to art and poetry," says Golden, "but in fact, Mineko was too naturally clever to resort to anything so artificial. For example, when she and her family came to visit us in Boston, I took her to Harvard Yard to see the place; it happened to be an hour or so after commencement ceremonies had ended. We sat together on a bench while I explained the meaning of the different colored gowns—black for undergraduates, blue for master's degrees, and red for PhDs—when an older man stumbled by, clearly a bit drunk. Mineko turned to me and said, 'I guess that man's nose just got a PhD.' That comment strikes me as so characteristic of Mineko. She became such an exceptionally successful geisha partly because of her cleverness—though her great beauty had a good deal to do with it as well. In establishing Sayuri's voice in the novel, I considered it essential to find some quality of cleverness that would help her rise out of the mire in which most geisha have no choice but to spend their lives. So, in this sense, I did draw on my knowledge of Mineko to create Sayuri. However, the story of Sayuri's life in no way relates to Mineko's."

The original story of Sayuri's life was written in the third person, in part because certain Japanese customs would have to be explained to an American audience by a narrator. Readers found that approach to be "dry," so Golden trashed his second draft and started his third, this time from a first-person perspective. Of course, that created quite a dilemma. Why would a Japanese character think to explain simple Japanese customs in detail? Why would she assume that her audience was American? Those questions inspired Golden to insert into his novel a translator, a decision on which he says, "I did, however, always try to keep in mind how things would be expressed in Japanese, and to select words and phrases that I felt would convey the same tone. But the translator's preface serves quite a different purpose. In writing a novel from the perspective of a geisha, I faced a number of problems. To begin with, how would Americans understand what she was talking about? Even fundamental issues like the manner of wearing a kimono or makeup couldn't be taken for granted if the audience wasn't Japanese. When I'd written the novel in third person, the narrator had had the freedom to step away from the story for a moment to explain things whenever necessary. But it would never occur to Sayuri to explain things—that is, it wouldn't occur to her unless her audience was not Japanese. This is the role of the translator's preface, to establish that she has come to live in New York and will be telling her story for the benefit of an American audience. That's also the principle reason why the novel had to end with her coming to New York."

MIDNIGHT'S CHILDREN

Salman Rushdie

1981

While penning his literary masterpiece, which won the "Booker of Bookers" Prize in 1993, Salman Rushdie chose not to consider the sensitivities of his audience, calling it "a terrible, horrible admission." He was well not to; *Midnight's Children* focused on the India he knew from personal experience—an India he felt was underrepresented in English literature prior to 1981. "Yeah, I did feel that what existed, certainly in English at that time—good as much of it was—didn't speak to me about the world I knew, the world I grew up in," said Rushdie in an interview with Gauri Viswanathan of the Southern Asian Institute at Columbia University. "The very manner of the novels was very calm, mild, classicist—kind of linguistically orthodox. And I just thought, India's not like that. India's turbulent and noisy and vulgar and crowded and unorthodox. It's a racket and it's a sexual assault—it's all of these things."

"One day in 1976—I'm no longer certain of the date—a young, unsuccessful writer wrestling with an enormous and still intractable story decided to start again, this time using a first-person narrator. On that day, much of what is now the beginning of *Midnight's Children* was written." So begins an essay Rushdie wrote for *The Guardian* in 2008, wherein he discusses his narrator's exploration of a newly independent India. Born in Bombay, Rushdie gives a description of India that is well founded. In perhaps his most enduring metaphor, he describes India as "a crowd." "How do you tell the story of a crowd? How do you tell the story of a multitude? The central narrative has to push its way through the crowd." So how did he do it? With his narrator, Saleem Sinai, of whom he writes, "I can still summon up the feeling of exhilaration that came over me as I discovered Saleem Sinai's voice, and in doing so discovered my own. I have always thought of that day as the moment I really became a writer, after a decade of false starts."

Saleem is the tool with which Rushdie paints an unfamiliar portrait of his India, one that feels alive and—though entirely foreign to Western readers—relatable. In an interview with *The Paris Review*, he says, "One of the things that has become, to me, more evidently my subject is the way in which the stories of anywhere are also the stories of everywhere else. To an extent, I already knew that because Bombay, where I grew up, was a city in which the West was totally mixed up with the East. The accidents of my life have given me the ability to make stories in which different parts of the world are brought together, sometimes harmoniously, sometimes in conflict, and sometimes both—usually both."

MRS. DALLOWAY

Virginia Woolf

———

1925

Written in the mid-1920s, Virginia Woolf's *Mrs. Dalloway* takes full advantage of the fact that it was published after James Joyce's *Ulysses*. Writes Woolf in her diary, "I . . . have been amused, stimulated, charmed, interested by the first 2 or 3 chapters—to the end of the Cemetery scene; [and] then puzzled, bored, irritated, [and] disillusioned as by a queasy undergraduate scratching his pimples. And Tom [T.S. Eliot], great Tom, thinks this is on a par with War & Peace! An illiterate, underbred book it seems to me: the book of a self-taught working man, [and] we all know how distressing they are, how egotistic, insistent, raw, striking, & ultimately nauseating. When one can have cooked flesh, why have the raw? But I think if you are anaemic, as Tom is, there is glory in blood. Being fairly normal myself I am soon ready for the classics again." And yet the very break from form that Woolf criticizes played a central role in making *Mrs. Dalloway* such a lasting work of literature.

It seems clear that Woolf didn't enjoy *Ulysses*, but she nonetheless employs some of the same concepts as Joyce's in her novel. The fluidity with which the book moves between thought and time; the fact that both are set in a single day in June; the presence of two primary narratives in each book—all aspects of *Mrs. Dalloway* that *Ulysses* may have inspired.

The character of Clarissa has clear influences as well—as Woolf modeled her after childhood friend Kitty Maxse, a high-society wife to a very prominent man. Woolf stated in a letter to her sister that Clarissa was "almost Kitty verbatim," and even thought about killing off the character, as Kitty herself died after falling over a staircase banister. She decided against it, instead creating a double for Clarissa named Septimus Smith—a World War I veteran who would go on to kill himself. Woolf instilled in Smith many of the same mental woes that she faced in her life, going as far as to have him hallucinate that birds are singing in Greek, a vision that she herself had experienced before.

NEVER LET ME GO

Kazuo Ishiguro

2005

"I'd always wanted to write a novel about my students, but I'd never got any further; I'd always ended up writing some other quite different novel." For Kazuo Ishiguro, writing *Never Let Me Go* was an exercise in repetition and futility. "Over the last fifteen years I kept writing pieces of a story about an odd group of 'students' in the English countryside," he said. "I was never sure who these people were. I just knew that they lived in wrecked farmhouses, and though they did a few typically student-like things—argued over books, worked on the occasional essay, fell in and out of love—there was no college campus or teacher anywhere in sight." Ishiguro had the subjects for his novel before he had the dystopian elements it's known for.

Thankfully, a chance occurrence offered him the direction he needed to write the novel. As he explains it, "Around four years ago I heard a discussion on the radio about advances in biotechnology. I usually tune out when scientific discussions come on, but this time I listened, and the framework around these students of mine finally fell into place. I could see a way of writing a story that was simple, but very fundamental, about the sadness of the human condition."

As for the setting? "I'd always seen the novel taking place in the England of the '70s and '80s—the England of my youth," said Ishiguro. "It's an England far removed from the butlers-and-Rolls-Royce England of, say, *The Remains of the Day*. I pictured England on an overcast day, flat bare fields, weak sunshine, drab streets, abandoned farms, empty roads. Apart from Kathy's childhood memories, around which there could be a little sun and vibrancy, I wanted to paint an England with the kind of stark, chilly beauty I associate with certain remote rural areas and half-forgotten seaside towns."

OH, THE PLACES YOU'LL GO!

Dr. Seuss

—

1990

Theodor Geisel, better known as Dr. Seuss, produced what is perhaps his most resonating work with *Oh, The Places You'll Go!* as he battled cancer late in life. The last of Seuss' published works that he had a hand in writing, the book offers great optimism and reassurance amid the dark and lonely times each individual encounters as they get older.

Geisel was no stranger to difficult times himself; he lived through the Great Depression, had his first manuscript (titled *And to Think That I Saw It on Mulberry Street*) rejected by between twenty and forty-three publishers (depending on the source), lost his first wife to suicide and himself suffered through oral cancer that would eventually take his life in 1991. Living through these experiences and still being able to lead a happy and successful life inspired him to write *Oh, The Places You'll Go!* as a way to say that everything is "98 and ¾ percent guaranteed" to work out. Says Susan Brandt, president of licensing and marketing at Dr. Seuss Enterprises, "You can feel him saying, 'Wait, I have one more thing to say. Listen to me; this is important.' "

RAGTIME

E.L. Doctorow

———

1975

"What comes first? Is it a character? You say a premise. What does that mean? Is it a theme?" This was a question posed to E.L. Doctorow in a 1986 interview with *The Paris Review*. His answer: "Well, it can be anything. It can be a voice, an image; it can be a deep moment of personal desperation. For instance, with *Ragtime* I was so desperate to write something, I was facing the wall of my study in my house in New Rochelle and so I started to write about the wall. That's the kind of day we sometimes have, as writers. Then I wrote about the house that was attached to the wall. It was built in 1906, you see, so I thought about the era and what Broadview Avenue looked like then: trolley cars ran along the avenue down at the bottom of the hill; people wore white clothes in the summer to stay cool. Teddy Roosevelt was President. One thing led to another and that's the way that book began: through desperation to those few images."

The story that followed, though conceptualized in reality, had its share of fictional elements. In fact, Doctorow employed *Ragtime*'s fictional realism as a way of getting back at groups he felt had hijacked the art of storytelling, as he says in a 1975 interview with the *New York Times*.

"Storytelling has been appropriated by sociologists and psychologists. Books about physical fitness and diet tell stories—with villains. Fat-around-the-middle is a villain. There is conflict and resolution. Even when they report the weather on television, they dramatize it; 'We'll have that story in a minute.' [The novelist] is pushed into a realm of personal experience, a very small preserve he is allowed to wander in. *Ragtime* is a novelist's revenge. It defies facts. Give 'em all sorts of facts—made up fats, distorted facts. I begin to think of *Ragtime* as fictive nonfiction. It's the reverse of Truman Capote. I see all those new journalists as guys on the other side . . . From the beginning, novelists have used strategies, have mixed up fact and fiction. That's the region where *Ragtime* is located, halfway between fiction and history."

STRANGER IN A STRANGE LAND

Robert Heinlein

1961

It was Robert Heinlein's wife, Virginia, who came up with the premise of *Stranger in a Strange Land*. An accomplished biochemist and engineer, she suggested introducing a space component to Rudyard Kipling's *The Jungle Book*. The concept—a boy grows up in a foreign environment—remained the same, only this remake would replace wolves with Martians. Over the next thirteen years, Heinlein slowly accumulated ideas and concepts for the novel, writing, "I had been in no hurry to finish it, as that story could not be published commercially until the public *mores* changed. I could see them changing and it turned out that I had timed it right."

In fact, Heinlein's desire to examine society's ethos was a major reason why he decided to write the book. In Michael Smith, his protagonist who comes to Earth for the first time as a twenty year old, Heinlein had the perfect tool to incite critical thinking about society's oldest institutions—including marriage, money, fear and religion. Said Heinlein in conversation with a fan, "I was not giving answers. I was trying to shake the reader loose from some preconceptions and induce him to think for himself, along new and fresh lines. In consequence, each reader gets something different out of that book because he himself supplies the answers . . . it is an invitation to think—not to believe."

THE GREAT GATSBY

F. Scott Fitzgerald

———

1922

"While I have every hope and plan of finishing my novel in June, you know how those things often come out, and even if it takes me ten times that long I cannot let it go out unless it has the very best I'm capable of in it, or even, as I feel sometimes, something better than I'm capable of." Fitzgerald wrote this in 1924 to his editor, Max Perkins. Fitzgerald's very best yielded a commercial failure, at least in the immediate sense, but it wasn't long before readers caught on to the novel's brilliance.

Fitzgerald's *This Side of Paradise* offered him the fame and access necessary to achieve good standing with the moneyed class of the Roarin' Twenties—whose parties inspired the ones hosted by Gatsby in his West Egg mansion. The origins of that mansion are cloudy, though a 2011 article in the *Los Angeles Times* suggests that it was based on Land's End, a Gold Coast Mansion where Fitzgerald had once attended a party. The origins of Nick Carraway and Jay Gatsby, however, are much clearer, as Fitzgerald writes himself into both. Nick was an Ivy-educated man, while Gatsby met the love of his life while stationed far from home in the military. Both were defining characteristics of Fitzgerald's life, as he himself writes on his Ivy League education: "My new novel appears in late March: *The Great Gatsby*. It represents about a year's work and I think it's about ten years better than anything I've done. All my harsh smartness has been kept ruthlessly out of it—it's the greatest weakness in my work, distracting and disfiguring it even when it calls up an isolated sardonic laugh." Fitzgerald met Zelda, his wife, while stationed in Camp Sheridan outside Montgomery, Alabama. Zelda was a debutante born into wealth, and Fitzgerald idolized the way that she lived; like Gatsby, he did much to prove himself worthy of her company.

In her *Careless People: Murder, Mayhem and the Invention of 'The Great Gatsby,'* Sarah Churchwell claims that the two murder victims in the novel were inspired by the Halls-Mills Case of the early 1920s, which saw the murder of a priest and his mistress garner nationwide attention. On how she made the connection, Churchwell tells *Signature*, "It's interesting the way that some people don't see the Halls-Mills case as paralleling *Gatsby* very satisfactorily because the details don't match up, but for me . . . the underlying themes are there. And so one of the things I was hoping was to suggest that all of the themes from *Gatsby* were in the air as Fitzgerald was writing. Not necessarily that it was a one-one correspondence with Hall-Mills, but Hall-Mills is representative of the kinds of stories that were around. It's not that I think that Fitzgerald was transcribing this case into his novel—that would be foolish— but rather that the case has these echoes of the deep themes of *Gatsby*. So for example, class resentment and social climbing . . . that there's actually a character in both stories who makes up a romantic past and a more aristocratic past. That this story about social climbing and class resentment is specifically about a woman who is seen as using an affair as a way to gain access to a better quality of life."

THE CRUCIBLE

Arthur Miller

———

1953

America was a scary place in the 1950s. Due process had been unofficially and knowingly suspended; Senator Joseph McCarthy served as judge, jury and executioner, wantonly pointing a finger at free-thinking liberals and locking them up at will for being communist sympathizers. Worried about falling victim of the very nature that he was trying to exploit, Arthur Miller attempted to tackle the enormity of the Red Scare without marking himself as a communist. His method? Capture the tone of the times by writing about a literal witch hunt, one during which "spectral evidence" was enough to convict and kill somebody. It was an apt comparison, as the Salem witch trials and the Red Scare are eerily similar; both dealt in baseless widespread fear, both acted on that hysteria, both saw convictions off allegations alone. In simpler terms, both are unfortunate chapters in United States history.

THE EXORCIST

William Peter Blatty

———

1971

"A coat on a hangar seemed to fly out of a closet . . . a Bible seemed to rise from a book-case . . . one day the kitchen table tipped over." Those words, written in Thomas Allen's *Possessed: The True Story of an Exorcism*, were used to describe a series of events that allegedly took place in the presence of the possessed fourteen-year-old boy that Peter Blatty's *The Exorcist* is based on. After an attempted exorcism at Georgetown University Hospital ended with a priest receiving one hundred stitches in his arm, the boy's family sought treatment in St. Louis, partly because of their strong ties to the city and partly because they found the word *Louis* spelled out in bloody scratches on the boy's chest.

What followed was a two-month battle between Jesuit priests and the demon that (supposedly) possessed the child, starting in a private home and ending at the Alexian Brothers Hospital. Said Allen during an event at Saint Louis University, "I feel he was possessed by something that was inside himself. I don't have the faith to say devils and diabolical possession. But then you look at Father Bowdern, who day after day for weeks is saying exorcism prayers over this boy, and when Blatty writes to him and says tell me about it . . . Father Bowdern writes back and says I can't tell you anything about it. I'm pledged to secrecy. But I'll tell you one thing. This was the real thing."

Blatty also found inspiration in British archaeologist Gerald Lankester Harding, stating that Harding "was the physical model in my mind when I created the character [of Merrin], whose first name, please note, is Lankester."

THE MARTIAN

Andy Weir

———

2011

Andy Weir's inspiration for writing *The Martian* was years in the making. The son of an electronics engineer and a particle physicist, his formative years were spent immersed in technology and all things sci-fi. He spent a lot of his twenties working as a computer programmer for AOL, a job he lost in 1999 when the then–tech giant merged with Netscape. Rather than take his talents elsewhere, Weir decided to shelve them and pursue another passion of his: fiction writing.

The pursuit didn't last very long as a full-time endeavor; Weir went back to the software industry in 2002 after producing two novels to little critical acclaim. It wasn't until 2009 that he decided to draw from his technical background and intense love of space in order to consider what a manned mission to Mars would look like. He started writing short pieces and publishing them on his website; after the work started to gain a following from the scientific community, Weir developed them into a novel and made it available as an e-book on Amazon for only ninety-nine cents. The rest, as they say, is history.

THE PICTURE OF DORIAN GRAY

Oscar Wilde

1890

Oscar Wilde needed look no further than his own social circles for literary inspiration, as the subject of his first and only novel was a writer by the name of John Gray. An individual of striking beauty, he looked as though he were made of "ivory and rose leaves"—a line that Wilde wrote to describe his Dorian. Further proof that John Gray inspired Dorian can be found in the character's very name. The Dorians, an ancient Greek tribe, were advocates for homosexuality. Both literary homosexuals, Wilde and Gray often found themselves in the same circles, where Wilde came to grow fond of the young poet.

Though it is widely accepted that one Gray inspired the other, Wilde explains it differently. He says, "Basil Hallward is what I think I am: Lord Henry is what the world thinks of me: Dorian is what I would like to be—in other ages, perhaps." Of course, the two sentiments aren't mutually exclusive.

THE SECRET GARDEN

Frances Hodgson Burnett

—

1911

"[It is] a charming place with a nicely finished park and a beautiful old walled kitchen garden," wrote Frances Hodgson Burnett in a letter describing Kent's Great Maytham Hall to her son Vivian. Already a very successful novelist and playwright, she began renting the charming estate in search of country living after a divorce that saw her heavily criticized by major news publications on both sides of the Atlantic. The estate quickly became home; she hosted many a party, accumulated a legendary wardrobe and wrote *In Connection with the DeWilloughby Claim* in the gazebo.

After calling the place home for roughly a decade, Burnett had to accept the sad reality that she would never have the money to own it herself. She wrote to her sister, "It was living at Maytham which meant England to me, in a way . . . That place belongs to me—it is the only place I ever felt was home . . . It seemed a sort of outrage that I was not living there. It seemed so what one needed—that sense of being able to go out of one big room into another—to go down corridors into room after room—to go upstairs and walk about."

Still, Burnett's love for the manor never faded. Instead it followed her to Long Island, where she built a home and began writing *The Secret Garden*—a story inspired by the manor and its walled kitchen garden. Working as the primary catalyst for character development, the garden is a healer in both a literal and figurative sense; it helps Mary, the protagonist, grow out of her horribly unpleasant demeanor and into a heroine, and it helps Colin regain his ability to walk as the story progresses.

Colin's character arc reveals another source of Burnett's inspiration: her strong belief using Mary Baker Eddy's Christian Science to address illness, rather than Silas Weir Mitchell's rest cure. The latter advocates social isolation, force-feeding and bed rest to address a health problem, while the former promotes positive thinking, prayer and social interaction. Reads a passage from Garden, "When new beautiful thoughts began to push out the old hideous ones, life began to come back to him, his blood ran healthily through his veins and strength poured into him like a flood." Clearly psychological, Colin's illness is an example of rest doing more harm than good, while positive thought and interaction serve as a wholly effective cure.

STEPPENWOLF

Hermann Hesse

———

1927

Unfortunately, many of the major themes in *Steppenwolf* were autobiographical, as Hermann Hesse suffered from severe depression. His first wife, Marie Bernoulli, also suffered from mental illness; after her schizophrenia led to a nearly crippling psychotic episode in 1919, Hesse acknowledged that the two had grown too far apart. He moved on from the marriage, relocating from Bern to Ticino to Montagnola, where he took up art, pursued his writing and experienced what he later called the happiest time of his life.

Feeling stable and hopeful, Hesse married Ruth Wenger in 1924, but the partnership quickly deteriorated. His resulting isolation and loneliness led to suicidal thoughts—all major themes in *Steppenwolf.*

A VISIT FROM THE GOON SQUAD

Jennifer Egan

———

2010

"The entry point for me was very much what it is for the reader," said Jennifer Egan, when asked about the genesis of her novel *A Visit from the Goon Squad.* "I was in a hotel bathroom, looked down and saw a wallet lying exposed in a woman's bag. I've had my wallet stolen many times and ways in my life—through carelessness, oblivion or just plain being a sucker—and when I saw that wallet, I thought, 'Oh no! Someone will take it!' Since I was the only person in a position to do so, my mind made one of the fictional leaps that I live for: Someone would take the wallet. Who? And why? I began writing from that moment, and the rest followed fairly intuitively; a peripheral character in one chapter would catch my eye, and I'd think, 'Who is that person? What does his or her inner world look like?' "

Egan's natural creative process provides the structure for *Goon Squad*, utilizing her unbound imagination to view the world from several perspectives. She moves across peripherals to give each chapter a new narrator—each appearing in the preceding chapter as a way to loosely connect the story.

Egan's ability to imagine the lives of strangers was only enhanced by her life in New York City. She says, "For me in fiction it's always been about what I can dream up, that feels far away from me. And seems to almost offer a way to be lifted out of my own life. So, walking around and looking at people for me is just this constant exercise of my mind reaching out and kind of imagining a life for them beyond the moment that I'm seeing, beyond the moment that I'm witnessing. And what I love about New York is that it just provides so much variety. So many different kinds of encounters happen in a single day, even just passing on the street or riding the subway. In a way I started *Goon Squad* not even realizing I was writing a book, I thought I was just writing a few stories to stall before starting this other book that I wanted to write—or thought I wanted to write—I still haven't written it. But, I think that for me that sense of someone catching my eye and being able to follow them into their lives is such a wish-fulfilment fantasy that the book is basically built around that. And I think that New York provides more fodder for that kind of wish-fulfilment fantasy than any other place I've lived. So there's the connection."

Goon Squad offers a perspective that most people only experience in their most empathetic moments: one that considers the viewpoints of others. Egan humanizes all of her characters, a storytelling device she took from watching *The Sopranos*: "I loved that it was polyphonic," says Egan, "with lots of narratives happening at once, I loved that the arc of the season, the basic story that a season was telling, was often not clear until the end. But the storytelling had such authority that we just sort of went along, not even knowing what was really on the table, exactly. I love the way they would make peripheral characters central, and kind of break open their inner lives, and I loved the way that they also used stereotypes and then dug under them to show really nuanced characters, so that people were both stereotypical and nuanced at the same time."

ALICE IN WONDERLAND

Lewis Carroll

1865

Hoping to entertain the younger sisters of his friend Harry Liddell on a boating trip from Oxford to Godstow, the mathematician formerly known as Charles Dodgson crafted a story about a whimsical world and a protagonist named Alice. The name was no doubt inspired by Carroll's infatuation with the young Alice Liddell, who was ten years old at the time of the boating trip. Writes historian Martin Gardner in *The Annotated Alice*, "A long procession of charming little girls (we know today that they were charming from their photographs) skipped through Carroll's life, but none ever took the place of his first love, Alice Liddell. 'I have had some scores of child-friends since your time,' he wrote to her after her marriage, 'but they have been quite a different thing.' "

Not only did Alice inspire the original story, she inspired Carroll to pursue it as something more than a one-off. She and her sisters pestered Carroll relentlessly for more stories about Alice, culminating with Alice requesting that they be written down. Carroll obliged, adding to the story as he wrote the manuscript and presenting it to Alice for Christmas in 1864. The book was titled *Alice's Adventures Under Ground*. Before sending the manuscript for publishing, Carroll would eventually change the title to *Alice's Adventures in Wonderland*, add the Mad Hatter's tea party scene and invent the Cheshire Cat character.

The Cheshire Cat can also trace its origins to the Liddells—the tree it calls home is said to be behind the Liddell's home at Christ Church College, Oxford. And to further the Liddell influence: The names of the three sisters in the Dormouse's story were cleverly derived from the names of the Liddell sisters.

Of course, Carroll drew on some of his own experiences as well. He was a conservative mathematician who rejected progression in his field, and some believe that his distaste for non-traditionalists influenced his writing. "One of the big developments that was going on at that time . . . was work by an Irish mathematician called William Hamilton," says *Weekend Edition* Math Guy Keith Devlin in a 2010 interview with NPR. "Carroll wasn't a fan of Hamilton's work, a new arithmetic called quaternions. Quaternions were numbers—not to deal with counting things, but to deal with understanding rotations. Back in Victorian times, when Hamilton himself was doing this work, he tried to understand his new arithmetic in physical terms. He said one of the four terms that was involved in these numbers had to be time. So time was inexplicably, inescapably bound up with these new numbers. What Hamilton said was that if you take this time parameter out of these new numbers, then the numbers would just keep rotating around—they won't go anywhere. It was just like the characters rotating round and round the tea party, round and round the table." If one interprets the dinner party scene this way, it becomes easy to see how the absence of Time (the character) is responsible for this constant rotation. Continues Devlin, "In fact, when the Hatter and the Hare try to squeeze the Dormouse into the teapot, they're trying to somehow get away from this complexity—throw away another of the parameters, if you like—so that life can resume as normal." The story's focus on size discrepancy was also based on something in Carroll's personal life: a neurological disorder now known as Alice in Wonderland Syndrome. The afflicted suffers from hallucinations that can distort the size of visual objects, making the sufferer feel bigger or smaller than they are.

Still, none of it would have been possible without Alice setting everything in motion. In 1932, Columbia University invited Alice Liddell to New York for a tea party in honor of Lewis Carroll's one hundredth birthday (he had long been deceased). Liddell's son implored his eighty-year-old mother to go, eliciting her famous response: "But oh my dear, I am tired of being Alice in Wonderland. Does it sound ungrateful? It is. Only I do get tired."

CALVIN AND HOBBES

Bill Watterson

———

1985

"So, what's it like in the real world? Well, the food is better, but beyond that, I don't recommend it."

In a commencement speech titled "Some Thoughts on the Real World by One Who Glimpsed It and Fled," given in 1990, Bill Watterson reflected on the time leading up to the explosion of *Calvin and Hobbes*. Fired from his position as an editorial cartoonist at the *Cincinnati Post* only several months after graduating college, he took a job in advertising that resulted in his being "starved for some life of the mind" after only a short time. The work was a means to an end, a soulless venture that did nothing to incentivize personality. More than anything, Watterson had trouble with the fact that he wasn't doing the work for himself—he was doing it because he had to.

So he decided to start doing cartoon work on the side. Said Watterson, "It's surprising how hard we'll work when the work is done just for ourselves. And with all due respect to John Stuart Mill, maybe utilitarianism is overrated. If I've learned one thing from being a cartoonist, it's how important playing is to creativity and happiness. My job is essentially to come up with 365 ideas a year. If you ever want to find out just how uninteresting you really are, get a job where the quality and frequency of your thoughts determine your livelihood. I've found that the only way I can keep writing every day, year after year, is to let my mind wander into new territories. To do that, I've had to cultivate a kind of mental playfulness."

That cultivation began with a comic strip called *Critturs*, which occasionally featured a side character and his stuffed tiger. The side character, named Marvin, and his stuffed tiger, Hobbes, were said to be the strip's strongest characters by comic strip syndicator United Feature Syndicate. So Watterson scrapped the other characters, changed Marvin's name to Calvin and built a comic strip around them. The strip was picked up in 1985 and ran for a decade, at which point he believed that he'd "done what I can do within the constraints of daily deadlines and small panels."

"Hobbes got all of my better qualities (with a few quirks from our cats)," Watterson wrote, "and Calvin my ranting, escapist side. Together, they're pretty much a transcript of my mental diary . . . it's pretty startling to reread these strips and see my personality exposed so plainly right there on paper. I meant to disguise that better."

GIOVANNI'S ROOM

James Baldwin

———

1956

It was in 1956 when James Baldwin, an African-American author with a history of writing about black characters, penned a novel about a homosexual white man in Paris, France. "I certainly could not possibly have—not at that point in my life—handled the other great weight," he said in a 1984 interview with *The Paris Review*. "The 'Negro problem.' The sexual-moral light was a hard thing to deal with. I could not handle both propositions in the same book. There was no room for it. I might do it differently today, but then, to have a black presence in the book at that moment, and in Paris, would have been quite beyond my powers."

Baldwin, who cites his time preaching from ages fourteen to seventeen as a major reason why he got into writing, was no stranger to tragedy.

His father died when he was young, and his best friend committed suicide by jumping off the George Washington Bridge. Worn down by the torment he had experienced in New York City, Baldwin moved to Paris, where he himself almost succumbed to sickness. He luckily found care and hospitality in a place that rarely afforded such things to black men, giving him the opportunity to hear about Lucien Carr. Says Baldwin, "David is the first person I thought of, but that's due to a peculiar case involving a boy named Lucien Carr, who murdered somebody. He was known to some of the people I knew—I didn't know him personally. But I was fascinated by the trial, which also involved a wealthy playboy and his wife in high-level society."

Lucien Carr inspired Giovanni, the man who has relations with David on the night before his execution. David, on the other hand, was likely inspired by Baldwin himself. Upon first moving to Paris, he fell in love with a Swiss man named Lucien Happersberger, with whom he lived for a brief time. His inability to depict a man who was both black and gay could be a nod to his real-life trouble with that duality, which made him a marginalized figure in American society. Regardless, Baldwin was way ahead of his time, as his depiction of a gay main character came well before the gay liberation movement.

GONE WITH THE WIND

Margaret Mitchell

———

1936

"For God's sake, Peggy, can't you write a book instead of reading thousands of them?" It's true—a husband's exhaustion led to one of the most famous works of literature in modern history. The emphatic suggestion came as a result of Mitchell's husband lugging books to and from Atlanta's Carnegie Library, hoping to keep his wife busy as she nursed an injured ankle back to health. He even bought a portable typewriter for Mitchell to write. Trying desperately to fight off the boredom that comes with going stir crazy, she began typing away at what would be a Pulitzer Prize–winning manuscript.

Inspired by the story of the Civil War in the South and Atlanta in general, Mitchell set out to write a book depicting the war's effect on the Georgians who lived through it. "That is the meaning of the title," said Mitchell, in a 1936 radio interview. "Naturally I would be glad if people thought that the book did tell the story of the whole South. But that isn't the kind of book I tried to write. It is a book about Georgia and Georgia people, especially North Georgia people . . . She [Scarlett O'Hara, the protagonist] lives through the terrible days of Reconstruction and the story carries her, and Atlanta, up to the time when the Carpetbaggers had been run out of Georgia and people could begin living their normal lives again."

MIDDLESEX

Jeffrey Eugenides

———

2002

Said Jeffrey Eugenides on coming up with the idea for *Middlesex*, "It's difficult to pinpoint the moment when *Middlesex* took root in my imagination. As far back as 1976, in a high school Latin class, I was introduced to the figure of Tiresias, who'd lived as both male and a female. We were reading Ovid's *Metamorphoses* and we came to the part where Zeus and his wife, Hera, have an argument as to which sex has a better time in bed. Zeus, somewhat surprisingly, says that women enjoy themselves more. Hera claims that men do. To adjudicate the matter, they ask Tiresias, who replies: 'If pleasures of love be as ten, then three times three belongs to woman. The rest belongs to man.' "

It took Eugenides nine years to write *Middlesex*

once he put pen to paper, as the topic was foreign to him and often led to long gaps of writer's block. One bit of inspiration (though it still took Eugenides ten years to get started from this point on) came from reading Richard McDougall's translation of *Herculine Barbin: Being the Recently Discovered Memoirs of a Nineteenth-Century French Hermaphrodite*. Said Eugenides, "On the face of it, Herculine's life story was an amazing one. A teenager at a French convent school, Herculine fell in love with her best friend. They began a love affair, which was eventually discovered by the school authorities. Doctors examined Herculine and declared her to be a man. It was the love story at the center of this memoir—a love story between two girls where one girl isn't exactly a girl—that most intrigued me. I expected the memoir to be fascinating, wildly dramatic as well as revelatory about experiences I myself had no clue about. Unfortunately, Herculine Barbin wrote very much like the convent schoolgirl she was. Her prose is melodramatic, sentimental. She's evasive about her anatomical details and unable—or unwilling—to describe her emotional states without resorting to platitudes or histrionics. The memoir frustrated my readerly expectations. I thought to myself, rather hubristically, that I'd like to write the story myself."

Eugenides would eventually do just that,

setting out originally to write a short work of fiction that read as the autobiography of a hermaphrodite. Eugenides wanted more than anything to avoid dehumanizing the protagonist by adhering to the traditions of mythology, so he made sure to research the biological facts. "I spent a lot of time those first months in a medical library at Columbia," he said. "It was there that I came across the condition I use in *Middlesex*, 5-alpha-reductase deficiency syndrome. The salient fact about this condition is that it's caused by a recessive genetic mutation. Populations who have the mutation tend to be isolated, often inbred. When I learned that, I began to think about the book in a different way. I no longer wanted to write merely a fictional autobiography of a hermaphrodite but a longer book—a comic epic—that would trace the transmigrations of a genetic mutation down through the bloodlines of a single family. The book would be told by the final inheritor of this gene, but it would encompass many things aside from this sexual metamorphosis. It would concern all kinds of transformations, national, racial, emotional, intel-lectual—you name it."

Eugenides broadened the scope of the book, shifting the narrative focus to a Greek-American family in which three generations have the deficiency syndrome. Of course, while it does touch on themes like race and intellect, the book is driven by the idea of sexual metamorphosis. "I remember being struck by the marvelous utility of this figure, Tiresias. Here was a guy who knew what it was like to be a woman. How amazing! And how useful, from a literary standpoint. If the novelist's job is to go into the minds of both women and men, if we value most of all the writers who are best able to do this, then telling a story from the point of view of Tiresias might gain the writer a measure of that longed-for omniscience."

MISERY

Stephen King

———

1989

"Well, I can't comprehend it now, either, but you do what you have to do," said Stephen King in an interview with *Rolling Stone* magazine. "And when you're an addict, you have to use. So, you just try to balance things out as best you can. But little by little, the family life started to show cracks. I was usually pretty good about it. I was able to get up and make the kids breakfast and get them off to school. And I was strong; I had a lot of energy. I would've killed myself otherwise. But the books start to show it after a while.

Misery is a book about cocaine. Annie Wilkes *is* cocaine. She was my number one fan."

King conceived of Annie at the height of his drug use, basing aspects of her personality on his addictive nature. Her refusal to leave, forcing Paul Sheldon to write his novel as she sees fit and leaving his life in ruin for a time can be linked to King's substance abuse. But Annie's origin story came from other sources as well. King writes, "The inspiration for *Misery* was a short story by Evelyn Waugh called *The Man Who Loved Dickens*. It came to me as I dozed off while on a New York-to-London Concorde flight. Waugh's short story was about a man in South America held prisoner by a chief who falls in love with the stories of Charles Dickens and makes the man read them to him. I wondered what it would be like if Dickens himself was held captive."

TWENTY THOUSAND LEAGUES UNDER THE SEA

Jules Verne

———

1870

One of the original and most influential works of science fiction, Jules Verne's *Twenty Thousand Leagues Under the Sea* is ironically influenced by one of literature's most famous mythological epics—Homer's *Odyssey*, from which Captain Nemo gets his name. In *The Odyssey*, Odysseus tells the cyclops his name is Utis, meaning "No-name." "Utis" translates to "Nemo" in Latin. To further the connection, both protagonists wander the seas as they experience the agony of their crew's demise.

Verne also references real people throughout the novel, including Commander Matthew Fontaine Maury, explorer Jean-François de Galaup, explorer Jules Dumont d'Urville and Ferdinand de Lesseps, who built the Suez Canal. The final three names are all associated with Galaup's failed attempt to circumnavigate the globe, as D'Urville found the remains and Lesseps was the trip's sole survivor.

RABBIT, RUN

John Updike

1960

The year was 1959, and John Updike's dis-illusion with middle America had just set in. "I suppose I could observe, looking around me at American society in 1959, a number of scared and dodgy men," said Updike in an interview with the National Book Foundation. "And I felt a certain fright and dodginess within myself. This kind of man who won't hold still, who won't make a commitment, who won't quite pull his load in society."

Feeling as though that specific characterization of the American man lacked representation in the literature of the mid-twentieth century inspired Updike to create Harry "Rabbit" Angstrom, the novel's protagonist. "I imagined him as a former basketball player. As a high school student I saw a lot of basketball and even played a certain amount myself, so the grandeur of being a high school basketball star was very much on my mind as an observed fact of American life. You have this athletic ability, this tallness, this feeling of having been in some ways a marvelous human being up to the age of eighteen, and then everything afterwards runs downhill. In that way he accumulated characteristics—even his nickname, 'Rabbit.' Rabbits are dodgy, rabbits are sexy, rabbits are nervous, rabbits like grass and vegetables. I had an image of him that was fairly accessible, and his neural responses, his conversational responses, always seemed to come very readily to me, maybe because they were in many ways quite like my own."

Updike's perceived misrepresentation was partly brought on by Jack Kerouac's *On the Road*. Says Updike, "Without reading it, I resented its apparent instruction to cut loose; *Rabbit, Run* was meant to be a realistic demonstration of what happens when a young American family man goes on the road—the people left behind get hurt. There was no painless dropping out of the '50s fraying-but-still-tight social weave. Arriving at so prim a moral was surely not my only intention: the book ends on an ecstatic, open note that was meant to stay open, as testimony to our heart's stubborn amoral quest for something once called grace."

THE AMAZING ADVENTURES OF KAVALIER AND CLAY

Michael Chabon

2000

"My father really made the middle years of the twentieth century in America come alive for me when I was a kid," said Michael Chabon. "He was full of lore about the radio shows, politicians, movies, music, athletes, and so forth, of that era. And since he was from Brooklyn, his memories and his view of that time had a very New York slant to them. The main thing I was trying to do in this book, I think, was simply transport myself into that time and that place the way my father had done for me when I was a little boy."

Chabon did exactly that, setting his story in New York City in the time before, during and after World War II. The rare perspective for a book set in that time—that of the individuals trying to find success in the United States while the country fights wars in Europe and the Pacific—was born out of Chabon's love of comic books as a child. Says Chabon, "I started writing this book because of a box of comic books that I had been carrying around with me for fifteen years. It was the sole remnant of my once-vast childhood collection. For fifteen years, I just lugged it around my life, never opening it. It was all taped up and I left it that way. Then one day, not long after I finished *Wonder Boys*, I came upon it during a move, and slit open all the layers of packing tape and dust. The smell that emerged was rich and evocative of the vanished world of my four-color childhood imaginings. And I thought, there's a book in this box somewhere."

Comic books experienced a golden age in the 1940s and 1950s stateside, making the story and the setting a natural and easy fit, especially considering Chabon's affinity for early to mid-twentieth-century United States history. Enter Josef Kavalier and Sammy Klayman, the novel's two protagonists, who find a creative niche and try to carve out their own American success stories. Each has distinguishing characteristics beyond the escapist character they create for their adventure stories; Joe is trying to get his family out of Nazi-occupied Prague, while Sammy seeks to define his sexual identity. Despite their unique properties and specific perspectives, Chabon claims that they're not based on any real person. Or as he says, "[Not] in any way that I'm aware of, at least." In fact, he claims not to know their absolute origin at all. "I have no idea where they came from. I suppose they initially took form, in the primordial soup of the first hours of the book's composition, as a vague, Mutt-and-Jeff pair, a big guy and a little guy, a Quixote and a Sancho . . . and then rapidly began to coalesce."

Of course, the origin of *The Amazing Adventure of Kavalier and Clay* goes all the way back to Chabon's father. "I don't know what the connection is to comic books, exactly, except that it was also a world my father introduced me to, and he himself had been a voracious reader of comics as a kid. At the time I was reading a lot of comics—the early 1970s—the comics published by National (DC) were giant things, eighty and one hundred pages in length, and typically they were filled out with reprinted stories from the '40s and '50s. So it was very easy for me to access and connect with at least this one aspect of my dad's own childhood. I guess it's no wonder the book is dedicated to my father, Robert Chabon."

THE AWAKENING

Kate Chopin

———

1899

Rediscovered in the 1960s as a legitimate piece of literature, *The Awakening*'s success was no longer bound to the absurdity of the times. Published in the 1890s, *The Awakening* touched on suicide and focused on a woman's place in society so much that its publication was met with discomfort and hostility. Society was on the precipice of major change at the time; women were challenging the mother-first mentality that had been thrust upon them, while men were worried about losing their political and economic control. *The Awakening* forced women readers to confront what limitations hampered their ability to live freely and forced male readers to confront the idea that women might one day achieve an equal standing in society. Tragically, Chopin found herself unable to continue writing after *The Awakening*, as her name had been tarnished to the point where her work was no longer publishable. She had no income and became consumed by health and family problems, eventually succumbing to a brain hemorrhage five years after *The Awakening* was published.

THE COLOR PURPLE

Alice Walker

———

1982

"My mother planted so many flowers around our shack that it disappeared as a shack and became . . . just an amazing place," said Alice Walker in a 2013 interview with the *Huffington Post*. "So my sense of poverty was always seen through the screen of incredible ingenuity and artistic power." Walker was born the daughter of two sharecroppers in Eatonton, Georgia, in the year 1944, when racism was very much the prevailing mentality of the deep American South. When she boarded a bus to leave for Spelman College in Atlanta in 1961, a white woman requested that the bus driver force her to the back of the bus, and he obliged. "I can refuse and sit in the front and get arrested in this little town," she recalled, "or I can stay on the bus, get to Atlanta, check into my college and immediately join the movement for civil rights."

Walker's repeated encounters with racism reflected the experiences of many individuals she knew, but were seldom represented in anything that she had read. "In most literature, the lives of the people I knew did not exist. My mother for instance was, you know, nowhere in literature. She was all over my heart, so why shouldn't she be in literature? People like my parents and my grandparents, the stories that I heard about their younger years were riveting. I started writing this novel longing to hear their speech. I was so determined to give them a voice, because if you deny people their own voice, there's no way to ever know who they were. And so they are erased."

Walker interviewed and transcribed the testimonies of sharecroppers facing eviction, using their stories and the stories of those she'd known growing up to write *The Color Purple*, her Pulitzer Prize–winning novel. "What I would like for people to understand when they read *The Color Purple* is that there are all of these terrible things that can actually happen to us, and yet life is so incredibly magical, abundant and present that we can still be very happy."

THE TALE OF PETER RABBIT

Beatrix Potter

———

1903

Inspired by her childhood pet rabbit, Peter Piper, Beatrix Potter originally wrote *The Tale of Peter*

85

Rabbit as a letter to a sick boy. Her audience? Five-year-old Noel Moore, the son of her former governess. Potter sent Moore Peter Rabbit's first adventure, accompanied by her own illustrations, as a way to help cheer him up as he battled his illness. It wasn't until ten years later, in 1902, that the story was finally published by Frederick Warne & Co, where it would go on to sell more than forty million copies.

THE GOLDFINCH

Donna Tartt

2013

"I was writing for a while not knowing what I was writing," said Tartt in reference to notes that she had been taking since 1993. "That's the way it's been with all my books. Things will come to you and you're not going to know exactly how they fit in. You have to trust in the way they all fit together, that your subconscious knows what you're doing."

What she was doing was writing some of the earliest pages of *The Goldfinch*, a Pulitzer Prize–winning novel about a painting by the same name. The painting is known today for surviving the very fire that killed the man, Fabritius, who painted it. "He died young," said Tartt. "Insofar as we know him, he was revolutionary. He was Rembrandt's most famous pupil, the great painter of his day. If you look at *The Goldfinch*, it's that quality of daylight. It's Rembrandt's technique, but not that golden, lit-from-within quality of Rembrandt. Fabritius used it to paint sunlight. Vermeer picked up on that. The quality of daylight that we love in Vermeer, he got from Fabritius. He was the link between Rembrandt and Vermeer. He was perfect to write about because he's so unknown that he's like something from Borges, this very famous painter who might exist and might not. So little is known about him, he's on the edge between fiction and nonfiction, legend and reality."

Once the idea to write *The Goldfinch* was in place, Tartt spent many mornings working in the New York Public Library, basing part of the story in the city and another in Amsterdam, a setting that she had always wanted to write into one of her novels. She added Las Vegas to the mix after taking a trip there during the early stages of the writing process. Nearly eight hundred pages later, she had a novel that explored, among other things, the art underworld. Says Tartt, "Rather than any specific story about art crime, I was more interested in a dark Amsterdam mood, a dark New York mood—and art seemed to be the tie between those two cities. As far as I remember, it wasn't really a conscious decision to take the art world as a subject but something that just seemed to spring organically from place. The destruction of the great Buddhas at Bamiyan was also something that bothered me greatly, and though I can't say how that affected my decision to write about crime in the context of art, I know that it did."

THE HOUSE ON MANGO STREET

Sandra Cisneros

___

1984

___

Published in 1984, *The House on Mango Street* focused on a Mexican-American family at a time when being American-Mexican was quite difficult. Racism toward people of Mexican descent was rampant, fueled in part by the United States government emphatically restricting illegal immigration and severely punishing employers who hired undocumented workers. The Mexican-American stereotype was being applied to everybody of such descent, without any consideration of decency or humanity. What resulted was, at the very least, a sense of discomfort felt by those affected.

When asked what the world was like when she created the novel's protagonist, Esperanza, Sandra Cisneros replied, "Well, I was fresh out of graduate school. I had started Esperanza in Iowa at the University of Iowa, feeling very displaced and uncomfortable as a person of color, as a woman, and as a person from a working-class background. And in reaction to being there I started *The House on Mango Street* almost as a way of claiming that this is who I am. It became my flag. And I realize now that I was creating something new. I was cross-pollinating fiction and poetry and writing something that was the child of both. I was crossing borders and I didn't know it."

Esperanza's fictional family is based largely on Cisneros' large one; in fact, she only downsized the fictional family because she was new to fiction and couldn't conceptualize writing and humanizing that many characters. Her use of the Cisneros family as inspiration for Esperanza's came despite the fact that her father didn't accept her being a writer until about two years before he died. He thought the practical path for success for a Mexican-American woman was to be a weather girl, mainly because it was the only visible success that Latinas had at the time.

Despite that lack of visible success in American media, Cisneros approached *The House on Mango Street* from a more personal perspective, saying, "I wanted to write something in a voice that was unique to who I was. And I wanted something that was accessible to the person who works at Dunkin Donuts or who drives a bus, someone who comes home with their feet hurting like my father, someone who's busy and has too many children, like my mother. I wanted this to be lyrical enough so that it would pass muster with my finicky classmates, but also be open to accept all of the people I loved in the neighborhood I came from."

THE HUMAN STAIN

Philip Roth

———

2000

On September 6, 2012, *The New Yorker* published an open letter that Philip Roth had written in an attempt to clarify the real inspiration behind *The Human Stain*. The letter begins with "Dear Wikipedia" and goes on to state the fact that site administrators could not consider Roth a credible source, citing their requirement of secondary sources to validate an edit to an entry. He was, of course, trying to make an edit to the Wikipedia page for his own novel, but again: "We require secondary sources."

Hence the open letter, which claims that the original Wikipedia entry included the line "allegedly inspired by the life of the writer Anatole Broyard." Roth goes on to clarify the actual inspiration, writing, "This alleged allegation is in no way substantiated by fact. *The Human Stain* was inspired, rather, by an unhappy event in the life of my late friend Melvin Tumin, professor of sociology at Princeton for some thirty years. One day in the fall of 1985, while Mel, who was meticulous in all things large and small, was meticulously taking the roll in a sociology class, he noted that two of his students had as yet not attended a single class session or attempted to meet with him to explain their failure to appear, though it was by then the middle of the semester. Having finished taking the roll, Mel queried the class about these two students whom he had never met. 'Does anyone know these people? Do they exist or are they spooks?'—unfortunately, the very words that Coleman Silk, the protagonist of *The Human Stain*, asks of his classics class at Athena College in Massachusetts. Almost immediately Mel was summoned by university authorities to justify his use of the word 'spooks,' since the two missing students, as it happened, were both African-American, and 'spooks' at one time in America was a pejorative designation for blacks, spoken venom milder than 'nigger' but intentionally degrading nonetheless. A witch hunt ensued during the following months from which Professor Tumin—rather like Professor Silk in *The Human Stain*—emerged blameless but only after he had to provide a number of lengthy depositions declaring himself innocent of the charge of hate speech."

THE HUNGER GAMES

Suzanne Collins

———

2008

When asked what inspired her to write *The Hunger Games*, Suzanne Collins responded, "One night, I was lying in bed, and I was channel surfing between reality TV programs and actual war coverage. On one channel, there's a group of young people competing for I don't even know; and on the next, there's a group of young people fighting in an actual war. I was really tired, and the lines between these stories started to blur in a very unsettling way. That's the moment when Katniss' story came to me."

The wartime aspect really resonated with Collins because of her father's service in the Vietnam War. "He was gone for a year," she said. "Even though my mom tried to protect us—I'm the youngest of four—sometimes the

TV would be on, and I would see footage from the war zone. I was little, but I would hear them say 'Vietnam,' and I knew my dad was there, and it was frightening. I'm sure that a lot of people today experience that same thing. But there is so much programming, and I worry that we're all getting a little desensitized to the images on our televisions. If you're watching a sitcom, that's fine. But if there's a real-life tragedy unfolding, you should not be thinking of yourself as an audience member. Because those are real people on the screen, and they're not going away when the commercials start to roll."

While the novel's foundation is based in historical reality, it is substantiated by an affinity for mythology. "It's very much based on the myth of Theseus and the Minotaur, which I read when I was eight years old. I was a huge fan of Greek and Roman mythology. As punishment for displeasing Crete, Athens periodically had to send seven youths and seven maidens to Crete, where they were thrown into the labyrinth and devoured by the Minotaur, which is a monster that's half man and half bull. Even when I was a little kid, the story took my breath away, because it was so cruel, and Crete was so ruthless. The message is, mess with us and we'll do something worse than kill you—we'll kill your children. And the parents sat by apparently powerless to stop it. The cycle doesn't end until Theseus volunteers to go, and he kills the Minotaur. In her own way, Katniss is a futuristic Theseus. But I didn't want to do a labyrinth story. So I decided to write basically an updated version of the Roman gladiator games."

THE OLD MAN AND THE SEA

Ernest Hemingway

1952

The idea that Ernest Hemingway had anything left to prove when he wrote *The Old Man and the Sea* in 1952 defies even the most basic logic, but it was that mentality that inspired him to prove that his best work wasn't behind him. It had been more than a decade since he published a novel to critical acclaim, and the narrative, at least as it pertains to the critics of the time, was that Hemingway could no longer produce work representative of his position among the literary greats.

Living in Havana, Cuba, during some of the 1930s and 1940s provided Hemingway with a unique perspective, from which he could observe the events that defined the ever-changing world. While dominant aspects of the forties and early fifties, like the rising tensions between the United States and the Soviet Union, are absent from the book, the rise of consumerism did serve to shape its plot. Fishing in Cuba was transitioning from culture to industry, as young professionals began utilizing new technology to ensure maximum profits. The act became much more individualistic while simultaneously becoming much less personal; no longer could an area and its people be defined by fishing while achieving success relative to the modern world.

Santiago was an embodiment of time passed, a composite of places visited and people met. Fishing was his identity; without it, his struggles against mortality, loneliness and poverty become much more prevalent and, in all likelihood, fatal. While Hemingway denied that his protagonist had any relation to people in his life, a Cuban named Gregorio Fuentes likely inspired some aspects of the character. The captain of Hemingway's boat Pilar, Fuentes was from the Canary Islands and had served as a fisherman for most of his life. He served as Hemingway's companion for thirty years before the author took his own life in 1961. Fuentes lived to be 104, passing away while getting ready for church in the same house he lived in while serving as Hemingway's chef and captain.

THE SOUND AND THE FURY

William Faulkner

1929

Widely recognized as one of the most success-fully innovative novels in twentieth-century American literature, *The Sound and the Fury* concerns itself with a Southern identity crisis post–Civil War. The crumbling aristocracy and bleeding wealth that followed the war and Reconstruction made it nearly impossible for Southerners to live up to what they considered historical greatness. In other words, the very values by which past Southern patriarchs and generals lived were no longer practical by the early twentieth century. So why does William Faulkner consider the perspective of the failed offspring of the South as they relate to their ancestors?

Faulkner himself was in a unique position. He was born in Mississippi to a prominent Southern family that had a number of ancestors fight in several different wars and hold several high political positions. Meanwhile, Faulkner never even finished high school. He knew what it was like to be haunted by past success that was irreclaimable—to be considered a failure based not on your reality but rather the reality of your ancestors. Of course, Faulkner was able to buck that fate early on—more than a century later and we talk about his literary prowess before we do any of his ancestors. Still, having a rich family history loom over him provided him the perspective necessary to write *The Sound and the Fury*, a novel celebrated today.

ANGELS IN AMERICA

Tony Kushner

———

1991

"Around November of 1985, the first person that I knew personally died of AIDS," Tony Kushner recalls. "A dancer that I had a huge crush on, a very sweet man and very beautiful. I got an NEA directing fellowship at the repertory theater in St. Louis, and right before I left New York, I heard through the grapevine that he had gotten sick. And then, in November, he died. And I had this dream: Bill dying—I don't know if he was actually dying, but he was in his pajamas and sick on his bed—and the ceiling collapsed and this angel comes into the room. And then I wrote a poem. I'm not a poet, but I wrote this *thing*. It was many pages long. After I finished it, I put it away. No one will ever see it. Its title was *Angels in America.*"

Kushner was wrapping up his graduate studies at NYU, where he attended the Tisch School of Arts, when he began shifting his focus from directing to writing. He rented out a twenty-eight-seat theater to stage a play he wrote called *A Bright Room Called Day*, which Oskar Eustis, dramaturge of the Eureka Theatre in San Francisco, happened upon after just missing the curtain for the play he'd intended to see. The play resonated with Eustis, evidenced by his inviting Kushner out West so that they could stage his work at the Eureka. After the West Coast showing went well, Oskar asked Kushner if he would be interested in doing a play on commission. Kushner was interested, and he wanted to call it *Angels in America.*

The result was a Pulitzer Prize–winning, seven-hour screenplay that had to be divided into two parts: *Millennium Approaches* and *Perestroika.* The original outline was designed for a two-hour play with an intermission in the middle, but in Kushner's own words, "The characters kept doing things they weren't supposed to. The problem with outlining is that you don't actually know yet who these people are. You learn who they are by writing about them." Those characters deal with major issues that defined the eighties, like Reaganism, homophobia, race, spirituality and the AIDS epidemic. The point, however, wasn't to make any kind of sweeping political statement; rather, it was meant to depict life for a homosexual man during the late twentieth century. "I set out to write about what it was like to be me," says Kushner, "a gay man in New York, in the mid-1980s, and it was not possible to do that without placing it in the middle of the epidemic. It also seemed like there was a huge shift in the political climate with President Reagan. The world I was born into was receding and something new and rather terrifying was taking its place."

ATONEMENT

Ian McEwan

———

2001

Responding to allegations of plagiarism in *Atonement*, Ian McEwan made clear where his inspiration for the book came in a 2006 essay he penned for *The Guardian*. He writes, " 'Stop me if I've told you this before,' was a sentence my father never uttered. He needed to relive his experiences, especially in the last year of his life. Perhaps after a sedentary postwar office job in the army, he sensed that the Dunkirk episode and his slow recovery from it was the most intense period of his life, the time when he felt most truly alive. When I came to write *Atonement*, my father's stories, with automatic ease, dictated the structure; after I finished the opening section, set in 1935, Dunkirk would have to be followed by the reconstruction of a 1940 London hospital. It is an eerie, intrusive matter, inserting imaginary characters into actual historical events. A certain freedom is suddenly compromised; as one crosses and re-crosses the lines between fantasy and the historical record, one feels a weighty obligation to strict accuracy. In writing about wartime especially, it seems like a form of respect for the suffering of a generation wrenched from their ordinary lives to be conscripted into a nightmare."

The claims came from a British paper called *Mail on Sunday*, which pointed to several phrases in the novel that looked as though they were taken out of the memoir of a wartime nurse. Those phrases were dug up as a result of countless hours spent researching the Nightingale nurses based at St. Thomas' in London, of whom there is very little information. "When all these elements are sixty years in the past," McEwan writes, "the quest for truth becomes all the more difficult and important." Bits of information began popping up—an occasional letter to or from home, the nuances of their daily routines, accounts of training sessions with the training doll named "George"—but everything ceased once the cases from Dunkirk began arriving at the hospital.

The breakthrough came when McEwan found *No Time for Romance*, the memoir of Lucilla Andrews that the British publication references in its accusation. The evacuation and treatment of the wounded from Dunkirk was recounted with what appeared to be extraordinary accuracy; to his surprise, Andrews describes a scene of somebody being yelled at for swearing that is eerily similar to the same account that his father would give when talking about his experiences there. McEwan writes, "What Andrews described was not an imaginary world—it was not a fiction. It was the world of a shared reality, of those War Museum letters and of my father's prolonged hospital stay. Within the pages of a conventional life story, she created an important and unique historical document. With painstaking accuracy, so it seemed to me, she rendered in the form of superb reportage, an experience of the war that has been almost entirely neglected, and which I too wanted to bring to life through the eyes of my heroine. As with the Dunkirk section, I drew on the scenes she described. Again, it was important to me that these events actually occurred. For certain long-outdated medical practices, she was my sole source and I have always been grateful to her. I have openly acknowledged my debt to her in the author's note at the end of *Atonement*, and ever since on public platforms, where questions about research are almost as frequent as 'where do you get your ideas from?' I have spoken about her in numerous interviews and in a Radio 4 tribute. My one regret is not meeting her. But if people are now talking about Lucilla Andrews, I am glad. I have been talking about her for five years."

BIRDSONG

Sebastian Faulks

1993

Writes Sebastian Faulks, "It was difficult to be precise about what I thought was missing, but in rough terms I think it was this: a full appreciation of the soldiers' physical experience; and, perhaps more importantly, a philosophical understanding of what it meant to be part of the first genocidal event of the century—the one that made the others imaginable." The years immediately following World War I were weighted by the trauma of ten million men dead; literature concerning the event was often of the autobiographical nature, the most reputable of which started popping up in the mid-1930s. The following decade saw a war the scale of which changed the face of wartime literature forever, and people began to forget about the war that had preceded it. "Within a few years of 1945," Faulks writes, "a considerable new war literature had sprung up, much of it concerned with flying and escaping from prisoner-of-war camps. Most of it was heroic in tone, as befitted a war in which the moral cause had been so much clearer . . . In the 1950s and 1960s, while cinema screens hummed with Spitfires, artistic interest in the First World War continued to dwindle."

The underrepresentation of World War I veterans in literature and film was made real for Faulks during a trip he took in 1988, accompanying a half dozen soldiers in their nineties to Flanders, a region of Belgium that saw some of the worst that the war had to offer. "Standing with these men in the mud at Aubers Ridge—the same mud from which they had collected the body parts of their friends in 1915—and holding their hands as they spoke about it, gave me a sense of connection and helped bring the war out of the 'Oh, What A Lovely . . . ' world and back to reality." That reality came to Faulks again in 2009, when the last living veteran of the war was buried with great ceremony and pageantry. Harry Patch, the deceased, served in that war for three months and hated everything that it stood for. And yet here was his burial being treated as though his service was that of a high-ranking military lifer. A "bad conscience," Faulks thought, "like a country belatedly waking up to the fact that for ninety years it had failed to extend to a generation of men the curiosity and care that had been their due."

Faulks respected those who served by keeping his research as authentic and relevant as possible, using only primary sources to substantiate his novel. After all, the book was "an attempt to offer a belated gesture of love and understanding to the men who were hurled into that catastrophic war."

CARRIE

Stephen King

——

1974

In his book *On Writing: A Memoir of the Craft*, King writes, "While he was going to college my brother Dave worked summers as a janitor at Brunswick High. For part of one summer I worked there, too. One day I was supposed to scrub the rust-stains off the walls in the girls' shower. I noticed that the showers, unlike those in the boys' locker room, had chrome U-rings with pink plastic curtains attached. This memory came back to me one day while I was working in the laundry, and I started seeing the opening scene of a story: girls showering in a locker room where there were no U-rings, pink plastic curtains or privacy. And this one girl starts to have her period. Only she doesn't know what it is, and the other girls—grossed out, horrified, amused—start pelting her with sanitary napkins . . . The girl begins to scream. All that blood! I'd read an article in *LIFE* magazine some years before, suggesting that at least some reported poltergeist activity might actually be telekinetic phenomena—telekinesis being the ability to move objects just by thinking about them. There was some evidence to suggest that young people might have such powers, the article said, especially girls in early adolescence, right around the time of their first—POW! Two unrelated ideas, adolescent cruelty and telekinesis, came together, and I had an idea."

Carrie was King's first published novel and remains one of his most famous to this day. Released in 1974, the novel's protagonist was inspired by two girls that he had known prior to their passing away; one was bullied in elementary school because she wore the same clothes to class every day, while the other came from a very religious family. He began forming the character and writing the story, only to trash the project after getting only a few pages in. He oversaw it through to the end only because his wife had pulled the pages from the wastebasket, read them, and wanted to know the rest of the story.

GOODNIGHT MOON

Margaret Brown

———

1947

Margaret Brown's ability to write from a child's perspective offered her unique opportunities to put her writing to use, though it wasn't one that she particularly cared for. "I hope to write something serious one day as soon as I have something to say," she said. "But I am stuck in my childhood, and that raises the devil when one wants to move on." Brown, who never married or had any children, grew up in a wealthy household with two parents whose busy lifestyles left little time for their children. Sustained by her desire to become a great novelist, Brown submitted several works to publishers to no avail. Pressured by her parents to start paying rent, she began to contribute to the textbooks for the school that she was working at. Her mentality was based in the idea that children connect more to what goes on in their world than they do the unknown. In other words, relatability was key. The idea for *Goodnight Moon* came to her in a dream, in which she remembered her ritual of saying goodnight to all of the items in her nursery as a little girl.

GREEN EGGS AND HAM

Dr. Seuss

1960

Described as having "limited vocabulary but unlimited exuberance of illustration" in a review by the *School Library Journal*, *Green Eggs and Ham* was the result of a bet between Dr. Seuss and his editor. He had just written *The Cat in the Hat*, a book that used 225 words, and was challenged by his editor to write one that was made up of only 50 or less. Seuss won the bet, turning his manuscript for *Green Eggs and Ham* in with a word count of exactly 50.

HOLES

Louis Sachar

1998

"I never start with a full idea of what I'm going to write," says Louis Sachar. "I usually just start with a piece of a character and then see what develops. In this case, I didn't start with a character; I started writing about Camp Greenlake and it developed from there. I suppose the initial inspiration for writing about the camp came from the heat of summers in Texas. At the time I began the book, we had just returned from the relative coolness of a vacation in Maine to the Texas summer. Anybody who has ever tried to do yard work in Texas in July can easily imagine Hell to be a place where you are required to dig a hole five feet deep and five feet across day after day under the brutal Texas sun."

INHERIT THE WIND

Jerome Lawrence and Robert Edwin Lee

———

1955

While still very much a work of fiction, Jerome Lawrence and Robert Edwin Lee's play *Inherit the Wind* traces its roots to a trial from 1925. The Scopes "Monkey" Trial was held in response to John T. Scopes teaching Darwin's theory of evolution to a high school science class, then a violation of Tennessee state law. The title itself comes from Proverbs 11:29 in the Bible, which reads, "He that troubleth his own house shall inherit the wind and the fool shall be servant to the wise of the heart," a passage that is actually read at the beginning of act 2. Of course, the play itself is fictional, as noted by the playwrights at the start of the play. The concept of creationism versus evolution was meant to speak to the realities of the United States in 1955; that is, the condemnation of communism and the rise of McCarthyism. In a 1996 interview for *Newsday*, Lawrence said, "We used the teaching of evolution as a parable, a metaphor for any kind of mind control. It's not about science or religion. It's about the right to think."

INVISIBLE CITIES

Italo Calvino

———

1972

Framed as a conversation between an older Kublai Khan and the explorer Marco Polo regarding the vastness of Khan's Mongol empire, *Invisible Cities* includes descriptions of fifty-five different cities that Polo claims to have explored. The descriptions are imaginative and fantastical; rather than try to map out the areas themselves, they focus on the major distinguishing factors of each place. The style of each chapter is somewhat similar to those of *The Travels of Marco Polo*, the work that inspired Italo Calvino's work. In *Travels*, Marco Polo describes the cities that he visited while journeying across Asia during the reign of the Mongol Empire. The authenticity of his travelogue is the source of much debate, though most people agree that the work contains much exaggeration.

JANE EYRE

Charlotte Brontë

1847

"I had never seen before—in this state of things having the charge given me of a set of pampered, spoilt, and turbulent children, whom I was expected constantly to amuse as well as to instruct. I soon found that the constant demand on my stock of animal spirits reduced them to the lowest state of exhaustion; at times I felt and I suppose seemed depressed." That brief passage is an excerpt from a letter Charlotte Brontë sent to friend Ellen Nussey while serving as a governess to the wealthy Sidgwick family. Unsurprisingly, Jane Eyre's hiring as a governess was based primarily on Bronte's own experiences—a running theme throughout the book.

The earliest of Brontë's life experiences seen in *Jane Eyre* is that of her two sisters, Elizabeth and Maria Brontë, who died from tuberculosis due to the poor conditions of their boarding school. Aside from naming two characters after her sisters, Brontë draws from this experience in writing Helen Burns' death from consumption— similarly related to the harsh conditions of a boarding school. To further the connection,

Brontë based the headmaster, Mr. Brocklehurst, on an evangelical minister named William Carus Wilson who ran the school the Brontës attended.

Charlotte's brother, Bramwell, also has a place in the book, as his decline into a fatal alcohol and opium addiction inspired the character John Reed, who also suffers from alcohol addiction. The love dynamic in *Jane Eyre*—that is, Jane falling in love with somebody who she later finds out is married—is based on both experiences had by both Brontë's brother and by Brontë herself. Her brother was guilty of having relations with a married woman, while Charlotte fell in love with a married professor named Constantin Heger.

The concept of a woman being kept captive was also close to Brontë. On a trip to North Yorkshire in 1839, Brontë visited Norton Conyers House, where she heard tell that a mentally ill woman was once held captive in the attic of the house—dubbed "Mad Mary's Room." The experiences of the woman inspired the fate of Bertha Mason, also kept in captivity due to the belief that she was mentally ill.

LITTLE WOMEN

Louisa Alcott

1868

Though it was an immediate success both commercially and critically, Louisa Alcott had no intention of writing *Little Women* despite multiple requests from her publisher that she do so. Feeling that they were an underserved audience, publisher Thomas Niles wanted to appeal to women with a book about women. When Alcott denied his request, saying that she wanted to continue writing short stories, Niles offered to publish her father, a renowned thinker who hadn't had much publishing success. Alcott ceded and sent Niles a dozen chapters a month later. While they both felt it lacked flavor and substance, all of the girls from whom they asked for feedback expressed interest in the story—and wanted more. It took Alcott just ten weeks to write the novel from start to finish, during which time she used her own life to inspire those of her characters.

The four sisters were all based on members of Alcott's family: she based Jo on herself; Beth was based on her sister Lizzie, who also contracted scarlet fever from an impoverished family; Meg was based on her sister Anna, whose wedding was similar to the one depicted in the novel and Amy was based on her sister May, an artist who was living in Europe. Their financial situation was similar as well, as Alcott's father refused to stray from his socialist ideology by taking wages, often leaving them without much food to eat. That reality is what led Alcott to start a career in writing, which took off after *Little Women* was published.

OUR LADY
OF THE FLOWERS

Jean Genet

———

1943

Put up for adoption at just seven months old, Jean Genet found himself staying with two different foster families at different points of his childhood. The second family enabled Genet's petty theft at a young age, leading him to embrace vagrancy and other misdemeanor acts. These acts landed Genet in the Mettray Penal Colony at just fifteen years old. After his release, he briefly served in the French Foreign Legion; from there he received a dishonorable discharge for engaging in a homosexual act, and immediately returned to a life of thievery while also working as a prostitute.

Genet was in and out of prison from that point forward, culminating with a life sentence that saw him lucky to avoid the death penalty. Jean Cocteau, Pablo Picasso and Jean-Paul Sartre, among others, had to petition then French president Vincent Auriol to suspend the sentence because they were so impressed with a novel that he had penned in prison, titled *Our Lady of the Flowers*. Originally written on brown sheets of paper meant for making bags, his manuscript was confiscated and burned by prison security. Genet was able to re-create the manuscript fairly easily, as most of it was taken from real life experiences. The book is even narrated from the perspective of somebody who is passing the time in prison, offering sexual tales in explicit detail as a way to aid his masturbation. Most of the characters were inspired by people Genet had encountered during his criminal years—societal outcasts, often homosexual, who possessed high sex drives. It is with these outcasts that Genet reevaluates society's morals, flipping them so that betrayal is virtuous and murder is sexual. As a result, the novel became a massive influence on the Beat generation, detailing sexual freedoms and self-reflexive language that generations of writers would come to embrace.

STORMBREAKER

Anthony Horowitz

———

2000

"When I was growing up, the James Bond films were a *very big* part of my life," said Anthony Horowitz when asked what inspired *Stormbreaker*. "I loved them passionately. And they had a very big impact on me. Alex Rider came about because, later in life, I began to feel that the Bond films had lost their magic. They didn't appeal to me anymore. And I think one of the reasons was that Bond *was just too old*. And that led me to wonder if it would be possible to reinvent those early films as seen through a fourteen-year-old. In other words, to go back to myself as a fourteen-year-old, seeing those films, and start again. And that was the inspiration."

THE DAY OF THE JACKAL

Frederick Forsyth

1971

Having spent three years of his life covering the Biafran war in West Africa as a freelance journalist, Frederick Forsyth thought it wise to compile all that he had seen in a book once he returned home to France. *The Biafra Story: The Making of an African Legend* was published in 1969 and sold terribly, leaving him unemployed and broke.

"I'm slightly mercenary: I write for the money," Forsyth said in an interview from 2010. "I feel no compulsion to write. If somebody said 'You're not going to write another word of fiction as long as you live' it wouldn't matter a damn." What was originally supposed to be a "one-off" meant to "clear his debts" would become *The Day of the Jackal*, a political thriller that spawned a series of thrillers for which Forsyth is now famous. The success of *Jackal* can, in part, be attributed to his investigative background; he would often hang out with French President Charles de Gaulle's bodyguards and was even able to report from the scene of his attempted assassination.

THE GIFT OF THE MAGI

O. Henry

1905

Seated alone at Pete's Tavern in New York City, William Porter, better known as O. Henry, wrote furiously over the span of a few hours in order to meet a tight deadline for his editor at the *New York Sunday World Magazine*. Though he was already a very famous writer, the resulting work would endure as one of the greatest love stories of all time.

While the ironic twist at the end of *The Gift of the Magi* was consistent with Henry's writing style, the love story was likely inspired by his own life; he was fiercely dedicated to his wife, Athol, whom he married while young and poor. Henry lost his job as a banker when he was accused of embezzlement and, a day before he was to stand trial, fled to Honduras. Free from United States extradition, Henry made plans to have Athol join him after a brief stay with her family in Texas, but she came down with tuberculosis and couldn't make the trip. Henry travelled back to the U.S. to see her, knowing that it would mean facing the law and likely going to prison. He was able to be with her until she passed before going to prison for three years.

THE LAST UNICORN

Peter S. Beagle

———

1968

After a 2014 screening of the movie his book inspired, Peter S. Beagle was asked what motivated his writing *The Last Unicorn*. He responded, "People always ask me about inspiration, and I always explain that it's never about inspiration, but always about desperation. As I said, I don't plan things. That particular summer I spent in a cabin in Massachusetts, with one of my three oldest friends . . . Phil was always the painter, just as I was always the writer. He had a lot of paintings that he wanted to get to, and I had published one book already and recently had another turned down, so I had some loose ends. I didn't know what I was going to be doing. So we drove up to Cheshire, Massachusetts on our motor scooters, and Phil would go out every day on his scooter to a particular spot, where he was working on an enormous landscape painting. The canvas was literally almost bigger than he was. And then there was me, in the cabin, not knowing what the hell I was going to be doing. Phil kept coming back with more paint on the canvas, and I wanted to have some pages to show him. After a couple of false starts, I started with the line 'The unicorn lived in a lilac wood, she lived all alone.' Ok, so now what? It was now what all the rest of the way. But I did manage to have pages written by the time Phil came back with more work on the canvas. We talked about that a few years ago . . . he told me 'I hated that damn landscape. I would've quit within a week, but you were back at the cabin writing this book.' So that's really how it happened; nothing to do with inspiration, everything to do with showing off."

THE FELLOWSHIP OF THE RING

J. R. R. Tolkien

———

1954

The most obvious and overarching inspiration for Tolkien's *The Fellowship of the Ring* came from the teachings of Catholicism, as he himself described the book as "a fundamentally religious and Catholic work, unconsciously so at first, but consciously in the revision." The battle of good versus evil, resurrection, self-sacrifice, salvation, mercy and death are all obvious evidence of Tolkien's claim, as are less obvious details like the setting being a monotheistic world under God the creator.

Tolkien drew particular inspiration from Nordic sources, particularly the literature he read while studying at King Edward's School in Birmingham. Tolkien's elves and dwarves were derived from the *Prose Edda* and the *Elder of Poetic Edda*, which actually gave Tolkien the idea that dwarves pre-dated the creation of man. *The Volsunga Saga* inspired the idea of the One Ring of Power, and Gandalf was influenced by Odin, a wandering Norse deity who promoted insight and justice. Finally, the collapse of the Bridge of Khazad-dûm and the fall of the Balrog in Moria can be traced to the Norse myth of the destruction of Asgard's bridge, and the demise of the fire giant Surt.

Tolkien also informed his writing with Old and Middle English literature, drawing particular inspiration from *Beowulf*. Aragorn channels much of Beowulf's character—both are concerned with the good of their people to the point of taking kingship for their sake only, both are accomplished fighters and both have a cloudy lineage. Tolkien also draws on *Pearl*, a Middle English poem in which the author describes the loss of his daughter. The poem's most notable influence? Referring to a loved one as "My Precious."

THE STRANGER

Albert Camus

1942

The year was 1942: Allied forces defeated the Japanese army at Midway, Britain brought the war to Germany for the first time and Albert Camus channeled a mentality shaped by the war into his premiere novel, *The Stranger*. The work focuses on Meursault, a character introduced just as he learns of his mother's passing. No grief or sorrow is displayed; in fact, he demonstrates little human emotion at all. He is eventually arrested for murder and, upon showing no remorse during his trial, is sentenced to public execution by guillotine. He rejects the opportunity to embrace God, realizes that his life has little meaning in the grand scheme of it all and accepts his fate.

Meursault's inability to feel remorse, and his idea that everything is meaningless, is representative of a popular philosophy shared by many intellects at the time of publishing—known today as the Absurdist movement. World War II left a lot of people feeling as though life had no meaning, as the Nazi regime tore through Europe and slaughtered millions of innocent people. The idea that something like this could be part of a plan was too implausible for a lot of people, including Camus. He began subscribing to the idea that life was meaningless and purposeless, guided by nothing except for our own actions. Meursault's indifference to the human condition embodies that concept.

THE WONDERFUL WIZARD OF OZ
Frank Baum

1900

In the words of L. Frank Baum, "[*The Wonderful Wizard of Oz*] aspires to being a modernized fairy tale, in which the wonderment and joy are retained and the heartaches and nightmares are left out." And while the goal of the novel was to appeal to children without eliciting nightmares, certain aspects of the book were inspired by the very nightmares that Baum had as a child. The Scarecrow was one such example, as his original iteration chased poor young Baum across a field while he slept, falling apart just before choking the author-to-be. The character resonated to the point where a much gentler version was integrated as one of the book's four central characters.

The Tin Woodman, on the other hand, had much less sinister origins: Baum's decision to contribute to a [department] store window display. Often captivated and inspired by the scenes he'd see behind glass, Baum successfully put together a figure that closely resembles the Tin Woodman from the book, funnel hat and all. Uncle Henry was based on his "passive but hard-working" father-in-law, the witches were inspired by the research of his witch-hunting mother-in-law and Dorothy's namesake was his wife's niece, who passed away as an infant.

Baum's disillusionment with Western culture inspired Emerald City, as both were preceded by baseless claims of infinite riches. However, there are no definitive answers regarding what inspired specific characteristics of the city, such as the castle or the yellow brick road. Some say that the castle was inspired by a building in Holland, Michigan, where he lived during the summers. Similarly, many believe that the yellow brick road was inspired by a road paved with yellow bricks in Peekskill, New York, where he attended a military academy. Australia is thought to be a possible source of inspiration as well, a fascinating and new area at the time of this book's publication. One certainty is that the name Oz came from the "O-Z" drawer on Baum's filing cabinet, as the author said so himself in an interview with *Publishers Weekly*.

For all of its whimsy, Baum wanted his book to be grounded and relatable—something that he learned to value while reading Lewis Carroll's *Alice's Adventures in Wonderland*. Though concerned that it might be hard for children to insert themselves into the story, Baum hoped that seeing a protagonist who looks like them would make it a bit easier. He incorporates real locations, like Kansas, for the same reason. He believed that a book's fantasy aspects become enhanced if viewed in a real-world context.

WALDEN

Henry David Thoreau

1854

"I went to the woods because I wished to live deliberately," said Thoreau about his inspiration to live the life depicted in *Walden*. "To front only the essential facts of life, and see if I could not learn what it had to teach, and not, when I came to die, discover that I had not lived. I did not wish to live what was not life, living is so dear; nor did I wish to practice resignation, unless it was quite necessary. I wanted to live deep and suck out all the marrow of life, to live so sturdily and Spartan-like as to put to rout all that was not life, to cut a broad swath and shave close, to drive life into a corner, and reduce it to its lowest terms, and, if it proved to be mean, why then to get the whole and genuine meanness of it, and publish its meanness to the world; or if it were sublime, to know it by experience, and be able to give a true account of it in my next excursion."

WHERE THE WILD THINGS ARE

Maurice Sendak

———

1963

Maurice Sendak was set to begin his second book when he realized, to his dismay, that he did not possess the ability to properly illustrate a horse. As a consequence, he decided that the title, "Land of Wild Horses," would no longer work, and changed it to "Wild Things"—an idea from his editor based on the Yiddish expression "vilde chaya," meaning "boisterous children." The book eventually became *Where the Wild Things Are* and featured caricatures of his relatives in place of the horses.

Sendak was born to a Jewish family that had emigrated from Poland to Brooklyn before Nazi forces invaded eastern Europe. He grew up detesting the weekly visits that his relatives paid him, so much so that he drew their caricatures as a way to pass the time whenever they were by. These caricatures would come to make up the beasts in his famous book. "They would lean over you with their foul breath," he said, "and squeeze you and pinch you, and their eyes are blood-stained and their teeth are big and yellow. Ahh! It was horrible, horrible."

THE WORLD ACCORDING TO GARP

John Irving

———

1978

The World According to Garp, a bestseller for several years after it was published, owes its conception to an ultimatum that John Irving gave his mother years earlier. Born out of wedlock, he was raised by a single mother and never knew who his biological father was. He was so desperate for any information about him that he made his mom an offer: either offer him some information regarding his biological father, or risk having him take creative liberties while depicting the situation in a book. His mother, rather indifferent to the whole idea, responded with, "go ahead, my dear."

A SEASON IN HELL

Arthur Rimbaud

———

1873

A Season in Hell came out in1873, the last year in which Arthur Rimbaud published any poetry. A key influencer of the eventual surrealist movement, his nine-part poem is presented to the reader as two different sides of one man's personality. He wrote the poem during an eventful time in his life, as he engaged in a homosexual relationship with poet Paul Verlaine that ended with Verlaine shooting Rimbaud with a revolver and getting incarcerated for two years. Though Rimbaud himself never said it, it is commonly believed that the relationship influenced some of his writing, particularly in regard to the two characters introduced in "Delirium 1: The Foolish Virgin." While that relationship may have helped substantiate his work in the short term, it went a long way toward crippling his career; *A Season in Hell* received little commercial success due to Rimbaud's sexual orientation, leading him to burn the manuscript and never write poetry again.

CATCH-22

Joseph Heller

———

1961

The origins of *Catch-22*, perhaps the greatest anti-war book of the twentieth century, can be traced back to a time when the literary world was desperate for something new to break up its staleness. So much so, in fact, that it took clashing mentalities between two of Joseph Heller's friends for him to not quit writing altogether. A British journalist quoted Heller as saying, "Conversations with two friends inspired me. Each of them had been wounded in the war, one of them very seriously. The first one told some very funny stories about his war experiences, but the second one was unable to understand how any humour could be associated with the horror of war. They didn't know each other and I tried to explain the first one's point of view to the second. He recognized that traditionally there had been lots of graveyard humor, but he could not reconcile it with what he had seen of war. It was after that discussion that the opening of *Catch-22* and many incidents came to me."

On the imaginative process that went into his writing, Heller stated, "I feel that these ideas are floating around in the air and they pick me to settle upon. The ideas come to me; I don't produce them at will. They come to me in the course of a sort of controlled daydream, a directed reverie. It may have something to do with the disciplines of writing advertising copy (which I did for a number of years), where the limitations involved provide a considerable spur to the imagination. There's an essay of T. S. Eliot's in which he praises the disciplines of writing, claiming that if one is forced to write within a certain framework, the imagination is taxed to its utmost and will produce its richest ideas. Given total freedom, however, the chances are good that the work will sprawl."

So describes the moment Heller conceived the opening line for *Catch-22*, after which many key aspects of the book became clear to him. "I didn't have the name Yossarian. The chaplain wasn't necessarily an army chaplain—he could have been a prison chaplain. But as soon as the opening sentence was available, the book began to evolve clearly in my mind—even most of the particulars . . . the tone, the form, many of the characters, including some I eventually couldn't use. All of this took place within an hour and a half. It got me so excited that I did what the cliché says you're supposed to do: I jumped out of bed and paced the floor. That morning I went to my job at the advertising agency and wrote out the first chapter in longhand. Before the end of the week I had typed it out and sent it to Candida Donadio, my agent. One year later, after much planning, I began chapter two."

THE HITCHHIKER'S GUIDE TO THE GALAXY

Douglas Adams

1981

"I got frantically depressed in Innsbruck," wrote Douglas Adams in a letter to Ken Welsh, the author of *Hitch-hiker's Guide to Europe*. "When the stars came out I thought that someone ought to write a *Hitchhiker's Guide to the Galaxy* because it looked a lot more attractive out there than it did around me." The idea came to him while drunkenly laying in a field in Innsbruck, taking time out of his hitchhiking trip around Europe to stargaze.

The genesis of the novel can be traced back to 1978, seven years after Adams' trip to Innsbruck, when the BBC played a radio show called *The Ends of the Earth*. The concept was simple: An alien explores earth for the purposes of writing a book, titled *The Hitchhikers Guide to the Galaxy*. Each episode ended with a unique destruction of the planet, a unifying occurrence in otherwise self-contained episodes. Publishers took notice and expressed interest in turning the series into a book, a notion that the BBC initially dismissed, writing, "In our experience, books and records of radio shows don't sell." They eventually ceded, and *The Hitchhikers Guide to the Galaxy* as it is known today was born.

Adams also integrated some inside humor in his writing, most notably by making the towel a staple in the hitchhiker's inventory. Regarding a vacation that he took to Greece with his friends, he wrote, "Every morning they'd have to sit around and wait for me because I couldn't find my blessed towel . . . I came to feel that someone really together, one who was well organized, would always know where his towel was."

PORTNOY'S COMPLAINT

Philip Roth

———

1969

Prior to its off-Broadway debut, the revue *Oh! Calcutta!* was meant to include a slideshow accompanied by a satirical monologue written by Philip Roth. The slideshow got scrapped before opening, but Roth didn't scrap his contribution; instead, he extracted a bit about masturbation and started to build a novel around it. He packaged a chapter under the name *Whacking Off* and sold it to the *Partisan Review*, for whom he would write the remainder of the novel. Progress was slow at first, as Roth's knowledge that his ex-wife would receive half of the book's royalties gave him a case of writer's block. Her death in 1968 seemed to have cured him, as production of the novel, eventually titled *Portnoy's Complaint,* went smoothly from there on out.

THE POISONWOOD BIBLE

Barbara Kingsolver

1998

"This story came from a long-term fascination with politics and culpability," said Barbara Kingsolver, "and my belief that what happened to the Congo in 1961 is one of the most important political parables of a century. I'd thought about this story for a very long time, ever since the early '80s when I read Jonathan Kwitny's *Endless Enemies*, a stunning non-fiction account of that piece of history. Here's how I framed the question, to myself: nearly every industrialized country has arrived at its present prosperity by doing awful things, extracting wealth from some unfortunate locale, whether in the form of tea or diamonds, cheap labor, or even human slaves. Most of us alive today didn't participate in those decisions, but we do benefit materially from this history. How do we think about that, if at all? England has a strong tradition of postcolonial literature, but here in the U.S., we can hardly even say the word 'postcolonial.' We were a colony ourselves; we didn't have colonies, we're not like that. If you can overlook an agricultural economy originally built on slave labor, and the odd coup our CIA has organized here and there, to control economic interests in Chile's copper, Congo's cobalt, and so on. We still would really like to think of ourselves as the global good guys. Who wouldn't? Denial is one path to redemption, but it leaves certain holes, and the possibility of repeat offense. I'm keen to look at history, and study truth in all its facets. I think this is one of the ways novelists can earn our keep, morally speaking. So I decided to dive into the heart of darkness and write about paths to redemption. It's a large ambition. I waited many years to begin. I'd have waited a hundred, but realized I'd be dead before I was really wise enough to write this book, so I'd better give it a shot."

The undertaking for *The Poisonwood Bible* was enormous, as the novel's many components required comprehensive research. Kingsolver did research on the social and political atmosphere of Africa and the Congo in the mid-twentieth century, which included utilizing memoirs that detailed what missionary life was like there. That soon evolved into taking research trips to Western and Central Africa, where she hoped to get a feel for the cultural nuances that only firsthand research could yield. Wanting her American characters to be authentic as well, Kingsolver "purchased thirty pounds of *Life*, *Look* and *Saturday Evening Post* magazines from 1958–1961" that she used to learn the vernacular of the mid-twentieth-century U.S. teenager.

Kingsolver also drew from her own experience of living in a Congolese village as a child for a year. "My father worked for fifty years as a physician," she writes, "dedicated to medically underserved populations. Mostly he practiced in rural Kentucky, but occasionally he took our family to live in other places, where 'medically underserved' is an understatement. We spent 1963 in a Congolese village where most residents had never experienced electricity or plumbing, let alone western medical care. I was seven years old when we went. My parents were not missionaries, though we met some missionary families and benefited from their generosity on many occasions. My memories of playing with village children and exploring the jungle are acutely sensory and indelible. My parents were courageous to do the work they did, risking their own comfort and security to help address problems like leprosy and smallpox. But for me, it was just an adventure. I was a child, and understood only about a thimbleful of what was happening around me in the Congo. The thematic material of *The Poisonwood* is serious, adult stuff. I wrote the book, not because of a brief adventure I had in place of second grade, but because as an adult I'm interested in cultural imperialism and post-colonial history. I had to approach the subject in an adult way."

ARE YOU THERE GOD? IT'S ME, MARGARET

Judy Bloom

———

1970

A book she dedicated to her mother as thanks for introducing her to literature, Judy Bloom's *Are You There God? It's Me, Margaret* features a protagonist written in her own image. She writes, "For the first time since I'd started writing, I let go and this story came pouring out. I felt as if I'd always known Margaret. When I was in sixth grade, I longed to develop physically like my classmates. I tried doing exercises, resorted to stuffing my bra, and lied about getting my period. And like Margaret, I had a very personal relationship with God that had little to do with organized religion. God was my friend and confidant. But Margaret's family is very different from mine, and her story grew from my imagination. Margaret brought me my first and most loyal readers. I love her for that."

While the substance of the book was based on Bloom's personal experience, offering a clear path to its origins, its title was less thought out. Bloom simply decided to use the first line in the book: "Are you there God? It's me, Margaret."

THE METAMORPHOSIS

Franz Kafka

1915

"As Gregor Samsa awoke one morning from uneasy dreams he found himself transformed in his bed into a monstrous vermin." In what is considered one of the greatest opening lines in literary history, Franz Kafka took special care not to offer the reader much in the way of detail. He even forbade his publisher from putting an insect on the story's original cover! Why? Perhaps in keeping us from being able to fully visualize the monster, Kafka thought that he could keep our attention on the person who had transformed and away from what that person had transformed into.

A lot of *The Metamorphosis* was clearly inspired by Kafka and his family, specifically the relationship that he had with his father. A working-class shop keep, Kafka's father did not indulge in and was not particularly approving of the literature that his son would often retreat to while home. Abusive, strict and contradictory in his treatment of Franz, his impact on his son was lasting. In a published letter to his father, Kafka recalls an incident during which he, a young boy, cried for water until his father grew so irritated that he locked him outside on their balcony. Writes Kafka, "I was quite obedient afterwards at that period, but it did me inner harm. What was for me a matter of course, that senseless asking for water, and the extraordinary terror of being carried outside were two things that I, my nature being what it was, could never properly connect with each other. Even years afterwards I suffered from the tormenting fancy that the huge man, my father, the ultimate authority, would come almost for no reason at all and take me out of bed in the night and carry me onto the [balcony], and that meant I was a mere nothing to him."

Kafka's Gregor Samsa endures and represents a lot of what the author went through. His prolonged suffering at the hands of an abusive father, his initial fear of going outside and his general lack of confidence all invite the comparison between Kafka's life and the life of his protagonist. Even Samsa's prolonged death, which allows his family to feel the relief of freedom, rather than the shock caused by sudden death, is symbolic of the author's low self-esteem. That Samsa is thought of as a burden in death is the ultimate indicator that Kafka wrote a lot of his personality into his protagonist.

His being in a position to write the book at all was also the product of inspiration, though in a less direct way. He had returned from university in 1911 after his father had asked him to help a relative open a factory, an endeavor that took up much of his time and cost him his good health. As consequence, he battled with suicidal thoughts for a time after—until he met Felice Bauer in 1912 and quickly fell in love. The love letters he wrote to his future fiancée helped him to find his footing in writing again, allowing him to write *The Metamorphosis* in less than a month's time that same year.

PSYCHO

Robert Bloch

1959

A Milwaukee, Wisconsin, native, Robert Bloch drew from the story of one of the area's most notorious criminals in his transition from magazine contributor to serious novelist. The criminal, Ed Gein, partly inspired Norman Bates, the central character in *Psycho*. Of course, it's not a literal re-imagining of the character; Gein raided cemeteries upwards of forty times to harvest body parts that he would then fashion into paraphernalia, while Bates merely ("merely") dealt with a multiple personality disorder. Writes Bloch, "Thus the real-life murderer was not the role model for my character Norman Bates. Ed Gein didn't own or operate a motel. Ed Gein didn't kill anyone in the shower. Ed Gein wasn't into taxidermy. Ed Gein didn't stuff his mother, keep her body in the house, dress in a drag outfit, or adopt an alternative personality. These were the functions and characteristics of Norman Bates, and Norman Bates didn't exist until I made him up. Out of my own imagination, I add, which is probably the reason so few offer to take showers with me."

Originality aside, Bloch surely drew from Gein's relationship to his late mother. Bates would get drunk and dress as his mother, speaking to himself in her voice whenever he felt close to being found out, while Gein was literally crafting a suit out of a woman's skin so that he could "become his mother." The two also passed as normal people living normal lives in middle America until one murder led to their being found out.

Calvin Thomas Beck is also pointed to as a source of inspiration for Bates' character. Publisher of the magazine *Castle of Frankenstein*, he physically resembles Norman Bates and also has a close relationship with an overbearing mother who followed him everywhere. Said Noël Carter, wife of fantasy writer Linwood Carter, "Lin and I met at the end of 1962 and were married in '63, and I became very involved with science fiction and fantasy, and with all Lin's cronies. Among his cronies were Chris Steinbrunner from WOR-TV, a wonderful, dear friend, and an awful lot of people who had been around in the '50s. They were all older than I, and among the people in the group that sort of ebbed and flowed with time was Robert Bloch. And Bloch was fascinated by Calvin Thomas Beck. Calvin was also in that group, on the fringes of it, with his mother constantly in tow."

THE THIRTY-NINE STEPS

John Buchan

———

1915

While he was bedridden with a stomach ulcer, John Buchan penned *The Thirty-Nine Steps*, the novel from which he would gain the most fame. Buchan lived a long and diverse life; he worked as a lawyer, an editor, an administrator in various South African colonies, a writer of war propaganda for Britain during World War I and a correspondent in France for *The Times* before writing his masterpiece. Needless to say, he had plenty of experience to draw from—he'd even dabbled in writing adventure fiction previously, having written *Prester John* in 1910. That experience came in handy when creating Richard Hannay, the famous protagonist whom Buchan featured in many more novels afterwards. The character was based on his friend Edmund Ironside, a senior officer in the British Army who was commissioned to spy on German forces in South Africa, where he and Buchan met.

The novel's title was the product of a much more freak occurrence. Writes Buchan's son William on the nursing home where Buchan's ulcer was treated, "There was a wooden staircase leading down to the beach. My sister, who was about six, and who had just learnt to count properly, went down them and gleefully announced: there are thirty-nine steps."

The novel, while certainly his most famous, didn't immediately launch his career, as he enlisted in the British Army just after publishing its sequel, *Greenmantle*. No, Buchan would serve as a second lieutenant, a speechwriter, the Director of Information under Lord Beaverbrook and a publisher for a monthly war-centric magazine before producing the remainder of his work. In fact, his *The Thirty-Nine Steps* might not be the work for which he is best known, as he also served as the fifteenth Governor General of Canada from 1935 to 1940. Of course, anybody who loves Buchan for his thrillers has *The Thirty-Nine Steps* to thank for launching his novel-writing career.

THE WAY WE LIVE NOW

Anthony Trollope

1875

The decades-long stretch of financial instability brought on by the Panic of 1873 exposed much corruption and dishonesty in the ranks of economic leadership—especially in Western Europe. When Anthony Trollope returned from a trip abroad in the midst of the crisis, he was shocked at how much scandal surrounded the economic collapse, to the point where he decided to pen a response reflecting the new reality of the times. On why he wrote *The Way We Live Now*, Trollope writes, "Nevertheless a certain class of dishonesty, dishonesty magnificent in its proportions, and climbing into high places, has become at the same time so rampant and so splendid that there seems to be reason for fearing that men and women will be taught to feel that dishonesty, if it can become splendid, will cease to be abominable. If dishonesty can live in a gorgeous palace with pictures on all its walls, and gems in all its cupboards, with marble and ivory in all its corners, and can give Apician dinners, and get into Parliament, and deal in millions, then dishonesty is not disgraceful, and the man dishonest after such a fashion is not a low scoundrel. Instigated, I say, by some such reflections as these, I sat down in my new house to write *The Way We Live Now*."

1Q84

Haruki Murakami

———

2009

"My indignation against the incident remains undiminished," says Haruki Murakami. "But my interest was piqued by Yasuo Hayashi, who is on death row. He fled after killing eight people, the biggest number, in the Tokyo subway attack. Hayashi joined Aum without knowing exactly what he was getting into and committed murder after being brainwashed. I think capital punishment is the reasonable decision when we consider Japan's penalty system and bereaved families' anger and sorrow. But I fundamentally oppose capital punishment, and I felt a heavy sense of gloom when the death sentence was given. At that time I imagined the terror of being left alone on the other side of the moon where a Joe Blow unwittingly commits a felonious crime and ends up becoming a death row convict. I considered for years the meaning of this. This served as a starting point for my story." Murakami is speaking about a primary influence on *1Q84*, the terrorist attack in Tokyo subway in 1995. He had previously conducted interviews with a number of individuals who had survived the attack and published the results in *Underground*. Aum Shinrikyo, the doomsday cult responsible for the attacks, likely inspired the cult aspect of the book.

In revealing that he had "long wanted to write a near-past novel similar to George Orwell's futuristic novel *1984*," Murakami explains another heavy influence on *1Q84*. That reality becomes even more obvious when considering the fact that Q, in Japanese, is a homonym for the number nine. The inspiration makes sense; Murakami developed a taste for literature by reading Western authors such as Dickens, Capote, Fitzgerald, Vonnegut and Dostoyevsky. In fact, he wasn't able to find his voice at the start of *1Q84* until he made the decision to write the opening in English and translate it back to Japanese once he was finished. When asked if he felt any kinship with Orwell, he responded, "I guess we have a common feeling against the system. George Orwell is half journalist, half fiction writer. I'm 100 percent fiction writer . . . I don't want to write messages. I want to write good stories. I think of myself as a political person, but I don't state my political messages to anybody."

When speaking specifically about *1984*, Murakami says, "Most near-future fictions are boring. It's always dark and always raining, and people are so unhappy. I like when Cormac McCarthy wrote *The Road*—it's very well written . . . But still it's boring. It's dark, and the people are eating people . . . George Orwell's *1984* is near-future fiction, but this is near-past fiction. We are looking at the same year from the opposite side. If it's near past, it's not boring."

THE SECRET AGENT

Joseph Conrad

1907

"The origin of *The Secret Agent*: subject, treatment, artistic purpose, and every other motive that may induce an author to take up his pen, can, I believe, be traced to a period of mental and emotional reaction," writes Joseph Conrad. "The actual facts are that I began this book impulsively and wrote it continuously. When in due course it was bound and delivered to the public gaze I found myself reproved for having produced it at all. Some of the admonitions were severe, others had a sorrowful note. I have not got them textually before me, but I remember perfectly the general argument, which was very simple; and also my surprise at its nature. All this sounds a very old story now! And yet it is not such a long time ago. I must conclude that I had still preserved much of my pristine innocence in the year 1907. It seems to me now that even an artless person might have foreseen that some criticisms would be based on the ground of sordid surroundings and the moral squalor of the tale."

While a critical success, *The Secret Agent* sold rather poorly upon its release, with many citing its indecent themes as the primary reason. The terrorism aspect of the book resonates above all else, as his novel was often cited by the American media in the weeks after the September 11 attacks and was heralded by Ted Kaczynski, the Unabomber, who claimed to identify very strongly with "The Professor" character.

For Conrad, *The Secret Agent* was the answer to the question "what's next." He writes, "The inception of *The Secret Agent* followed immediately on a two years' period of intense absorption in the task of writing that remote novel, *Nostromo*, with its far-off Latin-American atmosphere; and the profoundly personal *Mirror of the Sea*. The first an intense creative effort on what I suppose will always remain my largest canvas, the second an unreserved attempt to unveil for a moment the profounder intimacies of the sea and the formative influences of nearly half my lifetime. It was a period, too, in which my sense of the truth of things was attended by a very intense imaginative and emotional readiness which, all genuine and faithful to facts as it was, yet made me feel (the task once done) as if I were left behind, aimless amongst mere husks of sensations and lost in a world of other, of inferior, values. I don't know whether I really felt that I wanted a change, change in my imagination, in my vision, and in my mental attitude. I rather think that a change in the fundamental mood had already stolen over me unawares. I don't remember anything definite happening. With *The Mirror of the Sea* finished in the full consciousness that I had dealt with honestly with myself and my readers in every line of that book, I gave myself up to a not unhappy pause. Then, while I was yet standing still as it were, and certainly not thinking of going out of my way to look for anything ugly, the subject of *The Secret Agent*—I mean the tale—came to me in the shape of a few words uttered by a friend in a casual conversation about anarchists or rather anarchist activities; how brought about I don't remember now."

The Greenwich Bombing of 1894 was the inspiration behind much of the novel itself, as the character Stevie is based on Martial Bourdin, the man who planned to carry out the bombing. The explosives that he was carrying detonated prematurely, killing him and leaving the motives for his attack unclear. On the subject, Conrad writes, "Presently, passing to particular instances, we recalled the already old story of the attempt to blow up the Greenwich Observatory; a blood-stained inanity of so fatuous a kind that it was impossible to fathom its origin by any reasonable or even unreasonable process of thought. For perverse unreason has its own logical processes. But that outrage could not be laid hold of mentally in any sort of way, so that one remained faced by the fact of a man blown to bits for nothing even most remotely resembling an idea, anarchistic or other. As to the outer wall of the Observatory it did not show as much as the faintest crack . . . This book is that story, reduced to manageable proportions, its whole course suggested and centered round the absurd cruelty of the Greenwich Park explosion."

ENDER'S GAME

Orson Scott Card

———

1985

"The basic idea of the battle room came to me when I was sixteen," Orson Scott Card writes. "My future sister-in-law, Laura Dene Low (she soon married my older brother, Bill), had urged me to read Asimov's *Foundation* trilogy, which blew me away. I found myself wanting to come up with a futuristic story myself, and my rudimentary understanding of science fiction at the time led me to assume that SF stories began by the author thinking of a futuristic idea (and it certainly is one way to come up with a story). Since I had been a Civil War buff for years, and because my brother Bill was in the army at the time (and the Vietnam War was at its peak), I speculated on how military training would be different in the future— especially war in space, when there were three dimensions to think about. It wouldn't be like flying airplanes, because in flying there's always a 'down' to orient yourself with. It would take drastic rethinking of the organization of objects in space and time . . . and so I came up with the battle room as a means of training soldiers for 3-D combat. Years later, when I wanted to write a story that was, completely and obviously, science fiction, I came back to that idea and realized that if the soldiers being trained were all little kids, the story would be much more powerful. But this, too, came out of the obvious truth that most of the time our soldiers are children, or we make them into children through training—we want them utterly dependent on their commanders for their understanding of reality, the way children are utterly dependent on their parents."

ROOM

Emma Donoghue

2010

"What inspired *Room*? The shock of mother-hood," writes Emma Donoghue. "Back in 2008 when I heard about Elizabeth Fritzl and her children emerging from their Austrian dungeon, our kids were four and one. My first thought was: how did she do that, how did she manage to mother—and mother well—in a locked room? But my second thought was: aren't there moments for every parent, and every child too, when that intimate bond feels like a locked room?"

Donoghue is referencing the Fritzl case, which saw a woman held captive by her father for twenty-four years before escaping in 2008. The victim of countless sexual assaults, Elizabeth Fritzl gave birth to seven children while in captivity, four of whom would stay locked away with her. Felix, just five years old at the time of their escape, inspired Donoghue's Jack character. "Having a child narrator is very helpful in terms of point of view, because children are little Martians who see everything afresh and askew. The real technical challenge of the novel was representing Ma as a three-dimensional character, through Jack's lens, which is a very limited one not only because of his age but because she constantly tells him comforting lies."

Of course, *Room* wasn't a simple reflection of the Fritzl case; Ma and Jack are the only characters held captive, as opposed to Elizabeth and her four children, and the captor in the novel isn't the father of the captive. Even Jack, while clearly inspired by Felix, was partially the product of the research that Donoghue conducted across a wide swathe of materials. She wrote, "Of course there's never been a real Jack—born into captivity but in perfect health, living in a best-case-scenario of confinement—so I had to research a weird variety of situations that I thought might overlap with his: not just kidnap survivors but prisoners in solitary confinement or mother-and-child prison units, refugees, hermits and mystics. The research I did on hidden and abused children was the most upsetting task I've ever set myself, and I only wish I could forget what I learned."

FIGHT CLUB

Chuck Palahniuk

1996

"Bookstores were full of books like *The Joy Luck Club* and *The Divine Secrets of the Ya-Ya Sisterhood* and *How to Make an American Quilt*. These were all novels that presented a social model for women to be together. But there was no novel that presented a new social model for men to share their lives."

The idea that a man's life should be a private matter was what inspired Chuck Palahniuk to write *Fight Club* in the first place, after not being asked where his post-fight bruises came from at work. He began writing the novel in 1995 while practicing a technique known as "dangerous writing," which means utilizing painful experiences for the purposes of literary inspiration. His first draft, which itself would eventually blossom into *Invisible Monsters*, failed to catch any attention from the publishing industry. He expanded the story into "*Fight Club*," then a short story he got published in a collection, before expanding it once more into *Fight Club: A Novel*, which he finished in 1996.

THE ROAD

Cormac McCarthy

———

2006

"Well it's interesting, because usually you don't know where a book comes from," said Cormac McCarthy. "It's just there, an itch you can't quite scratch. My son John, about four years ago he and I went to El Paso. We checked in to the old hotel there. And one night, John was asleep, and it was probably about two or three o'clock in the morning, and I went over and looked out the window at this town. There was nothing moving, but I could hear the trains coming through with that very lonesome sound, and I just had this image of what this town might look like in fifty or a hundred years. I just had this image of these fires up on the hill, everything being laid to waste, and I thought about my little boy. So I wrote those pages and that was the end of it. Then about four years later I was in Ireland and I realized that it wasn't two pages of another book, it was a book, and it was about that man and that little boy."

When asked if *The Road*, which he dedicated to his son John Francis McCarthy, was a love story to his son, he replied in the affirmative. "In a way I suppose it is. It's kind of embarrassing. I suppose it is, yeah." In fact, his son was the only reason that the concept occurred to McCarthy in the first place. "It would have never even occurred to me to try to write a book about a father and his son."

A GRIEF OBSERVED

C.S. Lewis

1961

Published under the pseudonym N.W. Clark, C.S. Lewis' *A Grief Observed* was an exploration of his mental and emotional state after the death of his wife of three years. Joylessness and grief plagued his life after her death, to the point where he allowed it to affect his spiritual being as well as his relationship with God. How, he thought, could God take an individual's life away at such a young age and leave another individual completely devoid of happiness? Why couldn't God help him achieve a sense of normalcy in a life now ridden with pain and remembrance? Lewis' prevailing emotion at the end of the novel is one of gratitude, for having ever been able to experience true love in the first place. *A Grief Observed* was made up of four notebooks that

Lewis kept after his wife passed, making the work particularly authentic and candid.

LIFE OF PI

Yann Martel

———

2001

"The premise came to me from reading a review of a Brazilian novel," said Yann Martel, "by a man named Moacyr Scliar, which I read about twelve years ago. And it struck me that that's a good premise, I could do something with that. Then I forgot about it. And then, about seven years later, I was in India, and India is a country with a lot of animals and a lot of religion. And I was a bit lost there, too. I was sort of wondering, 'What am I doing in life? I've written two books, but they haven't really done well.' So I was sort of looking for a story, not only with a small 's,' but sort of with a capital 's'—something that would direct my life. And while I was there, I remembered that premise, and I sort of said, 'man, I could really do something. Here, I'll tell my own story.' And suddenly, all these ideas started coming together. And the main thing that struck me is the idea of a religious boy—because we have to say that Pi is a practicing Hindu,

Muslim, and Christian—the idea of a religious boy in a lifeboat with a wild animal struck me as a perfect metaphor for the human condition. Humans aspire to really high things, right, like religion, justice, democracy. At the same time, we're rooted in our human, animal condition. And so, all of those brought together in a lifeboat struck me as being . . . as a perfect metaphor."

The novel Martel references deals with a Jewish man stuck in a boat with a panther, meant to be an allegory for the Holocaust. Martel's, as described above, is more of a religious metaphor, based in Pi's practice of three religions. The Tiger in isolation is meant to bring that to light. Of course, a book dealing with so many different aspects at once requires a lot of research; Martel had to read up on Hinduism, Islam, Christianity, animal psychology, zoo biology, and even cast-away stories to get a firm grasp on what he was writing. "It was wonderful," he said. "It was wonderful. But they all came together very well, and I think one of the qualities of the book is that it carried the research quite lightly. It doesn't seem like a book where I'm flogging, you know, the facts. They all came together in quite a seamless way."

Perhaps the oddest origin story, however, centers on the tiger's name, Richard Parker. Writes Martel, "People have asked me how the tiger in my novel *Life of Pi* came to be called

Richard Parker. I didn't just pull the name out of a hat. In fact, Richard Parker's name is the result of a triple coincidence. In 1884, the *Mignonette*, a yacht, set sail from Southampton, England, for Australia. She had a crew of four. In the South Atlantic, the seas were heavy. Wave after wave struck the vessel. Suddenly, she broke apart and sank. Captain, mate, hand, and cabin boy managed to scramble aboard a dinghy—but without water or provisions except for two cans of turnips. After nineteen days adrift, starving and desperate, the captain killed the cabin boy, who was unconscious and had no dependents, and the three remaining survivors ate him. The cabin boy's name was Richard Parker. His fate, in itself, is not particularly noteworthy. Cannibalism on the high seas was surprisingly common at the time. The reason Richard Parker—or, more accurately, 'the case of the *Mignonette*'—has gone down in history, at least in knowledgeable legal circles, is that upon their return to England, the survivors (they were rescued shortly after killing R.P. by a Swedish ship) were tried for murder, a first. Up until then, murder committed under duress, because of severe necessity, was informally accepted as justifiable. But with the *Mignonette*, the powers-that-be decided to examine the question more closely. The case went all the way to the Lords and set a legal precedent. The captain was found guilty of murder. To this day, the only excuse for murder remains self-defense, and any British legal team that tries to argue otherwise will get a lecture from the judge about the *Mignonette*. Murder committed in extreme circumstances for the sake of sustaining life remains illegal (though those who commit it usually get light sentences). That's one Richard Parker.

"Fifty years earlier, in 1837, Edgar Allan Poe published his only novel, *The Narrative of Arthur Gordon Pym*. It was a commission that quickly lost Poe's interest. He finished it with a mix of reluctance and slapdash hurry that is not a recipe for great literature. *Pym* is a sloppy work that would have vanished without a trace if weren't for its author's fame. In the story, the ship upon which Pym and a friend set sail from Nantucket overturns in a storm. Survivors cling to the hull. After several days, hunger and despair push Pym and his friend to eat a third man. His name is Richard Parker. Remember, Poe wrote *Pym* fifty years before the sinking of the *Mignonette*. And then there was the *Francis Speight*, a ship that foundered in 1846. There were deaths and cannibalism aboard. One of the victims was a Richard Parker. So many victimized Richard Parkers had to mean something. My tiger found his name. He's a victim, too—or is he?"

SOMETHING WICKED THIS WAY COMES

Ray Bradbury

1962

Ray Bradbury's passion for writing began at a carnival when he was twelve years old. It was there that he met Mr. Electrico, the carnival magician, who introduced him to the concept of eternal life and reincarnation. Claiming that he was the reincarnation of a friend that he had lost during World War I, Mr. Electrico lit the imaginative fire that would burn throughout Bradbury's writing career.

Something Wicked This Way Comes takes place in Green Town, based on Bradbury's hometown of Waukegan, Illinois, and the setting of his previous work, *Dandelion Wine*. That *Dandelion* is set during the summer inspired Bradbury to set *Something Wicked* in autumn, as it represented a sort of maturation for him. The title of the novel also draws from past literature, though not his own—Shakespeare's line in Macbeth, "By the pricking of my thumbs / Something wicked this way comes," was its inspiration.

The novel started as a short story that Bradbury and his friend, Gene Kelly, tried pitching to movie studios. When nobody bit, Bradbury repurposed the short story, then titled "The Black Ferris," into a novel in which Mr. Electrico would play the villain. He even added characters crafted in the likenesses of the people he had met at the carnival, like the Skeleton Man and the Illustrated Man.

THE WORM OUROBOROS

Eric Rücker Eddison

—

1922

Eric Rücker Eddison's imagination as a ten-year-old boy was responsible for perhaps his most successful work, *The Worm Ouroboros*. The book focuses on a classic medieval conflict, one that pits those hailing from Witchland against those from Demonland. The names, along with characters such as Fax Fay Faz, were conceived by a ten-year-old, hence their oddity. The original drawings actually appear in one of his notebooks, dated 1892, which contains the original inspirations behind characters like Goldry Bluszco and La Fireez. In fact, the notebook even has drawings depicting events that take place in the novel, such as Lord Corund being challenged by Lord Brandoch Daha and Gallandus getting murdered.

The theme of the book, however, was derived from something quite different from Eddison's old notebook: the myth of a snake swallowing its own tail. Like the snake, the story is destined to repeat itself time and time again. The great conflict ends, the characters realize that they are meaningless without it, they wish to have it back and their wish is granted. The title of the book also comes from the myth, which is called Ouroboros.

STARSHIP TROOPERS

Robert Heinlein

———

1959

Writing in the midst of the Cold War between the United States and the Soviet Union, Robert Heinlein thought that *Starship Troopers* might prove a good vehicle to properly convey his political views. Originally published in *The Magazine of Fantasy & Science Fiction* in two parts, his teen novel failed to gain any traction with publishers. G.P. Putnam's Sons finally bought the rights to the book, okaying any edits that might make the novel attractive to adults as well as teens. "Let the readers decide who likes it," said Peter Israel, a senior editor at Putnam's.

Robert and his wife created the "Patrick Henry League" in response to a newspaper advertisement calling for the suspension of nuclear weapons testing in the U.S.; they hoped to show support for the nuclear testing program, something both of them thought was in the best interest of national security. The decision to write *Starship Troopers* came when it became evident that Heinlein had some things to clear up, facing backlash from friends and peers over his support of the program. Where he landed on the political spectrum isn't totally clear, as he often contradicted himself and was inconsistent in the views that he held, but what was clear was that he believed that the military could serve a multipurpose function in society. In *Starship Troopers* we watch a military function in society, and in later works he shows us the different roles that an individual can play in the military. Such views may explain why he had such a strong response to the liberal outcry for President Eisenhower to cease nuclear testing.

NATIVE SON

Richard Wright

1940

"No American Negro exists," writes James Baldwin, "who does not have his private Bigger Thomas living in his skull." Bigger Thomas, the protagonist of Richard Wright's *Native Son*, is an African American boy living in poverty in Chicago's South Side. He becomes the servant to a rich white family, who give him a room to stay in and are generally kind people. The kindness makes Bigger uncomfortable, and in this unfamiliar dynamic he is unsure how to respond. After spending a night chauffeuring for their daughter and her boyfriend, he carries the drunken girl inside and, unable to resist, steals a kiss before placing her in the bed. The mother, a blind woman, walks into the room at that moment, startling Bigger to the point where he pushes a pillow over the daughter's face to keep her quiet. By the time the mother leaves the daughter has suffocated, leading him to burn the body and blame the disappearance on the boyfriend. While on the run, he rapes his girlfriend and kills her by hitting her with a brick, tossing her body and the rest of his money down an abandoned air shaft.

Native Son is not a murder story. Its intention is to show Bigger as a product of his environment—that is, poor, uneducated, violent and, above all, ignored. White readers initially disliked the novel, as they felt as though it confirmed their beliefs regarding African Americans. But the nature of Wright's book upends that notion; the very fact that Bigger is so unused to white kindness shows the reader that societal factors outside Bigger's control have placed him in a bad spot to begin with. His befriending Mr. Max at the end of the novel gives some indication that Bigger, with the proper infrastructure in place, could have been taught to express himself before it was too late. Said Frantz Fanon in his essay titled "The Fact of Blackness," "In the end, Bigger Thomas acts. To put an end to his tension, he acts, he responds to the world's anticipation."

Bigger Thomas is partly inspired by murderer Robert Nixon, who was executed in 1939 for murders that he had committed in Los Angeles and Chicago. Nixon, like Thomas, was an African American male who committed his murders with a brick, granting him the nickname the "Brick Moron." He was depicted by the media as being very stupid, as evidenced by the *Chicago Tribune* headline reading "Brick Slayer Likened to Jungle Beast," in which Nixon is said to be the "missing link" in human evolution. Like Thomas, Nixon was also executed for his crimes.

The title for the novel was actually thought up by Wright's friend, Nelson Algren, who was going to use it for what became his *Somebody in Boots*. Algren offered the title to Wright, who graciously accepted.

OF HUMAN BONDAGE

W. Somerset Maugham

—

1915

"This is a novel, not an autobiography, though much in it is autobiographical in nature, more is pure invention," says W. Somerset Maugham, who used bits from his own life to create his protagonist Philip Carey. After losing his mother to tuberculosis, Maugham moved in with his aunt and uncle, where he developed an affinity for literature and art—he even had a Monet, Renoir, Pissarro and Sisley in his personal collection, all painters whose names are mentioned in the novel. While Maugham didn't have Philip's clubfoot, he did have a stammer due to relentless bullying he suffered at The King's School in Canterbury. That stammer prevented him from being a clergyman, forcing him to take up medicinal studies instead—just like Philip.

The title *Of Human Bondage* came from part 4

of Spinoza's *Ethics*, titled "Of Human Bondage, or the Strength of the Emotions." Spinoza defines perfection by the aims and intention of a particular desire; Carey, of course, achieves satisfaction once he finally realizes what his aim had been. Spinoza defines bondage as the inability for a person to control their emotions. Wrote Maugham in the novel's foreword, "The impotence of man to govern or restrain the emotions I call bondage, for a man who is under their control is not his own master . . . so that he is often forced to follow the worse, although he see the better before him."

THE OUTSIDERS

S.E. Hinton

———

1967

Unimpressed by the literature of the 1960s for its inability to relate to young people, Susan Hinton took matters into her own hands. She explains, "I'd wanted to read books that showed teen-agers outside the life of 'Mary Jane went to the prom.' When I couldn't find any, I decided to write one myself. I created a world with no adult authority figures, where kids lived by their own rules." She embarked on the endeavor as a fifteen-year-old, using rival gangs in her high school as inspiration for the Greasers and the Socs in *The Outsiders*. The gangs were so bad, in fact, that they had to use separate entrances when arriving to school each morning. Still, Hinton acknowledges that it was "rough all over." Her decision to tell the story from the perspective of a Greaser wasn't meant to vilify the Socs, but rather to humanize the lower-class characters.

Hinton also put a lot of thought into telling the story from a man's perspective, as she writes, "I started using male characters just because it was easiest. I was a tomboy, most of my close friends were boys, and I figured nobody would believe a girl would know anything about my subject matter. I have kept on using male characters because (1) boys have fewer books written for them (2) girls will read boys' books, boys usually won't read girls', and (3) it is still the easiest for me." Despite her writing "for boys," Hinton's publisher still advised her to use her initials as they thought that a novel written by a man would sell better.

The novel's setting is entirely inspired by Hinton's experience in Tulsa, Oklahoma, where she still lives today. The high school, Curtis house and drive-in were all real places that she frequented growing up. Even the altercation at the drive-in was inspired by a real experience she had watching a couple fighting at the front of the audience.

Hinton derived her style from the likes of Shirley Jackson, Charles Dickens, Will James and Ray Bradbury, all of whom produced great works of literature that she consumed growing up. She wrote two unpublished novels before penning *The Outsiders*, one of which her mother threw in the trash before Hinton rescued it. "When I was writing she'd come into my room, grab my hair and throw me in front of the TV," she said. "She'd say, 'You're part of this family—now act like it.' I hate TV now." Hinton sought refuge at her grandmother's farm, where she could play with her aunt's horse. She dreamt not of literary success but of owning a horse of her own. "I would tell myself, 'It'll get better,' " she said. "Hang on."

CLOUDY WITH A CHANCE OF MEATBALLS

Judi Barrett

———

1978

"I thought of the sentence 'Henry walked outside and got hit in the head with a meatball,' " said Judi Barrett when asked by a classroom what inspired her to write *Cloudy with a Chance of Meatballs.* "I don't know why I thought of it. I have no idea. I thought 'Well that was kind of funny,' and I started to play around with the idea of weather and food. I like to play with words, so I did pea soup fog and strawberry traffic jam, which didn't make it into the book. So I started to figure out weather and food, and then the prediction of cloudy with a chance of meatballs, which . . . I don't know how it came to me. It's a wonderful thing that happened. But I don't remember. The other thing that happened to me was that my mother, and keep in mind that I was a very bad eater, she was always concerned that I wouldn't eat enough or that I would eat too fast. So when she fed me, she would say to me after each spoonful 'Now chew and swallow.' 'Now chew and swallow.' So that I wouldn't gulp my food down. So that's where the town of 'Chew and Swallow' came from."

THE JUNGLE

Upton Sinclair

―――

1906

"I aimed at the public's heart, and by accident I hit it in the stomach," said Upton Sinclair upon seeing the reception to his novel *The Jungle*. Perhaps the best-known muckraker in American history, Sinclair went undercover in the meat-packing plants in Chicago for almost two months to get a feel for how workers were being utilized and treated. His initial goal was to pen a newspaper article that spoke to the mistreatment of immigrants in industrialized cities. Newspaper aside, he manages to do all of those things. The harsh working conditions, general hopelessness, low wages and long hours laid out in *The Jungle* led Jack London to call the situation "wage slavery," as the people in power were getting rich off the backs of poor, underpaid workers. But, in part because Sinclair's accurate descriptions of the workers didn't make them very likeable to the readers, the conditions of the food factories became the main story. The public was disgusted and captivated by Sinclair's horrific descriptions of men contaminating their food—some by falling into meat grinders themselves.

SOPHIE'S CHOICE

William Styron

1979

Sexuality and profanity aside, *Sophie's Choice* continues to be a source of controversy due to the way author William Styron portrays the Holocaust. Viewing the event from a non-Jewish perspective, he attempts to steer the conversation away from anti-Semitism and toward general evil, citing the fact that more than just the Jewish were victims of the mass killings, particularly Slavic Christians. In "The Holocaust According to Williams Styron," Alvin Rosenfeld speaks to Styron's point, writing "(1) while Styron acknowledges Jewish suffering under the Nazis, he insists on seeing Auschwitz in general or universalistic terms, as a murderous thrust against 'mankind' or 'the entire human family;' (2) in line with the above, he sees his own role as 'correcting' the view that the Holocaust was directed solely or exclusively against the Jews by focusing attention on the many Christians, and particularly the Slavs, who also perished in the camps; (3) . . . Auschwitz was 'anti-Christian' as well as 'anti-Semitic,' and hence assertions of Christian guilt are misplaced and perhaps even unnecessary; (4) since he rejects historical explanations of Christian anti-Semitism as causative, Styron is drawn to the view, set forth by Richard Rubenstein and others . . . that in its essential character Auschwitz was a capitalistic slave society as much as or even more than it was an extermination center; and (5) viewed against European examples of barbarism and slavery, epitomized by Auschwitz, the American South's treatment of the blacks looks pretty good and ' . . . seems benevolent by comparison.' "

The novel's title can likely be traced all the way back to Albert Camus, who described four human dilemmas in his 1947 essay "The Human Crisis." One of the four involved a Greek mother, who was forced by Nazis to choose which one of her three children they should kill.

AN AMERICAN TRAGEDY

Theodore Dreiser

1925

It was 1905 when Chester Gillette took a job at his uncle's factory in Cortland, New York. There he met Grace Brown, with whom he soon began a sexual relationship that led to her pregnancy. Brown was always operating under the assumption of marriage, and news of the pregnancy merely intensified her pleas. Jealousy brought her back to Cortland after a brief stint at home, desperate for an answer. Gillette refused to commit one way or the other. He decided to take her on a trip to the Adirondack Mountains, where he clubbed her to death with a tennis racket on a rowboat. He left her body and his hat behind, trekked through the woods and checked in at a nearby hotel. They quickly caught and convicted Gillette of murder and sentenced him to death by electric chair. The case grew to captivate the nation, and Gillette was killed on March 30, 1908.

Clyde Griffiths, the main character of *An American Tragedy*, was derived from the story of Chester Gillette. Both come from religious families, both take jobs at their uncle's factories, both impregnate a co-worker and are expected to marry, both murder said co-worker on Big Moose Lake and both die by electric chair. The differences are trivial; Clyde kills Roberta Alden with a camera instead of a tennis racket and rows back to shore rather than leaving her on the lake. Clyde even shares the same initials as Chester, C.S., which could be a nod to Chester checking into a hotel under a fake name with accurate initials in order to match the monogram on his bag.

APPOINTMENT IN SAMARRA

John O'Hara

1934

The title of *Appointment in Samarra* is derived from an ancient Mesopotamian tale, which is retold by W. Somerset Maugham and included in the novel itself. The tale describes a servant who, upon receiving a threatening gesture from Death at the marketplace, returns to his master and describes the scene. He flees to Samarra to hide from Death, while the master travels to the marketplace to confront Death. When asked why she made the threatening gesture, Death responds, "That was not a threatening gesture, it was only a start of surprise. I was astonished to see him in Baghdad, for I had an appointment with him tonight in Samarra." While defending his use of the title, John O'Hara said that it represents "the inevitability of Julian English's death."

AT SWIM-TWO-BIRDS

Brian O'Nolan

———

1939

Brian O'Nolan's idea to turn the characters against the writer first appeared in his short story titled "Scenes in a Novel," from which a passage reads, "The book is seething with conspiracy and there have been at least two whispered consultations between all the characters, including two who have not yet been officially created . . . Candidly, reader, I fear my number's up." The idea was expanded and brought to a larger scale in *At Swim-Two-Birds*, which features a line of writers who all create other characters within the novel. He created multiple lines of fiction, with his protagonist occupying the most immediate one. Dermot Trellis, a writer-character created by the protagonist, is tortured by his characters until the protagonist writes him out of the story, having just resolved his central conflict as well.

Early Irish literature is referenced throughout the story; O'Nolan studied the subject in college, familiarizing himself with the poetry and stories that he references throughout. The immediate line of fiction is somewhat autobiographical, as O'Nolan and his protagonist were both Irish writers who did so religiously while at university. O'Nolan also developed an affinity for satire, having taken a liking to the works of Huxley, Cabell and Joyce, hence the novel's satirical tone.

AMERICAN PSYCHO

Bret Easton Ellis

1991

"I didn't really care how many copies it was going to sell," said Bret Easton Ellis in a 2016 interview with *Rolling Stone Magazine*. "I really didn't care who connected with it." The author was responding to a question on whether he was surprised that his Patrick Bateman character resonated with so many people. Rather than try to create a character that appealed to the masses, Ellis wrote Bateman as an embodiment of what he was going through as a young gay man in the 1980s. He writes, "I created this guy who becomes this emblem for yuppie despair in the Reagan Eighties—a very specific time and place—and yet he's really infused with my own pain and what I was going through as a guy in his twenties, trying to fit into a society that he doesn't necessarily want to fit into but doesn't really know what the other options are. That was Patrick Bateman to me. It was trying to become a kind of ideal man because that seemed to be the only kind of guy that was 'accepted.' Bateman keeps saying 'I want to fit in.' I felt that way too. It's very surprising and completely shocking that a novel that I was writing in 1987, 1988 and '89 is being referenced now."

When asked whether or not his father influenced Bateman at all, Ellis responded, "I used him as a scapegoat, in some ways. The character was much more about me. I didn't feel comfortable talking about that for a long time because of the outcry over the book and I thought, 'Oh, God. Why get into that now, since that book was so misunderstood?' So using my father became an easier way to talk about the book. And in some ways, my father had traits similar to Patrick Bateman. I saw him being affected by the new '80s, male cosmetic overhaul. I was an artist, more liberal than he was, and certainly an outsider in terms of being gay. He was popular, white, privileged, Republican—all these things that Bateman was that I didn't necessarily feel like I was. I was more interested in the metaphor and how it connected to me."

The "new '80s" Ellis refers to is the general shift of male mentality in regards to health, wellness and appearance. That shift, referred to as the "dandification of the American male" by Ellis, was what the book itself was really about. "Beginning in the '80s, men were prettifying themselves in ways they weren't [before]," says Ellis. "And they were taking on a lot of the tropes of gay male culture and bringing it into straight male culture—in terms of grooming, looking a certain way, going to the gym, waxing and being almost the gay porn ideals. You can track that down to the way Calvin Klein advertised underwear, a movie like *American Gigolo*, the re-emergence of *Gentlemen's Quarterly*. All of these things really informed *American Psycho* when I was writing it. So that seemed to me much more interesting than whether he is or is not a serial killer, because that really is a small section of the book."

THE BLIND ASSASSIN

Margaret Atwood

———

2000

In a 2013 essay for *The Guardian*, Margaret Atwood explains the story behind creating her central character. She writes, "Writing *The Blind Assassin* was a start-and-stop process. My first idea was to write about the generations of my grandmother and my mother, which together spanned the entire twentieth century. They lived through the first world war and the second world war, both of which made a huge impact in Canada. Canada went into the first war in 1914 and the second one in 1939, two months before my birth, and the percentage of young Canadian men killed in those wars was very high. The sense of loss is commemorated in towns across the country, almost all of which have prominent war memorials; which is why the erection of such a memorial is a central event in the novel. But neither my grandmother nor my mother was devious enough to take the lead in the novel I proposed to write, which involved quite a bit of lying. Neither of these women told lies; at difficult moments they changed the subject and talked about the weather. But my Iris Chase was predestined to be a liar, at least in matters that concerned her dead sister, Laura."

Atwood had plans to tell Iris's story through Laura, killing off Iris instead. She lacked any interest in the character, however, and decided to write Iris' story in the third person, as if she were alive. She finally landed on giving Iris complete control and writing the story from the first person. Aspects of the final version, like the steamer trunk, were derived from the parts of the scrapped versions, like the hat box and the suitcase. In fact, making the object itself a steamer trunk was an acknowledgment to Atwood's own steamer trunk at home, passed down from her own mother. "It is now mine," Atwood says, "although I have painted it to get rid of the rust."

When it comes to choosing Port Ticonderoga for her setting, Atwood writes, "It is a blend of Stratford, Ontario, which has a summer theatre festival; Saint Mary's, which has a quarry; Elora, which has a gorge; and Paris, Ontario, which is a port on a main river, and, like the others but more so, had some beautiful nineteenth-century architecture. Such towns once supported a wide array of mills and manufacturers, including button factories; thus, the Chase family business. And many of these prospered in the early twentieth century, but faltered and failed during the great depression, as does the Chase enterprise."

THE MOVIEGOER

Walker Percy

1961

When asked what moved him to write *The Moviegoer* in a 1987 interview with *The Paris Review*, Walker Percy responded, "The spark might have come from Sartre's Roquentin in *Nausea* sitting in that library watching the Self-Taught Man or sitting in that café watching the waiter. Why not have a younger, less perverse Roquentin, a Southerner of a certain sort, and put him down in a movie house in Gentilly, a middle-class district of New Orleans, not unlike Sartre's Bouville . . . After the war, not doing medicine, writing and publishing articles in psychiatric, philosophical, and political journals, I was living in New Orleans and going to the movies. You can't make a living writing articles for *The Journal of Philosophy and Phenomenological Research*. The thought crossed my mind: Why not do what French philosophers often do and Americans almost never—novelize philosophy, incarnate ideas in a person and a place, which latter is, after all, a noble Southern tradition in fiction."

HEART OF DARKNESS

Joseph Conrad

———

1902

Originally published in 1899 as a three-part series in *Blackwood's Magazine*, Joseph Conrad's *Heart of Darkness* was very much based in his own life experience. His novel, described by Conrad as "a wild story of a journalist who becomes a manager of a station in the (African) interior and makes himself worshipped by a tribe of savages," was inspired by his experiences serving on a steamer on the Congo river in the 1890s. He assumed control of the ship when the captain became too sick and successfully navigated it to one of the company's stations. He would remain in Africa for a few more years, keeping detailed journals that accompanied him on his travels. Those journals would provide source material for Conrad once he began writing *Heart of Darkness* later that decade.

Not detailed in Conrad's journal, however, is the source of inspiration for Kurtz, the novel's antagonist. Some believe that the inspiration came from individuals who were part of the Emin Pasha Relief Expedition, which was among the last major European expeditions to travel into inner Africa. Others believe that it was a Belgian soldier named Léon Rom who inspired the character. Still others point to Georges-Antoine Klein, a colleague aboard the steamer. Conrad never disclosed his inspiration for the character.

DUNE

Frank Herbert

1965

Taken by the massive sand dunes in Florence, Oregon, Frank Herbert once wrote to his agent that they could "swallow whole cities, lakes, rivers and highways." The U.S. Department of Agriculture was attempting to provide integrity to the dune structure by planting large patches of grass throughout, inspiring an article that Herbert wrote, "They Stopped the Moving Sands." The article was never completed but inspired him to continue researching the subject, as evidenced in his three-part series *Dune World*, which was published in the science-fiction magazine *Analog*. The following year, in 1965, Herbert wrote a five-part series titled *The Prophet of Dune*, published in the same magazine. He tried to get an expanded and revised version of the series published as one novel, but the idea was soundly rejected across the industry. Only Chilton Books, better known for printing manuals, agreed to take it on. In his dedication, Herbert wrote, "To the people whose labors go beyond ideas into the realm of 'real materials'— to dry-land ecologists, wherever they may be, in whatever time they work, this effort at prediction is dedicated in humanity and admiration."

CLOUD ATLAS

David Mitchell

———

2004

When asked how he came up with the structure of *Cloud Atlas* in an interview with *The Paris Review*, David Mitchell responded, "The first time I read Calvino's *If on a Winter's Night a Traveler*, I didn't know what I was dealing with. I thought we'd be going back to the interrupted narrative later on in the book, and I very much wanted to. Finishing the novel, I felt a bit cheated that Calvino hadn't followed through with what he'd begun—which was, of course, the whole point of the book. But a voice said this: What would it actually look like if a mirror were placed at the end of the book, and you continued into a second half that took you back to the beginning? That idea was knocking around in my head since I was eighteen or nineteen years old and, by my third novel, had arrived at the front of the queue."

Mitchell wrote *Cloud Atlas* as six separate novellas, the first and last of which involve Adam Ewing, on whose origins Mitchell says,

"Ewing drew into focus, rather than popped. I spent a few months reading nineteenth-century things," said Mitchell, in the same interview. "Lots of Melville, and Richard Henry Dana's *Two Years Before the Mast*. I was also reading Jared Diamond's *Guns, Germs, and Steel*, and I found the bit about Moriori, the inhabitants of the Chatham Islands east of New Zealand, and that was irresistible. I wanted to work out a way of getting that story in, and I read about someone in San Francisco whose name was actually Ewing, someone lost to history—except that one of the last Moriori told his story to him."

Much of the novel takes place in the South Pacific and was likely inspired by Mitchell's time living in Japan, as he moved there from Europe when his love interest's visa expired. They started a family and, after realizing that Mitchell could provide for them by writing full time in Europe, moved back after several years.

The cannibalism, however, is a theme in many of Mitchell's books. He explains, "A writer has a relatively small family of themes, and however hard you try to write about something else, they reemerge like indestructible whack-a-moles. One of my serial-repeating themes is predacity—and cannibalism is an ancient and primal manifestation of predacity. I remember watching an animal documentary in school, where a cheetah successfully pursued an antelope. As the cheetah ripped the antelope to shreds, a cute girl called Angela said, 'Oh Miss, that's cruel.' The teacher answered, 'Yes, Angela, but nature is cruel.' That was an early encounter with ethical relativism. Yes, an innocent antelope got ripped to shreds—but what about poor Mrs. Cheetah and her six adorable cheetah cubs? Did I want them to get so thin and hungry that the hyenas pick them off one by one? Then what about the poor baby hyenas? And on we go . . . arriving, eventually, at questions like, 'What is cruelty?' and not long after, 'What is evil?' As a novelist I want answers in order to motivate, plausibly, the antagonists who bedevil my protagonists."

GULLIVER'S TRAVELS

Jonathan Swift

———

1726

Legend has it that Jonathan Swift began writing *Gulliver's Travels* around the same time that he and other authors were forming the Scriblerus Club, roughly 1713. The club, which was based in London and lasted only as long as its founders did, formed with the intention of writing satire—something they were able to do with the help of their created persona, Martinus Scriblerus. Different authors were assigned different duties, with Swift given the task of writing Scriblerus' memoirs in addition to writing satire in the "Traveler's Tales" literary subgenre. The resulting work was *Gulliver's Travels*, which was so anti-Whig that Swift had his manuscript copied so that his handwriting couldn't be used as evidence against him. After cutting some of the more sensitive scenes from the book and adding a few in favor of the government, the publisher, who had received the manuscript in secret, published *Gulliver's Travels* anonymously in 1726.

WIDE SARGASSO SEA

Jean Rhys

—

1966

Wide Sargasso Sea, written by Jean Rhys and published in 1966, is meant as a prequel to Charlotte Brontë's 1847 classic *Jane Eyre*. In *Jane Eyre*, the protagonist falls for a wealthy landowner who, unbeknownst to her, is married. He believes that his wife is insane and keeps her locked away in the attic. The plot of *Sargasso Sea* is an account of that marriage prior to Jane entering the picture, starting with the wife's childhood in Jamaica. The heritage of the protagonist, Antoinette Cosway, can likely be attributed to Jean Rhys' background. A Dominican-born British author, she understood the dynamic between somebody from the Jamaica area and somebody from England better than most. A Creole heiress, Cosway is the subject of an arranged marriage that forces her to leave her island home to live with her new husband. He renames her "Bertha," the name of the wife in *Jane Eyre*, and keeps her confined in a locked room. Held captive, away from home and without her Jamaican identity, Bertha begins to descend into madness.

Rhys' decision to write *Sargasso Sea* likely intended to right a wrong, or at least shine a light on one—that is, the unequal power balance between married man and woman. Antoinette's digression does everything to display that imbalance. Once a Creole heiress, Antoinette loses her home, her name, her freedom and, eventually, her sanity. All thanks to an arranged marriage with a man who cheats on her while she is locked away.

THE SHELTERING SKY

Paul Bowles

1949

"Everyone is isolated from everyone else," says Paul Bowles in a 1981 interview with *The Paris Review*. "The concept of society is like a cushion to protect us from the knowledge of that isolation. A fiction that serves as an anesthetic . . . The transportation of characters to such settings often acts as a catalyst or a detonator, without which there'd be no action, so I shouldn't call the settings secondary. Probably if I hadn't had some contact with what you call 'exotic' places, it wouldn't have occurred to me to write at all." Bowles is referring to his time in Tangier, where he "wrote in bed in hotels in the desert." Having received a contract for a novel with an advance, the move came as a result of both his wanting inspiration and his growing distaste for making music, of which he said, "I was a composer for as long as I've been a writer. I came here because I wanted to write a novel. I had a commission to do it. I was sick of writing music for other people—Joseph Losey, Orson Welles, a whole lot of other people, endless." He achieved both, writing years later, "Whatever one writes is in a sense autobiographical, of course. Not factually so, but poetically so." He penned *The Sheltering Sky* while living in Tangier, drawing on personal experience and surroundings to do so. The title came from the song "Down Among the Sheltering Palms," which he listened to every summer as a child.

The two central characters, Port and Kit, were loosely inspired by Bowles and his wife Jane. Bowles said, "The book was conceived in New York in 1947, and 80 percent of it was written before Jane ever set foot in North Africa in 1948, so there's no question of its being related to experience. The tale is entirely imaginary. Kit is not Jane, although I used some of Jane's characteristics in determining Kit's reaction to such a voyage. Obviously I thought of Port as a fictional extension of myself. But Port is certainly not Paul Bowles, any more than Kit is Jane." Of course, their constant moving about inspired by one of Bowles' long-held mentalities: to move is to be free—to avoid self-confrontation. "Moving around a lot is a good way of postponing the day of reckoning. I'm happiest when I'm moving. When you've cut yourself from the life you've been living and you haven't yet established another life, you're free. That's a very pleasant sensation, I've always thought. If you don't know where you're going, you're even freer."

THE BIG SLEEP

Raymond Chandler

1939

Raymond Chandler's *The Big Sleep* followed a creative process for which the author is now known: his "cannibalizing" previous works he had written. In this case, Chandler took two short stories that he had published in the *Black Mask* magazine, "Killer in the Rain" in 1935 and "The Curtain" in 1936, as well as little bits from two other short stories titled "Finger Man" and "Mandarin's Jade," and combined them into one novel. "Killer in the Rain" and "The Curtain," in particular, had similar father-daughter dynamics to that in *The Big Sleep*.

Chandler prioritized characterization over plot consistency, so while finished work is rich in detail, the novel ends without solving the murder—a hole that comes with his "cannibalizing" technique. When asked by filmmaker Howard Hawks which character killed the chauffeur, Chandler replied that he had no idea.

TO THE LIGHTHOUSE

Virginia Woolf

——

1927

Virginia Woolf spent many a childhood summer in a rented house in St Ives, Cornwall, where her family vacationed every year. The house was called Talland House, of which Virginia writes in a 1921 diary entry, "Why am I so incredibly and incurably romantic about Cornwall? One's past, I suppose; I see children running in the garden . . . The sound of the sea at night . . . almost forty years of life, all built on that, permeated by that: so much I could never explain."

The house, which is still standing, overlooks Porthminster Bay and the Godrevy Lighthouse— the very lighthouse that inspired the novel. The summer visits were an annual tradition until her mother died suddenly in 1895, when Virginia was only thirteen years old. The unexpected loss resulted in many nervous breakdowns, which only intensified after her father's death a few years into the new century. *To The Lighthouse* is a nod to happier times, inspired by Woolf's family vacations. Upon reading her sister's work, Vanessa Bell said that it was like seeing her mother raised from the dead. The setting of Hebridean Island was strikingly similar to St. Ives, down to the gardens leading to the sea. Even Woolf's own characteristics can be found in the character Lily Briscoe, who paints the same way that Woolf writes.

THE CAT IN THE HAT

Dr. Seuss

1957

"In the classroom boys and girls are confronted with books that have insipid illustrations depicting the slicked-up lives of other children," writes John Hersey, in his article titled "Why Do Students Bog Down on First R? A Local Committee Sheds Light on a National Problem: Reading." "All feature abnormally courteous, unnaturally clean boys and girls . . . In bookstores anyone can buy brighter, livelier books featuring strange and wonderful animals and children who behave naturally, i.e., sometimes misbehave . . . Given incentive from school boards, publishers could do as well with primers . . . Why should [school primers] not have pictures that widen rather than narrow the associative richness the children give to the words they illustrate—drawings like those of the wonderfully imaginative geniuses among children's illustrators, Tenniel, Howard Pyle, 'Dr. Seuss', Walt Disney?"

William Spaulding, the director of Houghton Mifflin's education division, was taken by this article and agreed with its criticisms. Wanting to act on his newfound mentality, he commissioned Theodor Geisel to write a children's book, exclaiming to him over dinner, "Write me a story that first-graders can't put down!"

Geisel, otherwise known as Dr. Seuss, was given a list of about 350 words with which to write his book, the idea being that the average six-year-old would already know the vocabulary. Of the 350 words, Seuss was to use 225, a limitation that made conceiving the book very difficult—after all, Seuss was more interested in wordy paragraphs that included completely made up vocabulary. Frustrated, he decided to build his story around the first two words on the list that rhymed, hence *The Cat in the Hat*. Some of the Cat's characteristics can be attributed to a woman named Annie Williams, the "small, stooped woman wearing 'a leather half-glove and a secret smile.'" She was an elevator operator in Houghton Mifflin's Boston office and the inspiration for the Cat's smile and gloves.

THE VERY HUNGRY CATERPILLAR
Eric Carle

1969

On the genesis of *The Very Hungry Caterpillar*, Eric Carle once said, "One day I was punching holes with a hole puncher into a stack of paper, and I thought of a bookworm and so I created a story called 'A Week with Willi the Worm.'" His editor, Ann Beneduce, suggested changing the animal to make the protagonist more likeable. Carle settled on a butterfly, recalling, "That's where it all began."

BECAUSE OF WINN DIXIE
Kate DiCamillo

2000

"The book is a direct result of two things," Kate DiCamillo responded when asked how she came up with the idea for *Because of Winn Dixie*. "(1) It was the first time in my life I had been without a dog for an extended amount of time. (2) I wrote the book during the worst winter in Minnesota, and during the worst winter in Minnesota you just want to go back to Florida, which I couldn't afford to do, but I could write a book that would take me there." Amazingly, out of those two simple desires came this classic story.

THE HUNT FOR RED OCTOBER

Tom Clancy

1984

In 1975, Captain of the Third Rank Valery Sablin led a mutiny on board the *Storozhevoy*, a Soviet Navy anti-submarine ship. Wanting to protest the corruption that plagued Brezhnev-era Russia, Sablin planned to move the ship to the Bay of Riga, where it could take political asylum and broadcast a signal to all of Russia vocalizing what he believed were commonly held beliefs— that socialism was in danger, communism was gone and authority was corrupt. Sablin detained the ship's captain, along with any officers that didn't want to go along with the plan, in separate compartments below the main deck. He delivered a rousing speech to the rest of the men on the ship and set out under the cover of night, disabling radar services to avoid detection. The Soviets learned of the mutiny and committed half of their Baltic fleet, as well as sixty warplanes, to the effort of stopping the ship, which stalled out just more than forty miles from Swedish waters. Sablin was convicted of treason and was executed, while his second-in-command served an eight-year prison sentence.

While Tom Clancy's Marko Ramius defects from the Soviet Union in part because of his wife's death, he's similar to Sablin in that the political atmosphere also played a role in his defection. While writing *The Hunt for Red October*, his first novel, Clancy often referred back to this story in an effort to believably convey Marko's mindset during his defection.

THE MALTESE FALCON

Dashiell Hammett

———

1929

The Maltese Falcon is another example of an author "cannibalizing" their work as means to a greater end. In this instance, Dashiell Hammett took pieces of his "The Gutting of Couffignal" and "The Whosis Kid," both published in the *Black Mask* magazine, and incorporated them into his new novel. *The Maltese Falcon* was published in novel form in 1930, but it was originally published in the *Black Mask* magazine as a five-entry series.

The novel borrows from Hammett's experience as a private detective for the Pinkerton Detective Agency in San Francisco, where he met many people who inspired characters in the novel. Hammett's protagonist, however, was completely made up, despite sharing a name with the author (whose birth name is Samuel). Hammett writes, "Spade has no original. He is a dream man in the sense that he is what most of the private detectives I worked with would like to have been, and, in their cockier moments, thought they approached."

THE ADVENTURES OF HUCKLEBERRY FINN

Mark Twain

———

1884

In his autobiography, Mark Twain writes, "In Huckleberry Finn I have drawn Tom Blankenship exactly as he was. He was ignorant, unwashed, insufficiently fed; but he had as good a heart as ever any boy had. His liberties were totally unrestricted. He was the only really independent person—boy or man—in the community, and by consequence he was tranquilly and continuously happy and envied by the rest of us. And as his society was forbidden us by our parents the prohibition trebled and quadrupled its value, and therefore we sought and got more of his society than any other boy's."

Tom grew up with Twain in Hannibal, Missouri, the son of an alcoholic sawmill laborer who produced very little income he didn't use to fuel his addiction. Pap Finn, Huck's father, was based partly on Tom's father and partly on Jimmy Finn, the homeless town drunk. Tom, motherless and essentially without a father, was granted the kind of freedom that Huck Finn's character embodies.

THE CALL OF THE WILD

Jack London

———

1903

"It was in the Klondike I found myself," wrote Jack London on his 1897 trip during the height of the Klondike Gold Rush. After dropping out of school at age fourteen, London travelled around the country as a hobo, eventually returning to

California to finish his high school education and attend the University of California in Berkeley. He left after one year, travelling to the Klondike by way of the Chilkoot Pass in Alaska, and staked claims with the rest of his group to eight gold mines in the area. He spent about a year there before contracting scurvy, forcing him and his group to raft two thousand miles down the Yukon River to St. Michael, where he worked on a boat in order to get home to San Francisco.

London's time in Alaska provided him the inspiration necessary to write *The Call of the Wild*. The dog Buck was inspired by a St. Bernard-Scotch Collie owned by his friend Marshall Latham Bond and his brother Louis Whitford Bond; the book's dog component was a product of there always being a lot of them at the camp, as horses were unable to survive the climb to the gold mines. Dogs were more versatile and could transport materials while navigating the steep White Pass, meaning that there were always a lot of them around. The Bond family also inspired another aspect of the novel—the ranch house in the beginning of the book was written in the image of the Bond family ranch.

The book wasn't meant to be a story about Alaska, as an editor at the San Francisco Bulletin had told London that stories about nature generated very little interest. Rather, it was meant to be a short companion piece to London's

Bâtard, a story about a dog that kills its master. Wanting to "redeem the species," London began writing *The Call of the Wild*, but in his own words, "it got away from me, and instead of four thousand words it ran thirty-two thousand before I could call a halt." The story originally ran in four installments in *The Saturday Evening Post* before being published as a novel by Macmillan in 1903.

THE PIGMAN

Paul Zindel

1968

"I was living in a fifty-room empty castle on Staten Island," responded Paul Zindel when asked what inspired him to write *The Pigman*. "I was minding it for a real estate firm. I was thirty years old at the time. One day, a teenage boy trespassed across the grounds. I went out to scold him, but he turned out to be one of the most interesting young men I'd ever met. He told me a lot of the exciting adventures that appeared in *The Pigman* . . . I modeled Lorraine after a girl who was a student in one of the chemistry classes that I was teaching at Tottenville High School. She was a girl who used to cry anytime anything about death, dying, or war was mentioned. I thought, what a wonderful adventure it would be to team those two life models for me into a story in which they met an eccentric, old mentor figure. Mr. Pignati was based on an Italian grandfather that I knew."

For Zindel, *The Pigman* was his imagination's best attempt to expand on the real-life characters who fascinated him. Of course, in his own words, "For any characters to come alive you have to put something of yourself into them—so a piece of the Pigman, and John, and Lorraine, is really me. I used to love telling jokes and pulling pranks and wondering about everything from life to death. I played in graveyards and tasted chocolate-covered ants and loved talking to animals at the zoo. My son, David, loves doing a lot of the crazy things I did. He started talking with a monkey in a zoo in Berlin and it started screaming at him. Even the graffiti in *The Pigman* came from my own experience. It was written on a desk in one of the classrooms where I taught. 'HELP ME! A ROTTEN SCIENCE TEACHER HAS GIVEN ME A DRUG TO TURN ME into a teeny, weeny tiny mosquito!'"

A CONFEDERACY OF DUNCES

John Kennedy Toole

———

1980

The lighter historical side of *A Confederacy of Dunces* saw John Kennedy Toole fill his pages with experiences had while in New Orleans. He completed his undergraduate education at Tulane University before studying English at Columbia University in New York, which he paid for in part by teaching at Hunter College during his time off. He returned to Louisiana to teach before being drafted into the army, where he began writing his novel. His novel heralded as one of the most accurate descriptions of New Orleans in literary history, Toole had a wealth of information to draw upon from his time spent in the city. In New Orleans, Toole worked as a hot tamale cart vendor and had a stint working at a family-owned and -operated cloth factory—both experiences he worked into his novel. His protagonist, Ignatius J. Reilly, was based a little bit on himself and a little bit on a professor friend named Bob Byrne, a smart and eccentric man who lacked any form of professionalism.

Then there is the novel's darker historical side.

Toole passed away before seeing his manuscript published, taking his own life on March 26, 1996, at just thirty-one years old. His mother, grief-stricken and depressed, found a copy of *A Confederacy of Dunces* atop an armoire in his old bedroom and believed it had the potential to prove to people just how talented her son was. Seven publishers rejected it over a five-year period, about which she said, "Each time it came back I died a little." She decided to seek out Walker Percy in 1976, having learned that he was a staff member at Loyola University in New Orleans. Several unanswered phone calls and letters later, she filled the doorway to his office, demanding that he read the manuscript. Percy described the event in the book's foreword, writing, "The lady was persistent, and it somehow came to pass that she stood in my office handing me the hefty manuscript. There was no getting out of it; only one hope remained—that I could read a few pages and that they would be bad enough for me, in good conscience, to read no farther. Usually I can do just that. Indeed the first paragraph often suffices. My only fear was that this one might not be bad enough, or might be just good enough, so that I would have to keep reading. In this case I read on. And on. First with the sinking feeling that it was not bad enough to quit, then with a prickle of interest, then a growing excitement, and finally an incredulity: surely it was not possible that it was so good." It would be three more years before it was published to critical acclaim, as Toole was posthumously awarded the Pulitzer Prize for Fiction in 1981.

LEAVES OF GRASS

Walt Whitman

1855

Leaves of Grass started off as a short collection of twelve unnamed poems, no more than ninety-five pages in length, per Whitman's intention that the book be pocket-sized. "That would tend to induce people to take me along with them and read me in the open air: I am nearly always successful with the reader in the open air," he said. Having received one of the eight hundred first editions, Ralph Waldo Emerson wrote to Whitman, "I find it the most extraordinary piece of wit and wisdom America has yet contributed . . . I am very happy in reading it, as great power makes us happy." The letter started, "I Greet You at the Beginning of a Great Career."

It was in response to an 1844 essay written by Emerson, called "The Poet," that *Leaves of Grass* was written. Emerson recognized the fact that the United States was undergoing drastic changes, and called out the need for a unique poet who could emulate those changes in their work. Whitman downplayed Emerson's role slightly, saying, "I was simmering, simmering, simmering; Emerson brought me to a boil." But upon receiving Emerson's letter of praise, Whitman expanded the collection to 384 pages in 1856, the first of seven expansions that would occur between then and 1891, when the ninth and final edition was put into publication. Dubbed the "deathbed edition," Whitman wrote to a friend, "L. of G. at last complete—after thirty-three [years] of hackling at it, all times & moods of my life, fair weather & foul, all parts of the land, and peace & war, young & old."

On the collection's final publication, *The New York Herald* published an announcement, reading, "Walt Whitman wishes respectfully to notify the public that the book *Leaves of Grass*, which he has been working on at great intervals and partially issued for the past thirty-five or forty years, is now completed, so to call it, and he would like this new 1892 edition to absolutely supersede all previous ones. Faulty as it is, he decides it as by far his special and entire self-chosen poetic utterance." The collection had grown significantly across editions, going from twelve in 1855 to four hundred in 1892. It is ironic that such an iconic collection is titled *Leaves of Grass*, as "grass" is an industry term for works of little value and "leaves" are the pages on which they are printed.

TO KILL A MOCKINGBIRD

Harper Lee

1960

To Kill a Mockingbird's most visible influences shine through in Harper Lee's characters, beginning with Atticus Finch. Lee wrote Finch in her father's image; like Finch, Amasa Coleman Lee was also a defense lawyer. In his final case, he defended two black men on murder charges, but they were convicted, hanged and mutilated. The trial upset Lee so much that he quit criminal law altogether. But there were many other influences as well. Lee often acknowledged that she based Dill on Truman Capote, Harper Lee's childhood friend with whom she bonded over long literary discussions. Lee lived down the street from a family that lived in a boarded-up house, a likely source of inspiration for the Radleys, while Tom Robinson could have been based on any number of black men killed for what they allegedly did to white women, with accusations ranging from rape to simple flirting. Maycomb, Alabama, was also inspired by Lee's hometown of Monroeville, Alabama. Scout was, to an extent, written in her likeness, as both were tomboys who had brothers four years older than they were.

THE NARRATIVE OF ARTHUR GORDON PYM OF NANTUCKET

Edgar Allan Poe

1838

While it's not immediately obvious, those who have studied Edgar Allan Poe's *Arthur Gordon Pym* have noted the fact that the novel seems to be influenced heavily by the author's life. Both Pym and Poe are known by their full names and have similar last names, while the "Gordon" in Arthur Gordon Pym can likely be attributed to Poe's affection for poet George Gordon Byron. Pym leaves Martha's Vineyard, an area that Poe had at one point called home, and arrives at the island of Tsalal on January 19, Poe's birthday. Augustus, a character many believe to be based on Poe's brother who served in South America aboard the USS *Macedonian*, dies on the same day as his presumed inspiration. Even Pym disguising himself from his grandfather can likely be traced back to Poe's disdain for familial obligation, particularly as it pertained to his foster father John Allan.

THE AGE OF INNOCENCE

Edith Wharton

1920

The first novel written by a woman to receive the Pulitzer Prize for Fiction, Edith Wharton's *The Age of Innocence* speaks to both the personal and national shift in the early twentieth century. Originally published in the *Pictorial Review* as a four-part series, Wharton's work is written from the perspective of a high-society woman in New York City, a place and time where decorum and routine ruled the day. "I found a momentary escape," writes Wharton, "in going back to my childish memories of a long-vanished America . . . it was growing more and more evident that the world I had grown up in and been formed by had been destroyed in 1914."

Wharton, who was in Europe during World War I and experienced mechanized warfare first-hand, was forced to reconcile the fact that this new age of destruction meant that the world she had known her entire life had changed forever.

She channelled that reconciliation into *The Age of Innocence*, which she started just after President Roosevelt's death—the point at which the transition to a new world was most palpable. The title, while sometimes interpreted as a nod toward the hypocrisy displayed by New York City's elite at the turn of the century, clearly speaks to a time long gone that can never be recaptured.

THE PHANTOM TOLLBOOTH

Norton Juster

———

1961

While discussing *The Phantom Tollbooth*, Norton Juster tells NPR, "Like most good things that have happened in my life, *The Phantom Tollbooth* came about because I was trying to avoid doing something else. It was 1958, and after three years in the Navy I returned to New York City to work as an architect. I had also received a grant to do a book on cities for children. I started with great energy and enthusiasm until I found myself waist-deep in stacks of 3-by-5 note cards, exhausted and dispirited. This is not what I wanted to do. In order to stop thinking about cities, I had to start thinking about something else. I had been an odd child: quiet, introverted and moody. Little was expected from me. Everyone left me alone to wander around inside my own head. When I grew up I still felt like that puzzled kid—disconnected, disinterested and confused. There was no rhyme or reason in his life. My thoughts focused on him, and I began writing about his childhood, which was really mine."

FEAR AND LOATHING IN LAS VEGAS
Hunter S. Thompson

1971

Hoping to interview attorney and activist Oscar Zeta Acosta in an environment free from the racism and bigotry that polluted early-1970s Los Angeles, Hunter S. Thompson decided to take *Sports Illustrated* up on their offer to have him pen photo captions for a desert race in Las Vegas. Ironically enough, the same publication would later reject a 2,500-word manuscript born from the trip—Thompson's *Fear and Loathing in Las Vegas.*

Thompson's initial goal was to interview Acosta, a Mexican-American political activist, about the killing of Mexican-American journalist Rubén Salazar, who had been shot with a tear gas grenade by the LAPD from close range while protesting the Vietnam War. However, in Thompson's own words, "The pressure was so heavy . . . I found it impossible to talk to Oscar alone. We were always in the midst of a crowd of heavy streetfighters who didn't mind letting me know that they wouldn't need much of an excuse to chop me into hamburger. This is no way to work on a very volatile and very complex story. So one afternoon I got Oscar in my rented car and drove him over to the Beverly Hills Hotel—away from his bodyguards, etc.—and I told him I was getting a bit wiggy from the pressure; it was like being on stage all the time, or maybe in the midst of a prison riot. He agreed, but the nature of his position as 'leader of the militants' made it impossible for him to be openly friendly with a gabacho."

What followed was the first of Thompson and Acosta's two trips to Vegas, where Thompson began putting the Salazar story together while working on a side project detailing the observations he had during the trip. "Oscar had to get back for a nine o'clock court appearance on Monday," writes Thompson. "So he took a plane and I was left alone out there—just me and a massive hotel bill that I knew I couldn't pay, and the treacherous reality of that scene caused me to spend about thirty-six straight hours in my room at the Mint Hotel . . . writing feverishly in a notebook about a nasty situation I thought I might not get away from. These notes were the genesis of *Fear and Loathing*. After my escape from Nevada and all through the tense work week that followed (spending all my afternoons on the grim streets of East LA and my nights at the typewriter in that Ramada Inn hideout) . . . my only loose and human moments would come around dawn when I could relax and mess around with this slow-building, stone-crazy Vegas story. By the time I got back to the Rolling Stone Hq. in San Francisco, the Salazar story was winding out at around nineteen thousand words, and the strange Vegas 'fantasy' was running on its own spaced energy and pushing five thousand words—with no end in sight and no real reason to continue working on it, except the pure pleasure of unwinding on paper. It was sort of an exercise—like Bolero—and it might have stayed that way if Jann Wenner, the editor of *Rolling Stone*, hadn't liked the first twenty or so jangled pages enough to take seriously on its own terms and tentatively schedule it for publication—which gave me the push I needed to keep working on it."

Thompson and Acosta returned to Vegas a month after their first trip, reporting on the National District Attorneys Association's Conference on Narcotics and Dangerous Drugs for *Rolling Stone*. While there, they sought to substantiate the latter half of *Fear and Loathing*, putting particular emphasis on the idea of the American Dream. Once he had put the full manuscript together, *Rolling Stone* published it as a two-part article titled "Fear and Loathing in Las Vegas: A Savage Journey to the Heart of the American Dream."

"Fear and Loathing in Las Vegas is a failed experiment in Gonzo Journalism," writes Thompson. "My idea was to buy a fat notebook and record the whole thing, as it happened, then send in the notebook for publication—without editing. That was what I felt, the eye and mind of the journalist would be functioning as a camera . . . But this is a hard thing to do, and in the end I found myself imposing an essentially fictional framework on what began as a piece of straight/crazy journalism . . . although it's not what I meant it to be, it's still so complex in its failure that I feel I can take the risk of defending it as a first, gimped effort in a direction that what Tom Wolfe calls 'The New Journalism' has been flirting with for almost a decade."

THE BONFIRE OF THE VANITIES

Tom Wolfe

1987

Like so many others, Tom Wolfe was fascinated with the New York City of the 1980s. The resurgence of Wall Street after a bad decade, the city's seedy underbelly slowly bubbling to the surface through crime and homelessness, and increasingly high racial tension made the 1980s the perfect time to capture the city on paper.

Wolfe travelled with homicide squads in the Bronx and sat in on criminal court cases in Manhattan to research his book, which he believed would work best if published piece-by-piece in a bi-weekly or monthly magazine. That way, he reasoned, deadlines would pressure him into writing, and he'd get to emulate the style of Victorian-era writers he idolized. Jann Werner paid Wolfe $200,000 to publish his work in *Rolling Stone*, which ran sections of *The Bonfire of the Vanities* bi-weekly for thirteen months.

The book's conflict begins with a white bond trader on Wall Street hitting a black man with his car, assuming that the group had approached him with intent to harm. Such an instance conceivably had historical accuracy, considering that high-profile cases of black men being killed in white neighborhoods occurred with shocking frequency. The character Myron Kovitsky, on the other hand, can trace his origins back directly to Burton B. Roberts, a famous judge in the Bronx.

ANIMAL FARM

George Orwell

1945

As a vocal critic of excessive government power, George Orwell's socialist mentality came from years of witnessing the elitism of British imperialism in India, having been born in Bengal. Orwell's strain of socialism, born out of genuine thought, rather than dogmatic allegiance, led him to question the Soviet Union's system. Although the country's name was Union of Soviet Socialist Republics, Joseph Stalin did little to appeal to international socialist thinkers like Orwell. While fighting in the Spanish Civil War, Orwell saw "how easily totalitarian propaganda can control the opinion of enlightened people in democratic countries." Stalin, having overturned the semi-feudal system that spread power amongst the tsars in favor of a single dictatorship, was the embodiment of that observation. Orwell condemned the Soviets as such, believing that they portrayed socialism in a very negative light.

In *Animal Farm*, Napoleon is made to represent Joseph Stalin, while Snowball represents Leon Trotsky. As chaos reigned under the rule of Vladimir Lenin, his allies began competing for his position, with Stalin and Trotsky emerging as frontrunners. Stalin consolidated power behind the scenes to best Trotsky, expelling him from Russia in 1936. Fear and famine plagued Russia under Stalin's rule; in order to secure his people's support, Stalin created unity out of hatred by using Trotsky as his scapegoat. Like Stalin, Napoleon secures power and exiles Snowball, still blaming him when the windmill falls.

As for his use of animals, Orwell writes, "I saw a little boy, perhaps ten years old, driving a huge carthorse along a narrow path, whipping it whenever it tried to turn. It struck me that if only such animals became aware of their strength we should have no power over them, and that men exploit animals in much the same way as the rich exploit the proletariat."

THE ALCHEMIST

Paulo Coelho

———

1988

"When I finally feel I'm ready to embark on a new book, I always go through the following cycle that takes me from two weeks to a month," says Paulo Coelho in an interview with *The Guardian*. "Before going to bed I have everything planned: I will wake up early and dedicate myself solely to the novel I'm writing. The only thing is, when I wake up I decide to browse through the net, then it's time for my walk. When I come back I quickly check my mails and before I know it it's already 2:30 p.m. and time to have lunch. After which I always take a sacrosanct nap. When I wake up at 5 p.m. I come back to my computer, check another set of emails, visit my blogs, read the news. Then it is already time for dinner—and at this point I'm feeling extremely guilty for not fulfilling my goal of the day. After dinner, I finally sit at my desk and decide to write. The first line takes a bit but quickly I'm submerged in the tale and ideas take me to places that I never thought I would tread. My wife calls me to go to bed but I can't, I need to finish the line, then the paragraph, then the page . . . It goes on like this until 2–3 a.m. When I finally decide to go to bed, I still have many ideas in my mind, that I carefully note down on a piece of paper. I know though that I'll never use this—I'm simply emptying my mind. When I finally rest my head on my pillow I make the same oath—that the next day I'll wake up early and that I'll write the whole day long. But this is useless: the next day I wake up late and this cycle starts all over again." Coelho put this exact strategy to work when writing *The Alchemist*, as he claims that it only took him two weeks to write the book from start to finish. As for the inspiration behind the book? There wasn't any. As Coelho said, "The book was already written in my soul."

THE LORD OF THE FLIES

William Goulding

―――

1954

William Goulding gathered inspiration for his *Lord of the Flies* from R.M. Ballantyne and his novel *The Coral Island*, in which three boys are left stranded on an island after a shipwreck. Like *Lord of the Flies*, the book features an all-juvenile cast of characters who are isolated on a foreign island; unlike *Lord of the Flies*, the conflicts that the children face deal with external factors, whereas Goulding's work deals with conflict as a product of mental corruption. Goulding's Ralph, Piggy and Jack are said to resemble Ballantyne's Ralph, Peterkin and Jack, a similarity embraced by giving his characters similar names. Goulding goes as far as to explicitly mention *Coral Island* in his text, writing the naval officer's line of dialogue in regards to the children chasing Ralph at the end of the novel: "a jolly good show, like the Coral Island."

A PRAYER FOR OWEN MEANY

John Irving

1989

"Suddenly one of my friends mentioned a name that drew a blank with me—a Russell some-body," recalls Irving. "Then another one of my friends reminded me that, in Sunday School, we used to lift up this little boy; he was our age, about eight or nine, but he was so tiny that we could pass him back and forth over our heads. I was amazed. I said one of the stupidest things I've ever said. 'But he was too *small* to go to Vietnam!' My friends looked at me with pity and concern. 'Johnny,' one of them said, 'I presume he *grew*.' That night I lay awake in bed, pondering the 'What if . . . ' That is the beginning of every novel for me. What if he didn't grow? I was thinking." The Sunday School scene would be written into the book, while the subject of his memory would inspire John Irving's protagonist in *A Prayer for Owen Meany*.

Irving sought to capture the toll that the Vietnam War had on his generation, both physical and mental. The physical ranged from dying in combat to disfiguring yourself to avoid being drafted. The mental dealt more with losing a fellow soldier, a relative who was serving or a lifelong friend whose life was no longer. "That was exactly what I was looking for," said Irving in a speech to Yale students. "Someone who is a victim of the war, but not the victim you see coming from Vietnam. [Owen Meany] definitely is a victim of that war, as our country continues to be a victim of that war . . . The last thing you expect is to lose someone of your age. I lose people of my age all the time. But if you lose a friend at your age, it changes your life." The idea that a Vietnam War victim may not have served, coupled with his learning about Russell's death in the war, inspired Irving to write *A Prayer for Owen Meany*.

A HANDFUL OF DUST

Evelyn Waugh

1934

"The idea for [the short story] came quite naturally from the experience of visiting a lonely settler . . . and reflecting on how easily he could hold me prisoner," writes Waugh. "Then, after the short story was written and published, the idea kept working in my mind. I wanted to discover how the prisoner got there, and eventually the thing grew into a study of other sorts of savage at home and the civilized man's helpless plight among them." Waugh's "The Man Who Liked Dickens," the short story that would inspire *A Handful of Dust*, was conceived after a South American man named Mr. Christie told him, "I was expecting you. I was warned in a vision of your approach." The two had dinner that night, at which point Christie spoke of the "Fifth Kingdom" and his having seen it. Waugh found himself stuck in Boa Vista days later and, due to boredom, began writing the short story based in part on his recent experience.

Noting the autobiographical elements of *A Handful of Dust*, critic Cyril Connolly called it "the only book which understands the true horror of the withdrawal of affection in an affair from [the point of view of] the innocent party." Prior to his trip to South America, Waugh had attempted to reconcile his marriage, which had fallen apart after his wife told him that she was in love with their mutual friend John Heygate. While derivations of his ex-wife and former friend may be absent from the book, many of the other characters were inspired by some of Waugh's actual friends. Mr. Todd was written in the image of Mr. Christie, Dr. Messinger resembles W.E. Roth, with whom Waugh was going to travel to the interior of South America before backing out and Thérèse de Vitré was inspired by his platonic friend Teresa Jungman. The novel was originally published as a five-part series in *Harper's Bazaar* in 1934, before being published in book form later that year.

The book's title, *A Handful of Dust*, came from a line in T.S. Eliot's *The Waste Land*, which reads, "I will show you fear in a handful of dust." The novel's feeling of emptiness is reflected in the section of Eliot's poem containing this line, titled "The Burial of the Dead."

BREAKFAST AT TIFFANY'S

Truman Capote

—

1958

The inspiration behind Capote's Holiday Golightly character, named Connie Gustafson in his earlier drafts, is the source of much speculation. Many women claimed to be the model for Capote's character, including writers Doris Lilly and Maeve Brennan, actress Carol Grace, socialites Gloria Vanderbilt and Oona O'Neill and models Dorian Leigh and Suzy Parker (who were also sisters). Even Nina Capote, Truman's mother, shares some similarities with Holiday. Both were born in the South, left their husbands to move to New York City and achieved favorable social standing while dating wealthy men. Aside from his mother, actress Joan McCracken likely has the most legitimate claim to the "Holly Golightly Sweepstakes," as Capote dubbed it. McCracken starred in the play *Oklahoma!,* from which Holly sings songs. She had also had a traumatized outburst when learning of her brother's death overseas, an event experienced by Holly in *Breakfast at Tiffany's.*

INFINITE JEST

David Foster Wallace

1996

Though David Foster Wallace began writing *Infinite Jest* at some point in the mid-1980s, consistent progress didn't begin until the 1990s. In an interview with *Salon*, he recalls, "I wanted to do something sad. I'd done some funny stuff and some heavy, intellectual stuff, but I'd never done anything sad. And I wanted it not to have a single main character. The other banality would be: I wanted to do something real American, about what it's like to live in America around the millennium . . . There's something particularly sad about it, something that doesn't have very much to do with physical circumstances, or the economy, or any of the stuff that gets talked about in the news. It's more like a stomach-level sadness. I see it in myself and my friends in different ways. It manifests itself as a kind of lostness. Whether it's unique to our generation I don't really know." He sought to write fiction that was human—that enlightened and touched the reader while embracing sentimentality. In an interview with the *Review of Contemporary Fiction*, Wallace laid out what he believed fiction should be, saying, "Really good fiction could have as dark a worldview as it wished, but it'd find a way both to depict this world and to illuminate the possibilities for being alive and human in it."

Originally titled *A Failed Entertainment*, David Foster Wallace took his new title from act v, scene 1 of Hamlet, which reads, "Hamlet: Alas, poor Yorick! I knew him, Horatio: a fellow of infinite jest, of most excellent fancy: he hath borne me on his back a thousand times; and now, how abhorred in my imagination it is!" In the scene, Hamlet is holding in his hand the skull of the court jester, Yorick, in as blatant an example of irony as a scene could possibly provide.

THE SOT-WEED FACTOR

John Barth

———

1960

In *The Sot-Weed Factor*, John Barth returned to an older form of novel-writing, embracing excess, irony and the metafictional rather than the conventional realism that his past works were known for. Those works, *The Floating Opera* and *The End of the Road*, were two of what was supposed to be a trilogy on nihilism, with *The*

Sot-Weed Factor slotted to be the third book in the series. Instead, it became a work in parodies, as Barth targeted the eighteenth-century genre of both the *Bildungsroman*, or formation novels, and *Künstlerroman*, or novels on the formation of an artist. Works like *Tom Jones*, *Tristram Shandy* and *Pocahontas* are rewritten in *The Sot-Weed Factor*, making the work incredibly unique for its time. The experience was, if nothing else, entirely unique for Barth, as it marked his discovery of postmodernism. "Looking back, I am inclined to declare grandly that I needed to discover, or to be discovered by, Postmodernism."

Barth owes one Ebenezer Cooke for the title of his novel, as he borrowed it from Cooke's 1708 poem of the same name. "Sot-weed" is a term for the tobacco plant, while a "factor" can be used to describe a middleman. On the subject, Barth writes, "*The Sot-Weed Factor* began with the title and, of course, Ebenezer Cooke's original poem . . . Nobody knows where the real chap is buried; I made up a grave for Ebenezer because I wanted to write his epitaph."

WATER FOR ELEPHANTS

Sara Gruen

2006

"I was actually two weeks into another novel and had just returned from a research trip to Hawaii," Sara Gruen says on the inspiration behind *Water for Elephants*. "I opened up a paper and found a vintage circus photograph . . . the negatives could capture an enormous amount of detail on hundreds of people at once. You could see every rhinestone and every beret, the wrinkles in the stockings, the fronds and the feathers. It just occurred to me at that moment that this situation is a fiction writer's dream. I mean, anything can happen, and believably. I started stabbing the paper and saying 'this, I'm doing this next!' And so I did."

Execution of this concept was made easier thanks to Gruen's love of animals, on which she says, "It seems natural to surround my fictional world with animals because my reality is full of them. When I'm sitting there conceiving a story, they just pop up . . . [I've got] three goats that I'm boarding, two horses, four cats and two dogs."

LUCKY JIM

Kingsley Amis

1954

"It was conceived, if that's the right word, way back in 1946, when I happened to visit Philip Larkin, who was on the library staff at Leicester University. The young man surrounded by bores whom for various reasons he doesn't dare to offend—that was all there. The contribution of Swansea, so to speak, was just to give me information about how things were run: what the faculty is, who the registrar is and what he does, what classes are like, what exam responsibilities are like, et cetera. But there's no character in the book, however minor, who was actually there at Swansea."

So says Kingsley Amis about the origins of *Lucky Jim*, a book that took him years to finish. As Amis explains, "Being busy and being lazy, which so often go together, my first year at Oxford after the war was spent celebrating not being in the army. Then I had to work hard for my final exams. At Swansea it took me some time to get to grips with the heavy work-load, and meanwhile there were also domestic responsibilities in the form of a wife and two young children who turned up very fast, one after the other. And another point was lack of a possible place to write in. The only requirement, I think, is a room to oneself, however small. Fortunately my wife received a small legacy and we got a house in Swansea which had such a room in it and instantly I began *Lucky Jim*. But that was a slow process: I had to redraft the whole thing. The first draft was very feeble, so I showed it to friends, particularly Philip Larkin again, who made very constructive suggestions. And then I started again from scratch, a thing I haven't done since. So it was not only delayed by external circumstances, but also, I think, by inexperience."

THE RED BADGE OF COURAGE

Stephen Crane

1895

Stephen Crane's literary career took off while he lived with his brother, Edmund, in Lake View, New Jersey. Having published *Maggie: A Girl on the Streets* to little fanfare in 1893, he went back to his freelance writing, which saw him contribute to a number of different New York

City newspapers. When not writing, he would spend his days relaxing at his friend's studio, perusing various issues of *Century Magazine* he had laying around. Much of the reading dealt with the Civil War, which Crane felt lacked any sort of emotion. "I wonder that some of those fellows don't tell how they felt in those scraps," said Crane. "They spout enough of what they did, but they're as emotionless as rocks."

Believing that he could bring some literary prowess to the stories, Crane decided to write on the subject of war himself, claiming that the story had been working itself out unconsciously since his childhood. He began writing *The Red Badge of Courage* in 1893, naming the protagonist after his sister-in-law's maiden name. The fifty-five-thousand-word manuscript was trimmed down so that it could be published in newspapers before being released as a novel, a strategy that worked well; the story was published in more than seven hundred different publications. A fifty-thousand-word manuscript was eventually published in October 1985.

THE ODYSSEY

Homer

---

late 8th century BCE

In "The East Face of Helicon: West Asiatic Elements in Greek Poetry and Myth," Martin West points out some significant similarities between *The Odyssey* and *The Epic of Gilgamesh*, to the point where it seems likely that the Mesopotamian poem inspired much of Homer's writing. The biggest similarity between the two works was the heros' journey to the ends of the earth, where the goddesses who guide them through the land of the dead are said to live. In the case of *The Odyssey* the goddess is Circe, while in *The Epic of Gilgamesh* it's Siduri—both of whom have ties to the sun.

Othenio Abel, a paleontologist, believes that the origins of the cyclops had to do with the ancient Greeks finding the skull of an elephant. Having never seen one before, it wouldn't be ridiculous to assume that many believed the giant nasal passage to be one single giant eye socket.

THE LONG GOODBYE

Raymond Chandler

1953

Self-heralded as the best book he had ever written, Raymond Chandler's *The Long Goodbye* was far and away his most personal novel. His time spent writing the book was plagued by depression and alcoholism, as his wife had slowly succumbed to an illness that left him in a drunken state for much of his life going forward. Chandler, perhaps as a sort of therapy, wrote aspects of himself in two of the novel's characters, Roger Wade and Terry Lennox. On a lighter note, Wade loves F. Scott Fitzgerald and shares much of Chandler's literary interests. On a darker note, he's an alcoholic writer who is desperate to be taken seriously. He knows that his best work is likely behind him and that many critics don't take his works in romantic fiction seriously, when really that's all he wants.

Lennox, like Wade and Chandler, is also an alcoholic. However, rather than representing the author's writer side, he reflects the side of him that served in World War I. For the sake of the story's time line, Lennox served in World War II; while the wars were different, the lasting effects were similar, as both never fully recovered emotionally. Lennox also spends a lot of time in England, where Chandler was raised and attended school, and took a liking for their general way of living and interacting. This made the transition to Los Angeles even more shocking for both the author and the character, as they each felt that the city lacked any desirable culture or nuance.

The Long Goodbye was Chandler's last piece of significant work, as his wife's death the year after it was published led him to attempt suicide and, after he had been stopped, live a life of alcoholism until his death five years later.

A CLOCKWORK ORANGE

Anthony Burgess

———

1962

Anthony Burgess substantiated most of *A Clockwork Orange* with his observations of youth culture and juvenile delinquency in early-1960s Britain. Having been abroad, Burgess was shocked by the cultural shift—the country he'd returned to no longer resembled the one he left behind. His decision to write the novel, however, was based on a personal tragedy that came years earlier: his wife's miscarriage. She had been beaten by a group of drunken American servicemen who were stationed in England during World War II and miscarried a short time later, most likely as a direct result.

Burgess doesn't offer one clear source of inspiration for the title *A Clockwork Orange*, though he does speak on it quite a bit. In an interview on the television program *Camera Three*, Burgess says, "Well, the title has a very different meaning but only to a particular generation of London Cockneys. It's a phrase which I heard many years ago and so fell in love with, I wanted to use it, the title of the book. But the phrase itself I did not make up. The phrase 'as queer as a clockwork orange' is good old East London slang and it didn't seem to me necessary to explain it. Now, obviously, I have to give it an extra meaning. I've implied an extra dimension. I've implied the junction of the organic, the lively, the sweet—in other words, life, the orange—and the mechanical, the cold, the disciplined. I've brought them together in this kind of oxymoron, this sour-sweet word." That answer confused a lot of people, as no record of the expression had appeared prior to the novel's publication. He also wrote in *A Clockwork Orange: A Play with Music* that the title was a metaphor for "an organic entity, full of juice and sweetness and agreeable odour, being turned into a mechanism."

THE RECOGNITIONS

William Gaddis

1955

"We come back to the Faust story and to the original Clementine *Recognitions*, which has been called the first Christian novel (I remember thinking mine was going to be the last one)," said William Gaddis in a 1987 interview with *The Paris Review*, "about his search for salvation, redemption, and so forth. And I had these notions of basing *The Recognitions* on the constant presence of the past and of its imposition of myth in different forms that eventually come down to the same stories in any culture. I think they titled the Italian edition *The Pilgrim* or *The Pilgrimage* or something like that. In a sense, it *is* that: a pilgrimage toward salvation."

Gaddis' crowning achievement started as a short parody of Johann Wolfgang von Goethe's Faust, a two-part tragedy considered to be one of the greatest works of German literature. It eventually evolved into a seven-year project, during which Gaddis' travels to Mexico, Central America and Europe influenced his writing. On the genesis of his novel, he said, "I think first it was that towering kind of confidence of being quite young, that one can do anything—'All's brave that youth mounts and folly guides,' as we're told in *As You Like It*. *The Recognitions* started as a short piece of work, quite undirected, but based on the Faust story. Then as I got into the idea of forgery, the entire concept of forgery became—I wouldn't say an obsession—but a central part of everything I thought and saw; so the book expanded from simply the central character of the forger to forgery, falsification and cheapening of values and what have you, everywhere. Looking at it now with its various faults, I suppose excess would be the main charge. I remember Clive Bell looking back on his small fine book, *Art*, 35 years after it was published in 1913, and listing its faults, finding it too confident and aggressive, even too optimistic—I was never accused of that!—but still feeling, as he said, 'a little envious of the adventurous young man who wrote it.' "

In writing *The Recognitions*, Gaddis also joined the ranks of authors who have written less than flattering reflections of themselves into their work. For Gaddis, Otto is that character. Sheri Martinelli, a famous poet and painter, was the inspiration for the character Esme, while Richard Nixon was written into the story in the form of the minister Dick. The book underwent a number of revisions in the five-year window between Gaddis finishing

the work and actually submitting it for publication, resulting in a 480,000-word manuscript.

MARY POPPINS

P.L. Travers

1934

One of P.L. Travers' lesser-known short stories
is believed to contain the real-life inspiration
behind her beloved Mary Poppins character,
though this has never been confirmed. In an
interview on BBC Radio in 1977, Travers
claimed that the name came from childhood
stories that she would tell her sisters when she
was younger, but provided no insight as to what
substantiated the character behind the name. It
appears as though inspiration came in the form
of her great-aunt Helen Morehead, otherwise
known as Aunt Sass, who would often say things
like "spit spot, into bed." Travers writes, "Her
remarkableness lay in the extraordinary and, to
me, enchanting discrepancy between her external
behavior and her inner self." Travers describes
Aunt Sass as having a "heart tender to the point
of sentimentality," while also being a "bulldog
with a ferocious exterior."

NAKED LUNCH

William S. Burroughs

———

1959

Meant to be read in any order, the loosely connected stories in William S. Burroughs' *The Naked Lunch* are traditionally called "vignettes" but are referred to by the author as "routines." These "routines" are a result of notes taken and short stories written over the span of many years, on which Burroughs tells *The Paris Review*, "I came back to Tangier and I started working on a lot of notes that I had made over a period of years. Most of the book was written at that time. I went to Paris about 1959, and I had a great pile of manuscripts. Girodias was interested and he asked if I could get the book ready in two weeks. This is the period that Brion is referring to when, from manuscripts collected over a period of years, I assembled what became the book from some thousand pages, something like that."

Burroughs' fascination with the world of the carnival helped connect many of his stories, as he gave many of his characters those origins. He says, "The carny world was the one I exactly intended to create—a kind of Midwestern, small-town, cracker-barrel, pratfall type of folklore, very much my own background. That world was an integral part of America and existed nowhere else, at least not in the same form. My family was southern on my mother's side. My grandfather was a circuit-riding Methodist minister with thirteen children. Most of them went up to New York and became quite successful in advertising and public relations. One of them, an uncle, was a master image maker, Ivy Lee, Rockefeller's publicity manager."

Of course, Burroughs was a member of Beat generation, joining writers like Ken Kesey and Jack Kerouac, whose literature was heavily influenced by their experience with drugs. Burroughs was no different, as he was addicted to morphine, majoun (a German opioid) and, most notably, heroin. These addictions enabled him to write himself into the book as protagonist William Lee and take the reader on a heroin-laced journey that explores the theme of addiction or, as Burroughs calls it, the "algebra of need."

Addiction not only gave his novel a narrative, it also inspired many characters, such as the *The Heavy Metal Kid*. "I felt that heavy metal was sort of the ultimate expression of addiction," says Burroughs. "That there's something actually metallic in addiction, that the final stage is not so much vegetable as mineral. It's increasingly inanimate, in any case. You see, as Dr. Benway said, I've now decided that junk is not green, but blue. Some of my characters come to me in dreams—Daddy Long Legs, for instance. Once, in a clinic, I had a dream in which I saw a man in this run-down clinic and his name in the dream was Daddy Long Legs. Many characters have come to me like that in a dream, and then I'll elaborate from there. I always write down all my dreams."

The same can be said for the character Hamburger Mary, on which Burroughs says, "There was a place in New York called Hamburger Mary's. I was in Hamburger Mary's when a friend gave me a batch of morphine syrettes. That was my first experience with morphine, and I built up a whole picture of Hamburger Mary. She is also an actual person. I don't like to give her name for fear of being sued for libel, but she was a Scientologist who started out in a hamburger joint in Portland, Oregon, and now has 11 million dollars."

His multiple drug addictions also put him in touch with the world he wanted to write about—the "underworld," as he calls it. "The old-time thieves, pickpockets, and people like that. They're a dying race," he says. "Very few of those old-timers left. Yeah, well, they were show business."

The title *Naked Lunch* can also be traced back to Burroughs' Beat generation contemporaries, as it was suggested by Jack Kerouac. In the novel's introduction, Burroughs writes, "The title means exactly what the words say: naked lunch, a frozen moment when everyone sees what is on the end of every fork."

TRAINSPOTTING

Irvine Welsh

1993

"*Trainspotting* was the book I had to do, basically to get it out of the way, in order to become a writer," writes Irvine Welsh. "I had been obsessed with books and literature for a while, and having failed at everything else, thought that I could give writing a go. But I had to understand my own personal journey and the issues I had come through first. What sort of a person was I? What could I bring to this? I knew that I could never do genre fiction; I wouldn't have the ability to write into a marketing hole. It would bore me to tears and be too much like the proper jobs I hated. It had to be about me expressing myself, without recourse to formulae.

"When I looked at my notes and doodlings in diaries over the years, I didn't have much to bring to the table. My life was essentially defined by, at best, mediocrity (I had risen to middle-management level in the public sector), and at worst failure. This latter element was with reference to recurrent drug issues, which have been discussed at length elsewhere. So I decided that this would be my starting point."

Despite living what he deemed a "rich inner life," Walsh resigned himself to working odd jobs in trade professions, believing that the wealthy wrote and the working class consumed their writing recreationally. A son of often-ill working class parents, Welsh relied on reading as a retreat from reality. Writes Welsh, "I went on a search, from Russian classics to Black American writing, to try to find a voice and set of social circumstances that chimed. I found it back home in Ayrshire when I picked up a copy of William McIllvaney's *Docherty*. Then came James Kelman's *The Bus Conductor* Hines and Alasdair Gray's *Lanark*."

While he agreed with the principles of the books, Welsh still felt as though it was inevitable that the rich would win the class war, instilling in him a fear that the poorest parts of Britain would become even poorer. His sense of hopelessness and confusion inspired him to put pen to paper, as he writes, "I started to write *Trainspotting*, as a way of making sense of my own life and times. When I wrote the book I was living in different circumstances from the characters in it. I had a good job, was married, and largely had my substance abuse issues under control. Acid house knocked me out of this comfort zone. Soon I was back out tearing it up at the weekends, energized by the power of that scene, but also with a newfound reflectiveness that the ecstasy 'comedowns' exacerbated. I knocked out a draft from old notes and diaries. It was way too long— about 250,000 words. I just chopped the ends off, and wrote a (I thought fairly cheesy) heist ending, in order to finish the book. I thought it would never be published, but the first person I sent it to took it on. I don't know how many languages it's been translated into or how much it has sold worldwide, but it has cast a big shadow and I've resigned myself to being called '*Trainspotting* author Irvine Welsh' for the rest of my life, even though I've written better books and will hopefully continue to do so. I just know that for the last decade a big grin has split my face twice a year when the royalty cheque hits the doormat. So being 'the *Trainspotting* guy' isn't so bad."

DEATH OF A SALESMAN

Arthur Miller

——

1949

"The first play I wrote was in Michigan in 1935. It was written on a spring vacation in six days. I was so young that I dared do such things, begin it and finish it in a week. I'd seen about two plays in my life, so I didn't know how long an act was supposed to be, but across the hall there was a fellow who did the costumes for the University theater and he said, 'Well, it's roughly forty minutes.' I had written an enormous amount of material and I got an alarm clock. It was all a lark to me, and not to be taken too seriously . . . that's what I told myself. As it turned out, the acts were longer than that, but the sense of the timing was in me even from the beginning, and the play had a form right from the start. Being a playwright was always the maximum idea. I'd always felt that the theater was the most exciting and the most demanding form one could try to master."

As it would turn out, that first play would go on to inspire Arthur Miller to write *Death of a Salesman* as an exploration of the dynamic between fathers and sons. However, Miller was unable to draw from his own relationship with his father, as they were always very close. "It's a very primitive thing in my plays," he says. "That is, the father was really a figure who incorporated both power and some kind of a moral law which he had either broken himself or had fallen prey to. He figures as an immense shadow . . . I didn't expect that of my own father, literally, but of his position, apparently I did. The reason that I was able to write about the relationship, I think now, was because it had a mythical quality to me. If I had ever thought that I was writing about my father, I suppose I never could have done it. My father is, literally, a much more realistic guy than Willy Loman, and much more successful as a personality. And he'd be the last man in the world to ever commit suicide."

Rather than use his father, Miller based Loman on individuals he knew very little about. He says, "Willy is based on an individual whom I knew very little, who was a salesman; it was years later that I realized I had only seen that man about a total of four hours in twenty years. He gave one of those impressions that is basic, evidently. When I thought of him, he would simply be a mute man: he said no more than two hundred words to me. I was a kid. Later on, I had another of that kind of a contact, with a man whose fantasy was always overreaching his real outline. I've always been aware of that kind of an agony, of someone who has some driving, implacable wish in him which never goes away, which he can never block out. And it broods over him, it makes him happy sometimes or it makes him suicidal, but it never leaves him. Any hero we even begin to think of as tragic is obsessed, whether it's Lear or Hamlet or the women in the Greek plays."

ALL QUIET ON THE WESTERN FRONT

Erich Maria Remarque

1929

Erich Maria Remarque's *All Quiet on the Western Front* is rare for its completely accurate depiction of the harsh and sometimes torturous life that came with serving in World War I. Most novels of that time romanticized war, painting pictures of heroes and good versus evil without detailing what actually makes up a war—the deaths of many people who were forced to serve their country without having much choice in the matter. Remarque's work, on the other hand, comes from the perspective of a German soldier who is badly hurt by shrapnel, leaving him wounded in a German army hospital for the rest of the war.

The novel also explored what it was like to return home from war, having seen and experienced things that could not be visualized by somebody who wasn't there. An inability to integrate back into civilian life was common but rarely acknowledged, and most people didn't know how big an issue it was. Remarque's intent in writing *All Quiet on the Western Front* was to present an accurate portrayal that didn't glamorize what it was to go to war.

His anti-war stance would cost him; as Hitler and the Nazi regime rose to power in the early 1930s, Remarque was condemned as being unpatriotic. After writing a sequel to *All Quiet*, he felt as though his life might be in danger, so he fled with his then wife to Switzerland. Tragically, Nazi forces killed his sister because of her relation to the author.

GREAT EXPECTATIONS

Charles Dickens

1861

In a letter to his biographer John Forster, Dickens details his new idea for a story, writing about a young protagonist who befriends a criminal, receives a fortune as an indirect result and then has to forfeit that fortune to the Crown. Forster later claimed that the protagonist and the convict that Dickens was describing were the earliest iterations of Pip and Magwitch, around whom the plot of *Great Expectations* revolved. The work was published at a rate of thirty-six weekly installments in *All the Year Round*, a publication founded by Dickens that grew in popularity as word spread of his ability. It was a huge commitment for the aging Dickens, though he never failed to take it seriously. He once took friends and family on a pleasure cruise under the guise of a relaxation trip, secretly taking notes of the riverbanks so that he could accurately write Magwitch's attempted escape.

Prior to the publication of *Great Expectations*, Dickens was encouraged to change the ending by his contemporary Edward Bulwer-Lytton, who told him that the ending was too sad. In another letter to Forster, Dickens wrote, "You will be surprised to hear that I have changed the end of *Great Expectations* from and after Pip's return to Joe's . . . Bulwer, who has been, as I think you know, extraordinarily taken with the book, strongly urged it upon me, after reading the proofs, and supported his views with such good reasons that I have resolved to make the change. I have put in as pretty a little piece of writing as I could, and I have no doubt the story will be more acceptable through the alteration." Safe to say, both Dickens and Bulwer knew what they were doing.

THE CURIOUS INCIDENT OF THE DOG IN THE NIGHT-TIME

Mark Haddon

2003

In an essay for *The Guardian*, Mark Haddon reveals an unexpected source of inspiration for him: Jane Austen. He writes, "The book most often in my mind was *Pride and Prejudice*. Jane Austen was writing about boring people with desperately limited lives . . . Her heroines were bound by iron rules about what they could do, where they could go and what they could say. Their futures depended on the single question of who they would marry. Was it going to be the baronet? Or were they going to fall for a cad in tight red trousers and be discarded in a boarding house in Bath? Yet Jane Austen writes about these humdrum lives with such empathy that they seem endlessly fascinating. And her first act of empathy is to write about them in the kind of book these women would themselves read—the romantic novel. This was what I was trying to do in *Curious Incident*. To take a life that seemed horribly constrained, to write about it in the kind of book that the hero would read—a murder mystery—and hopefully show that if you viewed this life with sufficient imagination it would seem infinite . . . The first thing I was doing was writing to entertain myself rather than the person I remember being at six, or eight. Second, yes, the book has simple language, a carefully shaped plot and invites you to enter someone else's life. And these, I think, are the aspects of the book that appeal most to younger readers. But the book, I hope, does something more than that. The legs aren't quite the same length. It isn't entirely comfortable. It's about how little separates us from those we turn away from in the street. It's about how badly we communicate with one another. It's about accepting that every life is narrow and that our only escape from this is not to run away (to another country, another relationship, a slimmer, more confident self) but to learn to love the people we are and the world in which we find ourselves."

FRANKENSTEIN

Mary Shelley

———

1818

In her preface of the 1831 edition of *Frankenstein*, Mary Shelley poses the question: "How I, then a young girl, came to think of, and to dilate upon, so very hideous an idea?" The conditions that fostered her idea were rooted in devastation, as the 1815 eruption of Mount Tambora had a years-long effect on the Earth's climate. The result was a volcanic winter that stretched into the summer of 1816, appropriately called the "Year Without a Summer," when Shelley and her then boyfriend visited Lake Geneva in Switzerland to stay with Lord Byron at Villa Diodati.

The poor weather forced them inside by a log fireplace, where they dabbled in ghost stories to pass the time. Each person was prompted to write their own ghost story, something that Shelley struggled with until they spent an evening chatting about life. She brought up the re-animation of corpses as a topic, one that would haunt her all night, as she wrote in the 1831 introduction. "I saw the pale student of unhallowed arts kneeling beside the thing he had put together. I saw the hideous phantasm of a man stretched out, and then, on the working of some powerful engine, show signs of life, and stir with an uneasy, half vital motion. Frightful must it be; for supremely frightful would be the effect of any human endeavor to mock the stupendous mechanism of the Creator of the world." She got to work, originally intending to write a short story before evolving the idea into a novel, one that was published in three volumes at the start of 1818. It wasn't until 1831 that the work would appear together in one volume.

INVISIBLE MAN

Ralph Ellison

1952

As *Time* essayist Roger Rosenblatt said, "Ralph Ellison taught me what it is to be an American." Ellison grew up in Oklahoma, a state with no slavery legacy and one that offered unprecedented accessibility for young African Americans in the early twentieth century. Though poor, he was still able to attend a good school and, ever the intellectual, sought out peers who he could learn from. That process served as his introduction to the various cultures surrounding him in Oklahoma City, a cultural familiarity that spawned a new kind modernism in *Invisible Man*.

Ellison's experiences growing up were not those of his African American literary contemporaries, giving him no basis from which to carry on the status quo of making the black protagonist uneducated and angry; rather, his character was educated and able to express himself, and existed in a setting rich with authentic black culture and traditions. Ellison wrote *Invisible Man* to show the reader a world in which African Americans influenced major American customs, such as musical genres like jazz and the blues. The title *Invisible Man* refers to the apparent cultural invisibility of African Americans at the time—an idea the novel is quick to discredit through the various people Ellison's narrator meets. The title also refers to the idea that African Americans were often denied a voice in society, rending them invisible.

IT

Stephen King

1986

On the genesis of *IT*, Stephen King writes, "In 1978 my family was living in Boulder, Colorado. One day on our way back from lunch at a pizza emporium, our brand-new AMC Matador dropped its transmission—literally. The damn thing fell out on Pearl Street. True embarrassment is standing in the middle of a busy downtown street, grinning idiotically while people examine your marooned car and the large greasy black thing lying under it. Two days later the dealership called at about five in the afternoon. Everything was jake—I could pick up the car any time. The dealership was three miles away. I thought about calling a cab but decided that the walk would be good for me. The AMC dealership was in an industrial park set off by itself on a patch of otherwise deserted land a mile from the strip of fast-food joints and gas stations that mark the eastern edge of Boulder. A narrow unlit road led to this outpost. By the time I got to the road it was twilight—in the mountains the end of day comes in a hurry—and I was aware of how alone I was. About a quarter of a mile along this road was a wooden bridge, humped and oddly quaint, spanning a stream. I walked across it. I was wearing cowboy boots with rundown heels, and I was very aware of the sound they made on the boards; they sounded like a hollow clock. I thought of the fairy tale called 'The Three Billy-Goats Gruff' and wondered what I would do if a troll called out from beneath me, 'Who is trip-trapping upon my bridge?' All of a sudden I wanted to write a novel about a real troll under a real bridge. I stopped, thinking of a line by Marianne Moore, something about 'real toads in imaginary gardens,' only it came out 'real trolls in imaginary gardens.' A good idea is like a yo-yo—it may go to the end of its string, but it doesn't die there; it only sleeps. Eventually it rolls back up into your palm. I forgot about the bridge and the troll in the business of picking up my car and signing the papers, but it came back to me off and on over the next two years. I decided that the bridge could be some sort of symbol—a point of passing. I started thinking of Bangor, where I had lived, with its strange canal bisecting the city, and decided that the bridge could be the city, if there was something under it. What's under a city? Tunnels. Sewers. Ah! What a good place for a troll! Trolls should live in sewers! A year passed. The yo-yo stayed down at the end of its string, sleeping, and then it came back up. I started to remember Stratford, Connecticut, where I had lived for a time as a kid. In Stratford there was a library where the adult section and the children's section was connected by a short corridor. I decided that the corridor was also a bridge, one across which every goat of a child must risk trip-trapping to become an adult. About six months later I thought of how such a story might be cast; how it might be possible to create a ricochet effect, interweaving the stories of children and the adults they become. Sometime in the summer of 1981 I realized that I had to write about the troll under the bridge or leave him—IT—forever."

MIDDLEMARCH

George Eliot

1871

George Eliot derived much of *Middlemarch* from a different story she had been working on, titled "Miss Brooke." She was in the process of writing a very different *Middlemarch* in August 1869, focusing on the Lydgate character, but had to stop writing during her stepson's battle with tuberculosis—a battle he would succumb to in October 1869. She started writing again in December of that year, revisiting "Miss Brooke" but unable to prevent parts of *Middlemarch* from creeping into the story. Despite the working title, "Miss Brooke" grew into the *Middlemarch* that is celebrated today.

As the novel's length grew to the point where a three-volume format was no longer an option, Eliot's publisher recommended cutting the work into eighths and publishing it bi-monthly—a process that generated so much demand that the final three installments were released every month instead.

THEIR EYES WERE WATCHING GOD

Zora Neale Hurston

1937

"Colored People of the United States: Solve the great race problem by securing a home in Eatonville, Florida, a Negro city governed by negroes," read the town's weekly paper. It was Eatonville, Zora Neale Hurston's hometown and the inspiration for the city of the same name in *Their Eyes Were Watching God*. Hurston crafted her setting not just by deriving its characteristics from the real Eatonville, but also by drawing from her experience travelling through the South to study folk culture as a student at Barnard College. She even borrowed from her reality when writing about the hurricane, as one swept through Florida in 1928 and dealt heavy damage to the state's infrastructure.

The dynamic of Janice and Tea Cake's relationship was written in the likeness of a love affair that Hurston had with one Percival Punter, who, like Tea Cake, was significantly younger than his lover. Punter was also similar to Tea Cup in that he occasionally crossed the line between dominant and violent during sex. Their relationship ended on rocky terms, as Hurston wrote that she had "tried to embalm all the tenderness of [her] passion for him." She sat down to pen *Their Eyes Were Watching God* a few weeks later, when the memories and nuances of their relationship were still fresh in her mind.

THE NAKED AND THE DEAD

Norman Mailer

———

1948

When writing *The Naked and the Dead*, Norman Mailer drew from his experiences with the 112th Cavalry Regiment during the Philippines Campaign in World War II. When asked in a 1964 interview with *The Paris Review* how the idea of the novel came to him, Mailer responded, "I wanted to write a short novel about a long patrol. All during the war I kept thinking about this patrol. I even had the idea before I went overseas. Probably it was stimulated by a few war books I had read: John Hersey's *Into the Valley*, Harry Brown's *A Walk in the Sun*, and a couple of others I no longer remember. Out of these books came the idea to do a novel about a long patrol. And I began to create my characters. All the while I was overseas a part of me was working on this long patrol. I even ended up in a reconnaissance outfit that I had asked to get into. A reconnaissance outfit, after all, tends to take long patrols. Art kept traducing life. At any rate, when I started writing *The Naked and the Dead* I thought it might be a good idea to have a preliminary chapter or two with which to give the reader a chance to meet my characters before they went on patrol. But the next six months and the first five hundred pages went into that, and I remember in the early days I was annoyed at how long it was taking me to get to the patrol."

Mailer expands on his preparation methods, saying, "For *The Naked and the Dead* I had a file full of notes and a long dossier on each man. Many of these details never got into the novel, but the added knowledge made me feel more comfortable with each character. Indeed, I even had charts to show which characters had not yet had scenes with other characters. For a book that seems spontaneous on its surface, The *The Naked and the Dead* was written mechanically. I studied engineering at Harvard, and I suppose it was the book of a young engineer. The structure is sturdy, but there's no fine filigree to the joints. Just spot-welding and riveting. And the working plan was very simple. I devised some preliminary actions for the platoon in order to give the reader an opportunity to get to know the men, but this beginning, as I said, took over two-thirds of the book. The patrol itself is also simple, but I did give more thought to working it out ahead of time."

THE CATCHER IN THE RYE

J.D. Salinger

1951

It seems as though Salinger, knowingly or not, had been building toward his masterpiece for some time, as certain aspects from his first and only published novel resemble those from short stories that he had written in years prior. In his "The Young Folks" there is an early version of Sally Hayes, the "Slight Rebellion Off Madison" is a short story that features Holden Caulfield ten years before he became a nationally recognized character, and "I'm Crazy" is a story told from Caulfield's perspective that resembles, both in style and substance, certain aspects of *The Catcher in the Rye*.

In writing the novel, Salinger also uses some of his experiences to fully develop Holden's story-line, one that occurs in the world post–World War II rather than in the 1930s and 1940s, when Salinger was growing up. Like the author, Holden has a bit of a discipline problem, to the point where he is constantly switching prep schools. Whereas Salinger was really forced to go to Valley Forge Military Academy in 1934, Holden was only threatened with military school. Holden also knows a student who goes to Columbia, the school where Salinger took a creative writing class and wrote "The Young Folks." Salinger's use of profanity in the text was in response to the conformity expected of the nation's youth after the war, an expectation that both Holden and Salinger (for a time, at least) were unable to meet.

THE DA VINCI CODE

Dan Brown

———

2003

Dan Brown relied on many sources to build *The Da Vinci Code,* but few more impactful than the works of Margaret Starbird, whose writing focuses on the Catholic Church's suppression of the "divine feminine." Brown said that her writing "is of particular interest to me because it fuses the diverse fields of symbolism, mythology, art, heraldry, psychology and gospel history." When asked whether Brown had ever contacted her, Starbird said, "He sent me an e-mail in probably early May of 2003, right after his book went to the top of the best-seller list, telling me that he had received all these media requests for information about Mary Magdalene and he didn't know what to do with them. So he sent them to me." Starbird's work on the union between Jesus and Mary Magdalene served as a major inspiration for *The Da Vinci Code*.

BEL CANTO

Ann Patchett

___

2001

Ann Patchett's *Bel Canto* came about as a result of her watching the Lima Crisis, otherwise known as the Japanese embassy hostage crisis, unfold over the span of several months on the news. The crisis began when terrorists from the MRTA movement took an entire party, being held by the Japanese ambassador to Peru, Morihisa Aoki, in celebration of Emperor Akihito's sixty-third birthday, hostage. They released most of the partygoers soon after, and after 126 days, the Peruvian Armed Forces conducted an operation in which all of the terrorists and one of the remaining hostages were killed.

The parallels between the plot of *Bel Canto*

and the crisis are obvious, as the very framework of the story comes directly from the terrorist attack. When asked what it was about the attack that suggested the novel to her in the first place, Patchett responded, "Well, I definitely have a theme running through all my novels, which is people are thrown together by circumstance and somehow form a family, a society. They group themselves together. So as I'm watching this on the news, it was as if I was watching one of my own novels unfold. I was immediately attracted to the story . . . When I was watching all of this unfold on the news—and the book is about 98 percent fiction—I thought, this is so operatic what's happening in Lima. The only thing that's missing from this story is an opera star hung up with the rest of these people, which is the nice thing about being a novelist instead of a journalist. When you see a story that is crying out for an opera singer, you just stick an opera singer into the story."

She did exactly that, basing the character Roxane Coss on Karol Bennett. "Karol and I were both fellows at the Bunting Institute at Radcliffe College in 1990–91," she says. "Physically, Karol and Roxanne are very similar, small women with huge personalities. Karol commanded any room she walked into. It was as if music surrounded her even when she wasn't singing. I admired her greatly. The funny thing is that now I know

Roxane so much better than I ever knew Karol. For Roxane's singing I mostly listened to Renée Fleming. I didn't have any recordings of Karol singing so I gave my character Renée Fleming's voice."

RESURRECTION

Leo Tolstoy

———

1899

With his pacifist, pro-anarchy and anti-marriage stances, Leo Tolstoy was known as much for embracing unpopular mentalities as he was for his renowned works of literature. His turn-of-the-century work *Resurrection* seeks to push those mentalities, as the novel highlights the injustices of the aristocracy and the hypocrisy of institutionalized religion. In fact, Tolstoy allocated the money that he was making from the book—which was originally published in the magazine *Niva* in weekly installments—toward resettling the Doukhobors, a spiritual Christian religious group that embraced the pursuit of inner spirituality without subscribing to an institution, a concept Tolstoy loved. He also sought to make people aware of the economic philosophy Georgism, which essentially advocated for no private ownership of land and the equal distribution of any value derived from the land.

THE PRIME OF MISS JEAN BRODIE

Muriel Spark

1961

In *The Prime of Miss Jean Brodie*, Muriel Spark writes about six ten-year-old girls who make up the "Brodie set," an elite group of girls to be taught by the unconventional Miss Brodie. Self-described as "in [her] prime," Miss Brodie teaches the girls about love, travelling and culture to the point where they begin to stand out from the students around them. Brodie's character was at least partially inspired by Spark's former teacher Christina Kay, of whom she writes, "What filled our minds with wonder and made Christina Kay so memorable was the personal drama and poetry within which everything in her classroom happened." Kay shone through Brodie's better qualities, while also inspiring some of her weirder ones; Kay would accompany Renaissance artwork on her classroom walls with paintings of Mussolini and fascist Italy.

MONEY

Martin Amis

1984

When asked about how he begins the process of writing a novel, Martin Amis responded, "The common conception of how novels get written seems to me to be an exact description of writer's block. In the common view, the writer is at this stage so desperate that he's sitting around with a list of characters, a list of themes, and a framework for his plot, and ostensibly trying to mesh the three elements. In fact, it's never like that. What happens is what Nabokov described as a throb. A throb or a glimmer, an act of recognition on the writer's part. At this stage the writer thinks, Here is something I can write a novel about. In the absence of that recognition I don't know what one would do. It may be that nothing about this idea—or glimmer, or throb—appeals to you other than the fact that it's your destiny, that it's your next book. You may even be secretly appalled or awed or turned off by the idea, but it goes beyond that. You're just reassured that there is another novel for you to write. The idea can be incredibly thin—a situation, a character in a certain place at a certain time. With *Money*, for example, I had an idea of a big fat guy in New York, trying to make a film. That was all. Sometimes a novel can come pretty consecutively and it's rather like a journey in that you get going and the plot, such as it is, unfolds and you follow your nose. You have to decide between identical-seeming dirt roads, both of which look completely hopeless, but you nevertheless have to choose which one to follow."

Born to Booker-prize winning novelist Sir Kingsley Amis, Martin began to enjoy literature in his formative years, as novelist and step-mother Elizabeth Jane Howard introduced him to the works of Jane Austen. He went from an "unusually unpromising" student to the top of his English class at Exeter College in Oxford, from which he graduated to a job at *The Times Literary Supplement*. Though his father's status as a critically acclaimed writer certainly fueled his getting into the field, Kingsley was never particularly interested in the work of his son. Says Martin, "I can point out the exact place where he stopped and sent *Money* twirling through the air; that's where the character named Martin Amis comes in." Kingsley felt as though crossing the line between fiction and reality was forbidden and that it was selfish of his son to do so. That said, living with a famous author can only be a net positive for an up-and-comer, which Martin himself admits. "I want to make it clear that it's been nothing but a help to me," he says. "Maybe it was more difficult for him, funnily enough; it took me a long time to realize that. I don't know how I'd feel if one of my little boys started to write, but I do know that I feel generally resentful of younger writers."

In *Money*, Amis wanted to reflect the experiences that he had as an English man coming to America, one that wasn't very well represented in the literature of the time. He says, "You know the usual Pooterish Englishman who goes abroad in English novels and is taken aback by everything. Well, not a bit of that in John Self. He completely accepts America on its own terms and is perfectly at home with it. A bit shocked at some things, like taxi meters on ambulances. Personally, I love New York. I did find though that my attitude changed overnight when I went there with my wife and child. I just thought, 'Well, it's a great place to be by yourself but when you've got your personal tribe with you, it's hard to relax.' Everyone's windmilling around in this neurotic state. Some are just not up to it and are coming apart at the seams. When you stroll alone down the streets of New York, you take this on as part of the deal. But when you're wheeling someone that's four months old, it's rather more of an undertaking. It was actually in Cape Cod that I really fell out of love with America, even as I was experiencing it at its best."

The character Lorne Guyland was derived from two very different sources: the name is meant to make fun of the way New Yorkers pronounce Long Island, while the character himself was inspired by Kirk Douglas, with whom Amis worked while writing for the movie *Saturn 3*.

AUSTERLITZ

W.G. Sebald

2001

Sebald's *Austerlitz* exists thanks to a program on BBC television called *Whatever Happened to Susi?* The program follows the true story of three-year-old twins Susi and Lotte Bechhöfer, who arrived in London by way of Kinder-transport, a system implemented to evacuate Jewish children from Germany before and during World War II. Their adopted parents gave them new identities, wiping their past clean so that the girls could start anew. When Lotte died of a brain tumor at age thirty-five, Susi discovered who her parents were; one a Nazi soldier and the other a Jewish woman who suffered death by gas in Auschwitz. The journey that follows is one of severe trauma, as Susi wants to know who she is and where she came from. That story inspired Sebald's titular character Jacques Austerlitz, whose circumstances mirror Susi's almost exactly.

TINKER TAILOR SOLDIER SPY

John le Carré

1974

A member of the British Secret Service and the Secret Intelligence Service in the 1950s and 1960s, John le Carré approached his espionage novels with an unusual amount of experience from his time in the field. No work reflects that perspective better than *Tinker Tailor Soldier Spy*, which deals with the discovery of the Cambridge Five, a group of moles found in the British Intelligence services. Le Carré was serving at the time, and modelled the character David Cromwell after himself, while Bill Haydon was inspired by a double agent named Kim Philby. Le Carré's career with the Service ended in 1964, due in large part to Philby compromising his identity to the Russians.

THE TROPIC OF CANCER

Henry Miller

1934

When asked about his writing process in a 1964 interview with *The Paris Review*, Henry Miller responded, "Who writes the great books? It isn't we who sign our names. What is an artist? He's a man who has antennae, who knows how to hook up to the currents which are in the atmosphere, in the cosmos; he merely has the facility for hooking on, as it were. Who is original? Everything that we are doing, everything that we think, exists already, and we are only intermediaries, that's all, who make use of what is in the air. Why do ideas, why do great scientific discoveries often occur in different parts of the world at the same time? The same is true of the elements that go to make up a poem or a great novel or any work of art. They are already in the air, they have not been given voice, that's all. They need *the* man, *the* interpreter, to bring them forth."

Miller found that voice in his breakthrough novel, in which his voice drove the narrative above all else. "Up until that point," he says, "you might say I was a wholly derivative writer, influenced by everyone, taking on all the tones and shades of every other writer that I had ever loved. I was a literary man, you might say. And I became a non-literary man: I cut the cord. I said, I will do only what I can do, express what I am—that's why I used the first person, why I wrote about myself. I decided to write from the standpoint of my own experience, what I knew and felt. And that was my salvation."

THE TIN DRUM

Günter Grass

———

1959

"As a child I was a great liar," recalls Günter Grass in a 1991 interview. "Fortunately my mother liked my lies. I promised her marvelous things. When I was ten years old she called me Peer Gynt. Peer Gynt, she said, here you are telling me marvelous stories about journeys we will make to Naples and so on . . . I started to write down my lies very early. And I continue to do so! I started a novel when I was twelve years old. It was about the Kashubians, who turned up many years later in *The Tin Drum*, where Oskar's grandmother, Anna (like my own), is Kashubian. But I made a mistake in writing my first novel: all the characters I had introduced were dead at the end of the first chapter. I couldn't go on! This was my first lesson in writing: be careful with your characters."

At twenty-five years old, Grass began writing *The Tin Drum* as a way to make fun of and express his disgust toward Germans who were easily seduced by Nazi ideas. "Homeland is something one becomes aware of through its loss," he says. "I wrote *The Tin Drum* partly to counter the view that these lands could be regained. My parents believed the lies of Adenauer, who said, 'If you vote for me, you'll be able to go back to your old homeland.' "

THE DIARY OF A NOBODY

George and Weedon Grossmith

———

1892

The Grossmith brothers were showmen from an early age, having put on a play when they were just seventeen and ten that included a burlesque version of *Hamlet*. George, who was seven years older than Weedon, began to establish himself as a comic piano sketch entertainer in his adult years, receiving critical acclaim and a few acting opportunities in the process. Between writing sketches and stage performing, George wrote short sketches for *Punch* magazine with his brother, basing his subjects on the characters he met while working as a court reporter for Bow Street Magistrates' Club—a job that he took as a young adult to follow in his father's footsteps. Those short sketches were published in book form in 1892 and titled *The Diary of a Nobody*.

THE GIRL WITH THE DRAGON TATTOO

Stieg Larsson

—

2005

In an essay for *The Daily Mail*, Kurdo Baski writes about his friendship with Stieg Larsson, author of *The Girl with the Dragon Tattoo*. He recalls an experience that Larsson had when he was younger, citing it as a major impetus behind Larsson's work and its themes. He writes, "However, one of the most pressing reasons why Stieg wrote his novels happened in the late summer of 1969. The location was a camping site in Umea, northern Sweden, where he was brought up. I have always avoided writing about what happened that day, but it is unavoidable in this context. It affected Stieg so deeply that it became a somber leitmotif running through his books.

On that day, fifteen-year-old Stieg watched three friends rape a girl, also called Lisbeth, who was the same age as him and someone he knew. Her screams were heartrending, but he didn't intervene. His loyalty to his friends was too strong. He was too young, too insecure. It was inevitable that he would realize afterwards that he could have acted and possibly prevented the rape. Haunted by feelings of guilt, he contacted the girl a few days later. When he begged her to forgive him for his cowardice and passivity, she told him bitterly that she could not accept his explanations. 'I shall never forgive you,' she said, gritting her teeth. That was one of the worst memories Stieg told me about. It was obvious, looking at him, that the girl's voice still echoed in his ears, even after he had written three novels about vulnerable, violated and raped women. It was probably not his intention to be forgiven after writing the books, but when you read them it is possible to detect the driving force behind them. As a result, the women in his novels have minds of their own and go their own ways. They fight. They resist. Just as he wished all women would do in the real world."

RIDDLE OF THE SANDS

Robert Erskine Childers

1903

Robert Erskine Childers was wary of the rising power of Imperial Germany as early as 1897, when he set off on the Baltic cruise that helped to inspire *Riddle of the Sands*. British preparedness for war is a central theme in the book, as Childers felt as though Britain's weaponry was outdated to the point where it would be a decided disadvantage during "conflicts of the future." His 1897 Baltic cruise, which he spent aboard the yacht *Vixen*, travelled along the East Frisia coast and allowed him to fill his logbook with information about new German naval installations. Though Childers was often falsely credited with inspiring Britain to build the naval base Rosyth, he was indeed given a job by the Director of Naval Intelligence when World War I began.

THE STRANGE CASE OF DR. JEKYLL AND MR. HYDE

Robert Louis Stevenson

1886

"In the small hours of one morning, [. . .] I was awakened by cries of horror from Louis. Thinking he had a nightmare, I awakened him. He said angrily: 'Why did you wake me? I was dreaming a fine bogey tale.' I had awakened him at the first transformative scene." Biographer Graham Balfour offers this quote from the wife of Robert Louis Stevenson in order to show how perhaps the exact moment the author thought up the novel.

Stevenson's writing had always shown the interplay of good and evil, as he had long been fascinated by different human personalities. He had written a play and a short story titled "Markheim" before dreaming up the first scene of his unquestioned masterpiece—a scene that drove Stevenson to write nonstop until the book was completed. Writes Stevenson's stepson, "I don't believe there was ever such a literary feat before as the writing of *Dr. Jekyll*. I remember the first disease of the world though it were yesterday. Louis came downstairs in a fever; read nearly half the book aloud; and then, while we were still gasping, he was away again, and busy writing. I doubt if the first draft took so long as three days."

Stevenson was ill throughout much of the writing process, from a fever to a hemorrhage that left him bedridden by the completion of his first draft. His wife, having always read and marked up her husband's initial drafts before he revised them, made a note that the book was really a grand allegory that had been written as a story. Upon reading this, Stevenson allegedly burned his entire manuscript to ashes, so as to keep himself from trying to salvage any of it. He started from scratch, this time writing an allegorical story as his wife had wisely suggested. The rewrite lasted a drug-fueled six days, during which Stevenson saw no improvement in his health. However, as his stepson noted, "The mere physical feat was tremendous and, instead of harming him, it roused and cheered him inexpressibly."

Stevenson likely drew inspiration for Dr. Jekyll from his friend, Dr. Eugene Chantrelle, a mild-mannered man who was found guilty of poisoning his wife and sentenced to death, having been believed to commit other murders as well. The author was shocked as he watched the trial unfold, as the man that he had known showed no signs or traces of having a murderous personality.

The name Jekyll was inspired by another friend of Stevenson's, Reverend Walter Jekyll, younger brother of landscape designer Gertrude Jekyll.

ALL THE PRESIDENT'S MEN

Carl Bernstein and Bob Woodward

1974

When Carl Bernstein and Bob Woodward came up with the idea to write *All the President's Men*, they imagined it as a narrative on the Watergate scandal and the events surrounding it. However, upon receiving word that Robert Redford had expressed interest in purchasing the rights to the film version of the book, they decided to change the narrative to focus more on their investigative roles during the scandal. The pair had, of course, been responsible for much of the original reporting on the Watergate scandal while working for *The Washington Post* in the early 1970s.

The title comes from a line in the Humpty Dumpty nursery rhyme, which reads, "All the king's horses and all the king's men / Couldn't put Humpty together again." It alludes to the fact that, despite all efforts, Nixon's resignation was inevitable once the Watergate tapes came to light.

LOOKING FOR MR. GOODBAR

Judith Rossner

———

1975

By the early 1970s, Judith Rossner's career had earned her a good deal of clout; she'd already successfully published three novels and had become very sought after. Among those looking to recruit her talents was Nora Ephron, then columnist for *Esquire*, who asked Rossner to write a piece for a special women's issue of the magazine. Rossner accepted, choosing to write about the murder of schoolteacher Roseann Quinn earlier that year.

The murder occurred on New Year's Day in 1973, when Quinn went to a bar across the street from her New York City apartment. She met a man and took him back to her place, where they smoked marijuana and attempted to have sex. According to John Wayne Wilson, her murderer, he was unable to achieve an erection and was ridiculed for it. When Quinn demanded he leave the apartment, he picked up a knife and stabbed her eighteen times. Her body was found two days later when a schoolteacher, concerned that she hadn't shown up in two days, went to check on her.

Worried that the subject matter might be too much for their readers, and that they would face legal ramifications if they published the story, *Esquire* axed the essay from the issue. Still intensely interested in the subject, Rossner opted to expand her research and write a book instead.

INTERVIEW WITH
A VAMPIRE
Anne Rice

———

1976

Anne Rice's four-year-old daughter Michelle was diagnosed with acute granulocytic leukemia in 1970, when Rice was attending a graduate program for creative writing at San Francisco State University. Michelle succumbed to the illness two years later, sending Anne into a deep depression that saw her turn to alcohol and abandon her studies. It wasn't until 1973 when, thanks to encouragement received from one of her husband's students, she began to re-work and expand on a short story she had written four years earlier. Five weeks later and the 30-page story had become the 338-page novel *Interview with a Vampire*, as she researched the subject by day and wrote the novel by night. The character Claudia was partly inspired by Rice's late daughter Michelle.

GORKY PARK

Martin Cruz Smith

1981

"You have unreal expectations . . . You overestimate your personal powers. You feel isolated from society. You swing from excitement to sadness. You mistrust the people who most want to help you. You resent authority even when you represent it. You think you are the exception to every rule. You underestimate the collective intelligence. What is right is wrong and what is wrong is right." This is a description of Pathoheterodoxy Syndrome, a fictional mental illness in Martin Cruz Smith's *Gorky Park*. Smith created the illness satirically, as he wanted to highlight the illogical practices employed by the Soviets after one of their own defected—that is, labeling Soviet dissidents as being mentally ill as a means of delegitimizing proponents of Western civilization and government.

A WRINKLE IN TIME

Madeleine L'Engle

1963

In *A Circle of Quiet*, L'Engle writes, "We drove through a world of deserts and buttes and leafless mountains, wholly new and alien to me. And suddenly into my mind came the names, *Mrs. Whatsit. Mrs. Who. Mrs. Which.*" Her revelation came during a ten-week camping trip that her family took across the country in the spring of 1959, prior to moving from Connecticut to New York City so that her father could try his hand at acting. This trip came about one year after L'Engle had sworn off writing for good, citing her inability to earn a living as a forty-year-old woman despite all of the time and effort that she put in. The trip inspired her to begin writing again and, about a year after the trip, *A Wrinkle in Time* was completed. Despite more than twenty-five rejections from publishers, likely due to the fact that L'Engle had written a female protagonist into a work of science fiction, Farrar, Straus & Giroux eventually published the novel in 1962.

THE BELL JAR

Sylvia Plath

1963

Originally published under the pseudonym "Victoria Lucas" in 1963, *The Bell Jar* was Sylvia Plath's first and only novel, published one month before she committed suicide. She began writing the novel in 1961, according to her husband, directly after publishing her collection of poetry titled *The Colossus*. Plath separated from her husband and moved to a smaller apartment, "giving her time and place to work uninterruptedly. Then at top speed and with very little revision from start to finish she wrote *The Bell Jar*," he said.

The novel, which at one point was titled "Diary of a Suicide," was semi-autobiographical; names and places reflect real people and places in Plath's own life and Esther, the protagonist, experiences a descent into depression much like Plath did in her own life.

FLOWERS FOR ALGERNON

Daniel Keyes

———

1966

When *Galaxy Science Fiction* magazine reached out to Daniel Keyes asking him to write a story, he already had one in mind. He submitted to them a shorter version of *Flowers for Algernon*, but when they requested that he change the ending to make it lighter, he refused and submitted the story to *The Magazine of Fantasy & Science Fiction* instead. The novelized version of the story faced the same problem, as Doubleday wanted the ending changed as well. Again Keyes said no and, after several more rejections, the book was finally published by Harcourt in 1966.

Flowers for Algernon can trace its origins back to 1945, when Keyes' parents insisted he pursue a career in medicine when he was much more interested in writing. Struggling to balance both efforts while maintaining what was then a tumultuous relationship with his parents led Keyes to an interesting concept: what if it were possible to increase a person's intelligence?

That concept began maturing while he taught English to special-needs students in the late 1950s. He witnessed severe regression in one of his students after he was taken out of regular classes and placed into Keyes'. In his own words: "When he came back to school, he had lost it all. He could not read. He reverted to what he had been. It was a heart-breaker." Another student asked him whether or not he'd be allowed to attend the regular classes if he studied hard to get smarter. These interactions further stimulated Keyes to ponder what an intelligence-enhancing procedure would look like.

Keyes also relied on experience to create the novel's characters, as several of them had roots in his day-to-day life. The scientists responsible for developing the surgery in the story, Nemur and Strauss, were based on graduate school professors that Keyes had met while studying psychoanalysis. The name Algernon was based on the poet Algernon Charles Swinburne, who is best known for his *Poems and Ballads*.

WHERE THE RED FERN GROWS

Wilson Rawls

1961

"Son," his father said, "a man can do anything he sets out to do, if he doesn't give up." Wilson

Rawls was unable to generate much interest in literature until his mother bought for him Jack London's *Call of the Wild*, a story that inspired him to one day write about the connection between a man and his dog. His father encouraged Rawls to pursue his dream, even if Rawls himself didn't believe he could do it.

While working construction in Mexico and Idaho, Rawls stored his manuscripts away at his parents' house. He burned them all when he met his fiancée, as he didn't want her to see him as a failure who never achieved his dream. Eventually he confessed this to her and, at her encouragement, rewrote one of his stories from memory in three weeks' time. Still horribly self-conscious about his work, Rawls gave the finished manuscript to her and left for town, staying there until he knew she'd have enough time to finish it. He called her on the phone and, fully prepared to hear her condemn the story, but instead he heard: "You get back out here to the house, I want to talk to you . . . this is the most wonderful dog and boy story I've ever heard in my life." He took her advice and expanded the manuscript, writing the whole thing without any punctuation, while his wife typed out the final copy for distribution.

VALLEY OF THE DOLLS

Jacqueline Susann

1966

Considered by many to be a roman à clef, Jacqueline Susann's *Valley of the Dolls* was the materialization of a goal that she had set for herself years earlier. The world of show business always interested her, as evidenced by her attempt to write a novel about it titled *Underneath the Pancake* with friend and actress Beatrice Cole. That book was followed by the idea for a novel called *The Pink Dolls*, which would detail the world of drugs and drug use as it pertained to show business. This idea eventually gave way to *Valley of the Dolls.*

Famous figures such as Dean Martin, Judy Garland and Ethel Merman were all sources of character inspiration for Susann's book, backing the theory that the book was a roman à clef, to which Susann said, "They keep calling it that. It'll only make my books sell, I don't care." She rejected the claim that her book was based largely on her actual life, insisting instead that she came up with a theme and then noticed people in her day-to-day interactions who seemed like they fit that theme.

THE THINGS THEY CARRIED

Tim O'Brien

1990

On why he wrote *The Things They Carried*, author Tim O'Brien says, "I wanted to write a work of fiction that would feel to the reader as if this had occurred or, in a way, is occurring as [they] read it. And, so, I would use every strategy I could think of, invention, and dialogue, and using my own name, dedicating the book to the characters, as a way of giving a reader a sense of witnessed experience. I was a soldier in Vietnam. But the stories in the book are, for the most part, invented. Yet, they're launched out of a world I once knew." O'Brien later confirmed that the book is a memoir of his experience serving in Vietnam, which is not a surprise, as he goes as far as to write himself into the story.

A STREETCAR NAMED DESIRE

Tennessee Williams

1947

Tennessee Williams, whose birth name was Thomas Lanier Williams III, was born to an alcoholic father and an often-hysterical mother in Columbus, Mississippi, in 1911. He and his family moved often, with each move bringing an increase in his father's alcohol consumption and in the frequency of his mother's panic attacks. The constant moving—they relocated sixteen times in ten years—forced Williams and his sister Rose to develop a strong relationship. Eventually, she had become his closest friend. Williams began making a name for himself as a teenager, winning a national essay contest and having his work published in *Smart Set* magazine. He attended the University of Missouri to study journalism and began writing plays, thanks in part to the inspiration he found in southern literary greats like Faulkner, Wolfe and Tate. He was, however, unable to graduate, as his father pulled him out of school and had him work at a shoe factory as punishment for his failing a ROTC program course.

After three years at the shoe factory, Williams enrolled at Washington College in St. Louis, where a theater group produced two of his plays. He then transferred to the University of Iowa, where he was studying when Rose began to experience the effects of mental illness. She underwent a prefrontal lobotomy, a failed procedure that left her institutionalized for the remainder of her life. Heartbroken, Williams bounced from city to city after graduation before moving to New York City, where he enjoyed further success as a playwright. His play *The Glass Menagerie* debuted in 1944 and was a huge success. It was a sign of things to come— Williams was only three years away from writing *A Streetcar Named Desire*.

The playwright clearly borrowed from his own life in creating both the characters and the story; most of the central characters appear to be modeled after himself, his mother and Rose, while Stanley Kowalski shares characteristics with Williams' father. Themes like depression and alcoholism also invite comparisons to Williams' life.

HIROSHIMA

John Hersey

1946

Granted access to things that very few people would ever see or experience, John Hersey wrote *Hiroshima* as a result of his time as war correspondent for *Life* and *The New Yorker*. He was on the ground for the invasion of Italy and Sicily before moving to the Pacific Theatre a year before the United States dropped two nuclear bombs on Japan, following Lt. John F. Kennedy through the Solomon Islands. He had an early look at Hiroshima after the bomb had been dropped, as he was commissioned by *The New Yorker* to write articles on the explosion based on witness accounts.

Originally published as a thirty-thousand-word essay, *The New Yorker* included Hershey's piece in the "Talk of the Town" section. At the bottom of the page appeared the writing "TO OUR READERS. *The New Yorker* this week devotes its entire editorial space to an article on the almost complete obliteration of a city by one atomic bomb, and what happened to the people of that city. It does so in the conviction that few of us have yet comprehended the all but incredible destructive power of this weapon, and that everyone might well take time to consider the terrible implications of its use. The Editors."

The article was an instant success, forcing the magazine to order reprints mere hours after the issue hit the shelves. Networks broadcasted readings as people were captivated by the sensationalism of the story; tales of melted eyeballs painted an image of mass destruction the likes of which nobody had ever seen.

The feeling began to sour after the essay was published in book form. The realization had set in that the United States had wiped from the face of the Earth entire cities of innocent people who had little to do with the war in the Pacific. The prevailing American notion that the Japanese credited the bombs for saving their country from its own government did some to alleviate the guilt, but the realization that nuclear warfare was now an option left with it a steady unease that remains to this day. That was the point of *Hiroshima*: to offer an honest account of horrors of war.

CURIOUS GEORGE

Hans Augusto Rey & Margret Rey

1941

The story of Curious George begins with the relationship between Hans and Margret Rey, the husband-wife duo responsible for creating America's favorite monkey. Born in Germany to Jewish families, they married in 1935 and moved to France, where the idea for George was conceived. Of course, his name wasn't originally George; it was Fifi, as the monkey was created in France and was therefore French. Though he was originally just a character that Hans had sketched, the couple made George (or Fifi) the central figure in a children's book at the suggestion of a publisher, using their own life experiences to come up with his adventures.

Though he was originally French, George didn't achieve mainstream success until the couple emigrated from France to America. They were given very little choice, as Nazi forces were approaching and the fall of the country was likely imminent. Hans and Margret fled on bikes to a ship that would take them overseas, bringing their manuscript with them.

THE SUN ALSO RISES

Ernest Hemingway

———

1926

Much of *The Sun Also Rises* was based on a single weeklong trip to Pamplona in 1925, where Hemingway's recently found passion, bullfighting, was celebrated each year. He and his wife, Hadley Richardson, had first explored the Festival of San Fermín in 1923, where they had so much fun that they decided to go back the following year. The couple traveled while Hemingway was stationed in Paris as a foreign correspondent for the *Toronto Star*, where he hoped to use his real-life experience to write fiction. As Hemingway himself said, a work of fiction can be based on real events if "what he made up was truer than what he remembered."

The third trip to Pamplona—and the one that inspired Hemingway's novel—had a dynamic very similar to that depicted in the story. Hemingway, attracted to a recently divorced member of the group named Duff, grew intensely jealous of the man who had just shared a romantic getaway with her, named Harold Loeb. By the end of the week, the two had engaged in a fistfight similar to the one that takes place in

Hemingway's novel. As this was all going on, Cayetano Ordóñez, a young matador, presented Hemingway's wife with the ear of the bull that he had killed. His likeness can be found in the Pedro Romero character, on which Hemingway states, "Everything that happened in the ring was true, and everything outside was fiction. Nino knew this and never complained about it."

Though he had set out to write a nonfiction work on the subject of bullfighting, Hemingway believed that the week he'd experienced was worthy of a novel. He had fourteen chapters written later that year, and a finished novel by 1926.

THE CASTLE

Franz Kafka

———

1926

Franz Kafka never wanted *The Castle* to be published; he had left instructions that his work was to be burned when he died. Max Brod, his friend, ignored these wishes and set out to have his work published, including an unfinished manuscript for *The Castle*. Kafka had written a letter to Brod in 1922 that mentioned giving up on the novel and having no intention to ever return to it, which would describe why the published work ends mid-sentence. Kafka had begun work on the novel in January of 1922 at the mountain resort of Spindlermühle, a setting very much like the one depicted in the story.

ALL THE LIGHT WE CANNOT SEE

Anthony Doerr

———

2014

When asked in a 2014 Goodreads interview whether the motivating question of *All the Light We Cannot See* was "Don't you want to be alive before you die?" Anthony Doerr responded: "Yeah, no question. My mom was a science teacher. She was a big part of my life. I went to the same school where she taught. I drove with her pretty far. We lived in rural Ohio in a tiny town outside of Cleveland called Novelty. I was at a Montessori school in Cleveland Heights. So we drove fifty minutes to school each way. She was always teaching us all kinds of things. I remember very clearly geologic time being one of the big lessons she taught us. She even had us take toilet paper rolls and unroll them and had us map out the various eras, like Cambrian, and figure out where humans would fit on this toilet paper timeline of the Earth. You realize, of course, that human life goes in the last square— and really goes in the last quarter of the last square. And your life can't really even fit if you draw this microscopic line down the final edge of the final square of toilet paper. I remember those lessons make you feel small. Then they make you feel—what an amazing thing we get to be on this Earth. I should take advantage of this tiny spark of light we have in our lives before it's over. Start thinking of all the species that have lived on Earth; 99 percent of them have gone extinct. Why do we think humans will be different? That was part of my worldview growing up: We're only here a short time. I don't really believe in reincarnation, so this is our one chance to kinda help people and see things and taste and fall in love with everything you can. So I think that's part of everything I work on."

WONDER

R.J. Palacio

2012

On her inspiration for *Wonder*, R.J. Palacio says, "I was inspired to write *Wonder* by a chance encounter I had with a child outside an ice cream shop about five years ago. The little girl, who might have been around seven or eight, was sitting next to me on a bench in front of the store. She was eating an ice cream cone, sitting with a friend or sibling and her mother. My older son was inside the store getting us milkshakes, and my younger son, who was about three, was sitting in his stroller facing me. He was distracted by something he was playing with, but I knew the moment he looked up, the moment he saw the girl, he would react in a way that might hurt the girl's feelings . . . My older son came out of the store carrying the three milkshakes, my younger son looked up and saw the girl, and before he could start crying hysterically, I got up quickly, spun his stroller around, grabbed my older son by the arm to pull him with me—which made him drop the milkshakes—and made a mad dash to try to get us as far away from that sweet little girl as possible, hoping she hadn't caught onto what had just happened. I'll never know if she did or not, to be truthful, but I do know that I heard her mom say, in about as calm and sweet a voice as you can imagine, 'okay, guys, I think it's time to go.' And my heart just broke for her. I wanted to go back and talk to her, to apologize, but I was so ashamed by the little scene we had just caused, and mortified, that I never did look back. And I was haunted by that encounter. I couldn't stop thinking about how it had all played out . . . The book just kind of came to me on that car ride home. I knew it would be from the point of view of a child with that face. I knew it would be a positive story, a story about kindness and the impact of kindness. In a way, it would be my atonement for that moment in front of the ice cream shop. To this day, I regret not having gone back to talk to that little girl and her mom. *Wonder* is my message to them."

THE HELP

Kathryn Stockett

———

2009

On writing her novel *The Help*, Kathryn Stockett says in a 2009 interview with *Time*, "I started writing it the day after September 11. I was living in New York City. We didn't have any phone service and we didn't have any mail. Like a lot of writers do, I started to write in a voice that I missed. I was really homesick—I couldn't even call my family and tell them I was fine. So I started writing in the voice of Demetrie, the maid I had growing up. She later became the character of Aibileen [in *The Help*]. I sent the story to my mother and she was sort of like, 'Hmm, that's good.' As I wrote, I found that Aibileen had some things to say that really weren't in her character. She was older, soft-spoken, and she started showing some attitude. That's [how another character] Minny came to be. After a while longer, I decided to make it a book."

EXTREMELY LOUD AND INCREDIBLY CLOSE

Jonathan Safran Foer

———

2005

"I think it's a greater risk not to write about [9/11]," Foer says. "If you're in my position—a New Yorker who felt the event very deeply and a writer who wants to write about things he feels deeply about—I think it's risky to avoid what's right in front of you." Jonathan Foer learned of the attacks when he was woken up by a phone call from a friend, who described to him what was happening, after which he said, "I think it's going to be a very strange day." When explaining why he chose to write a story based around 9/11 from the perspective of a child, Foer explains that he was working on a different story altogether, and began working on the side project to alleviate his boredom. As the story progressed it became the center of his focus, as he felt as though he was presenting an interesting perspective on an interesting topic.

WATERSHIP DOWN

Richard Adams

1972

When asked about the genesis of *Watership Down* in a 2007 interview with the BBC, Adams said, "One day we were going to Stratford-upon-Avon to see Judi Dench in *Twelfth Night*. Before I said anything in particular my elder daughter, who was eight at the time, said, 'Now daddy we're going on a long car journey, so we want you to while away the time by telling us a completely new story, one that we have never heard before and without any delay. Please start now!'"

What followed was an early rendition of *Watership Down*, which included central characters Hazel and Fiver. Adams went to bed each night already planning the events of the next day's story, becoming so engrossed in his narrative that his daughters actually had to ask him to start writing everything down. He obliged them, and eighteen months later he had his novel.

Adams' experience as a supply officer in the British Army proved valuable to his storytelling, as his fellow soldiers ended up inspiring many of the rabbits in Hazel's group. Says Adams, "There were about twelve or thirteen altogether, and they comprised a very strong team, much stronger than any I had yet come across. Apart from that, collectively, they have importance to this book, since later, from my memory, they provided the idea for Hazel and his rabbits in *Watership Down*." Adams' most important influence was Major John Gifford, who commanded the 250 company and inspired the novel's protagonist, Hazel-Rah. Adams writes, "Everything about him was quiet, crisp, and unassuming. He was the most unassuming man I have ever known. When giving any of his officers an order, he usually said 'Please,' 'Would you like to—?' or 'Perhaps you'd better—.' He could be extraordinarily cutting; at least one sensed it like that because a rebuke from him was so quiet and rare, and because everyone had such a high regard for him that you felt his slightest reproof very keenly."

The character of Bigwig was also inspired by a soldier—Captain Paddy Kavanagh, on whom Adams writes, "Paddy was a sensationalist; by temperament entirely the public's idea of a parachute officer; good-natured, debonair, generous, always in high spirits . . . a deviser of dares, afraid of nothing (including jumping), so it seemed. He once jumped with a kit bag on each leg, to show that it could be done: another time he jumped with a large wireless transmitter. He had a bucko sergeant, McDowell, and the two of them used to get up to some rare old larks. Once, Kavanagh was going to make his platoon crawl under live fire from a Bren gun, and began by setting them an example. After about a quarter of a mile he called to McDowell, on the gun, to aim closer. Afterwards, they found bullet holes in his airborne smock . . . Sometimes Kavanagh and McDowell would take the pin out of a live grenade and toss it between them until one or the other ('Sissy!') threw it down the pit or over the wall."

LET THE RIGHT ONE IN

John Ajvide Lindqvist

———

2004

A former street magician and comedian, John Ajvide Lindqvist didn't achieve substantial fame until *Let the Right One In* debuted in 2004. The story about a twelve-year-old boy and his relationship with an ancient vampire is set in Blackeberg, a suburb of Stockholm and Lindqvist's hometown. For Lindqvist, it was important to represent the place where he grew up in his literature: "Well, it was my first novel, that became this completely unlikely and unexpected success here in Sweden and I just originally started from wanting to depict the place where I grew up—Blackeberg, a suburb to Stockholm, like I did back when I was a stand-up comedian, I used to talk a lot about Blackeberg, or like a fictitious Blackeberg with rival gangs of senior citizens and well, what it was like there. And then I sort of returned there when I was going to write my first novel, to create a Blackeberg where I depicted it in such a way that it was going to be possible for a vampire to be living there. That a world where a vampire, a twelve-year-old vampire, would be able to exist and I wanted to approach my subject completely seriously and absolutely reject all . . . sort of 'romanticized' notions about vampires, or what we've seen earlier of vampires, and just concentrate on the question: If a child was stuck forever like, in a twelve-year-old existence and had to walk around killing other people and drink their blood to live—what would that child's existence really be like? If you disregard all the romanticized clichés. And then it struck me when I wrote the book that it would be an absolutely horrible existence. Miserable, gross and lonely. And hence, the way Eli is depicted."

THE EXECUTIONER'S SONG

Norman Mailer

—

1979

Discussing *The Executioner's Song* with *The Paris Review*, Norman Mailer says, "I'm smiling because you give it such a nice edge. My motives at the time of *The Executioner's Song* were not all that honorable. I'd been running into a lot of criticism of my baroque style, and it was getting to me. My whole thing became, you know—you asses out there, you think a baroque style is easy? It's not easy. It's something you really have to arrive at. It takes years of work. You guys keep talking about the virtues of simplicity—I'll show you. There's absolutely nothing to simplicity, and I'm going to prove it with this book, because I probably have the perfect material for showing that I can write a simple book. So I proceeded to do it. My pride in that book is that the best piece of writing is Gary Gilmore's letter about two-thirds in. I quoted it verbatim. No writing by me up to this point could be superior to that letter, because that letter makes him come to life, and suddenly you see this man was a man of substance, despite all. He might have been a punk, as he was called, he might have killed two people in hideous fashion, but by God, he had a mind and he had a sense of personal literary style, which was in that letter.

"One of my basic notions for a long, long time is that there is this mysterious mountain out there called reality. We novelists are always trying to climb it. We are mountaineers, and the question is, which face do you attack? Different faces call for different approaches, and some demand a knotty and convoluted interior style. Others demand great simplicity. The point is that style is an attack on the nature of reality.

"So I wrote the Gilmore book simply. Maybe it led me to think I could take a crack at Hemingway, but the fact of the matter is, when it comes to writing simply, I am not Hemingway's equal. My great admiration for Hemingway is not necessarily for the man, the character. I think if we had met it could have been a small disaster for me. But he showed us, as no one else ever has, what the potential strength of the English sentence could be."

THE PRINCE AND THE PAUPER

Mark Twain

———

1881

Twain's obsession with French and English history was all-encompassing; it was all he read after traveling through Europe in the latter half of the 1800s. Accounts of times past inspired an idea that caused him to stop writing *The Adventures of Huckleberry Finn* in order to explore it further. As he wrote, "My idea is to afford a realizing sense of the exceeding severity of the laws of that day by inflicting some of their penalties upon the King himself and allowing him a chance to see the rest of them applied to others." Twain does exactly that, telling the story of a prince and a commoner whose identical appearances allows them to switch positions for a time. Edward, the actual prince turned king, experiences the harsh living endured by his people and vows to end all unjust laws in his country.

A THOUSAND SPLENDID SUNS

Khaled Hosseini

2007

On how he chose a title for *A Thousand Splendid Suns*, Khaled Hosseini says, "It comes from a poem about Kabul by Saib-e-Tabrizi, a seventeenth-century Persian poet, who wrote it after a visit to the city left him deeply impressed. I was searching for English translations of poems about Kabul, for use in a scene where a character bemoans leaving his beloved city, when I found this particular verse. I realized that I had found not only the right line for the scene, but also an evocative title in the phrase 'a thousand splendid suns,' which appears in the next-to-last stanza. The poem was translated from Farsi by Dr. Josephine Davis."

As for the story itself, Hosseini wanted to make clear that his intent wasn't to inform the world what life was like in Afghanistan. "For me as a writer," he says, "the story has always taken precedence over everything else. I have never sat down to write with broad, sweeping ideas in mind, and certainly never with a specific agenda. It is quite a burden for a writer to feel a responsibility to represent his or her own culture and to educate others about it. For me it always starts from a very personal, intimate place, about human connections, and then expands from there. What intrigued me about this new book were the hopes and dreams and disillusions of these two women, their inner lives, the specific circumstances that bring them together, their resolve to survive, and the fact that their relationship evolves into something meaningful and powerful, even as the world around them unravels and slips into chaos. But as I wrote, I witnessed the story expanding, becoming more ambitious page after page. I realized that telling the story of these two women without telling, in part, the story of Afghanistan from the 1970s to the post-9/11 era simply was not possible. The intimate and personal was intertwined inextricably with the broad and historical. And so the turmoil in Afghanistan and the country's tortured recent past slowly became more than mere back-drop. Gradually, Afghanistan itself—and more specifically, Kabul—became a character in this novel, to a much larger extent, I think, than in *The Kite Runner*. But it was simply for the sake of storytelling, not out of a sense of social responsibility to inform readers about my native country. That said, I will be gratified if they walk away from *A Thousand Splendid Suns* with a satisfying story and with a little more insight and a more personal sense of what has happened in Afghanistan in the last thirty years."

THE GRAPES OF WRATH

John Steinbeck

—

1939

A series of articles published in the *San Francisco News* detailing the lives of migrant workers in California's Central Valley, "The Harvest Gypsies" was the start of what would eventually become Steinbeck's *The Grapes of Wrath*. The articles followed the workers during the Great Depression, a topic that had always interested Steinbeck and influenced a lot of his work. The workers' situation was unique, as the Dust Bowl forced many to migrate to California, leading to an excess of workers and extremely low pay. Steinbeck sought to document these conditions to see if they had any greater impact on California culture.

It is also believed that Steinbeck substantiated *The Grapes of Wrath* by using field notes taken by Farm Security Administrator Sanora Bobb, who was documenting the experiences of the migrant workers for a novel that she herself intended to write. Her supervisor shared the notes with Steinbeck, who drew inspiration from the stories she had documented in the notes.

Steinbeck's wife, Carol, suggested the title to him, having likely borrowed it from "The Battle Hymn of the Republic," in a lyric that reads, "Mine eyes have seen the glory of the coming of the Lord: He is trampling out the vintage where the grapes of wrath are stored; He hath loosed the fateful lightning of His terrible swift sword: His truth is marching on." That line is itself derived from the Bible, in Revelation 14:19–20. It reads, "And the angel thrust in his sickle into the earth, and gathered the vine of the earth, and cast it into the great winepress of the wrath of God. And the winepress was trodden without the city, and blood came out of the winepress, even unto the horse bridles, by the space of a thousand and six hundred furlongs."

1984

George Orwell

1949

Five years before *1984* was published, George Orwell penned a letter that indirectly outlined his reasons for writing one of the greatest dystopian novels ever. The letter begins: "You ask whether totalitarianism, leader-worship etc. are really on the up-grade and instance the fact that they are not apparently growing in this country and the USA. I must say I believe, or fear, that taking the world as a whole these things are on the increase. Hitler, no doubt, will soon disappear, but only at the expense of strengthening (a) Stalin, (b) the Anglo-American millionaires and (c) all sorts of petty fuhrers of the type of de Gaulle. All the national movements everywhere, even those that originate in resistance to German domination, seem to take non-democratic forms, to group themselves round some superhuman fuhrer (Hitler, Stalin, Salazar, Franco, Gandhi, De Valera are all varying examples) and to adopt the theory that the end justifies the means."

Orwell had noticed a concerning trend. Major world governments were moving toward a more central economy, precipitating a sort of caste system in their own countries. As Orwell saw it, this would ultimately lead to a singular ruling power, creating "a world of two or three great superstates which are unable to conquer one another," wherein "two and two could become five if the fuhrer wished it." This was perhaps Orwell's primary concern—that objective truths would begin to fail, starting with a country's own account of its history. He knew that historical accuracy didn't carry the same weight as a pro-government narrative, citing Hitler's claim that Jewish people started World War II as an example.

Despite his pessimism toward every world power, Orwell also observed that the Allied forces were not yet in the grips of totalitarianism. Believing that the English could move toward a more centralized system of government without killing democracy, he writes, "It is a choice of evils—I fancy nearly every war is that. I know enough of British imperialism not to like it, but I would support it against Nazism or Japanese imperialism, as the lesser evil. Similarly I would support the USSR against Germany because I think the USSR cannot altogether escape its past and retains enough of the original ideas of the Revolution to make it a more hopeful phenomenon than Nazi Germany. I think, and have thought ever since the war began, in 1936 or thereabouts, that our cause is the better, but we have to keep on making it the better, which involves constant criticism."

DOG SOLDIERS

Robert Stone

———

1974

"It's goddamn hard," said Robert Stone when asked about his writing process in a 1985 interview. "Nobody really cares whether you do it or not. You have to make yourself do it. I'm very lazy and I suffer as a result. Of course, when it's going well there's nothing in the world like it. But it's also very lonely. If you do something you're really pleased with, you're in the crazy position of being exhilarated all by yourself. I remember finishing one section of *Dog Soldiers*—the end of Hick's walk—in the basement of a college library, working at night, while the rest of the place was closed down, and I staggered out in tears, talking to myself, and ran into a security guard."

An admirer of and participant in the literary Beat scene, Stone took his time working on his novels, often noting in interviews that Ken Kesey had produced two novels in the time it took him to write one. It was Kesey who introduced Stone to LSD, which led him to begin taking other hallucinogens. Stone himself confirmed that his drug use informed some of his writing, while also noting that certain Beat contemporaries inspired some of his characters. On writing the character Ray Hicks, Stone said, "I didn't know him well. And I didn't travel on the bus. I saw the bus off and greeted the bus when it arrived on Riverside Drive. We went to a party where Kerouac and Ginsberg and Orlovsky and those guys were, and Kerouac was at his drunken worst. He was also very jealous of Neal, who had shifted his allegiance to Kesey. But Neal was pretty exhausted, too. I saw some films taken on the bus—Neal looked like he was tired from trying to keep up with the limitless energy of all those kids. Anyway . . . Kerouac at that party was drunk and pissed off, a situation I understand very well. The first thing I ever said to him was, 'Hey, Jack, have you got a cigarette?' And he said, 'I ain't gonna give you no cigarette, man, there's a drugstore on the corner, you can go down there and buy a pack of cigarettes, don't ask me for cigarettes.' That's my Kerouac story."

LOLITA

Vladimir Nabokov

1955

In *On a Book Entitled Lolita*, Nabokov writes, "As far as I can recall, the initial shiver of inspiration was somehow prompted by a newspaper story about an ape in the Jardin des Plantes, who, after months of coaxing by a scientist, produced the first drawing ever charcoaled by an animal: the sketch showed the bars of the poor creature's cage." The Russian author's *Lolita* remains one of the most controversial literary masterpieces of all time, as the novel's narrative is driven by Humbert Humbert's desire for the much younger Dolores Haze. The novel's pedophilia elements initially distracted critics from the author's mastery of the written word. In writing from Humbert's perspective, Nabokov creates an unreliable narrator who both repulses and fascinates the reader. Like the ape in Jardin des Plantes, Humbert is trapped by something that he cannot control and is painfully conscious of it. The character also shares some qualities with Nabokov, such as the fact that he's highly educated and quite proficient in language.

STRONG MOTION

Jonathan Franzen

1992

Says Franzen in an interview with *The Paris Review,* "A bunch of things had happened. My first book had been published, and my wife and I had fled to Europe; things were getting hard in the marriage. And, perhaps not coincidentally, I'd fallen under the spell of religious writers, particularly Flannery O'Connor and Dostoyevsky. My wife and I began touring cathedrals and looking at medieval sculpture and Romanesque churches. *Wise Blood, The Brothers Karamazov,* and the cathedral at Chartres are all examples of religious art, which is neither just religion nor just art; it's a special category, a special binding of the aesthetic and the devotional. O'Connor and Dostoyevsky venture intensely into the extremes of human psychology, but always with serious moral purpose. Because of the difficulties in my marriage, I was attracted to their search for moral purpose in emotional extremity. I imagined static lives being disrupted from without—literally shaken. I imagined violent scenes that would strip away the veneer and get people shouting angry moral truths at each other. I had the title *Strong Motion* very early on."

SARAH'S KEY

Tatiana de Rosnay

———

2006

On writing *Sarah's Key*, a novel that follows two parallel storylines dealing with the Vel' d'Hiv Roundup, Tatiana de Rosnay says, "I wrote this book ten years ago. I have always been interested by how walls can talk. One of my novels [*La Mémoire des Murs, The Memory of Walls*] describes the rue Nélaton. That is where the Vél d'Hiv roundup took place on July 16th 1942. I realized I didn't know the exact details of what happened that day. I was not taught about this event at school, during the '70s. It seemed to be shrouded by taboo. So I started researching. I was appalled by what I discovered concerning the roundup, about what happened to those four thousand Jewish children, and I knew I had to write about it. And that's how I imagined Julia's story taking place today, linked to Sarah's, back in the '40s. Through Julia's modern story, I could reveal the taboos and scars the Vel d'Hiv left in France, sixty years later."

THE BRIDGE OVER THE RIVER KWAI

Pierre Boulle

1952

Nine years before publishing *The Bridge over the River Kwai*, Pierre Boulle was captured by Vichy France loyalists on the Mekong River while serving as a secret agent for the Free French Mission during World War II. He was subjected to forced labor for the next two years, a time during which he worked on the Burma Railway, also known as the Death Railway. The Japanese, having recently lost the Battle of Midway in 1942 to Allied forces, needed a supply route to Burma that was less vulnerable to attack. A railway line from Bangkok to Burma seemed like the most logical alternative, so Japanese forces put their POWs to work despite their inability to accommodate such a large workforce.

The completion of the project came at a massive cost; an estimated 13,000 POWs died during its construction, as well as upwards of 100,000 workers of Asian decent who were forcibly drafted to work on the railway. Perhaps the most famous aspect of that project was Bridge 277, or "the bridge on the river Kwai." Stretching over a river that was then part of the Mae Klong, the bridge was the intended target for a number of Allied strikes, including several that eventually knocked it out of commission.

ON THE ROAD

Jack Kerouac

1957

On the Road is perhaps the most popular piece of writing to come out of the Beat generation and was written by perhaps the most popular author in that group, Jack Kerouac. The novel is known for being written in a very stream-of-consciousness style, on which Kerouac tells *The Paris Review*, "What style? Oh, the style of *On the Road*. Well as I say, Cowley riddled the original style of the manuscript there, without my power to complain, and since then my books are all published as written, as I say, and the style has varied from the highly experimental speed-writing of *Railroad Earth* to the ingrown toenail packed mystical style of *Tristessa*, the *Notes from Underground* [by Dostoyevsky] confessional madness of *The Subterraneans*, the perfection of the three-as-one in *Big Sur*, I'd say, which tells a plain tale in a smooth buttery literate run, to *Satori in Paris*, which is really the first book I wrote with drink at my side (cognac and malt liquor) . . . and not to overlook *Book of Dreams*, the style of a person half-awake from sleep and ripping it out in pencil by the bed . . . yes, pencil . . . what a job! Bleary eyes, insane mind bemused and mystified by sleep, details that pop out even as you write them you don't know what they mean, till you wake up, have coffee, look at it, and see the logic of dreams in dream language itself, see? . . . And finally I decided in my tired middle age to slow down and did *Vanity of Duluoz* in a more moderate style so that, having been so esoteric all these years, some earlier readers would come back and see what ten years had done to my life and thinking . . . which is after all the only thing I've got to offer, the true story of what I saw and how I saw it."

100 YEARS OF SOLITUDE

Gabriel Garcia Marquez

———

1967

"I was reading Garcia Marquez," said Carmen Balcells, Marquez's agent, in an interview with *Vanity Fair*, "one of the early books—and I said to Luis, 'This is so fantastic, Luis, that we have to read it at the same time.' So I made a copy of it. We both had enthusiasm for it: it was so fresh, so original, so exciting. Every reader says in his mind, of certain books, 'This is one of the best books I have ever read.' When that happens to a book again and again, all over the world, you have a masterpiece. That is what happened with Gabriel Garcia Marquez."

Balcells got in touch with Marquez and, after getting to know each other, got him a contract from Harper & Row for his next four books. Marquez then set off to Acapulco before stopping his car and turning everybody around, returning home to type out the work of fiction that had been inside him for twenty years. "It was so ripe to me," he said, "that I could have dictated the first chapter, word by word, to a typist." Eighteen months, 30,000 cigarettes and 120,000 pesos and he had his *100 Years of Solitude*, a novel that cost him most of what he owned to write and paid it all back a thousand times over. The idea that had been inside of him for all of that time was simple: a tale of a large family in a small village.

The parallels between Marquez's fictional Macondo and real hometown Aracataca are clear. Both towns experience a gradual decline into poverty, brought on in part by foreign fruit companies buying up valuable plantations in the area. Both had to deal with foreign settlers introducing technology that shocked and crippled the economic system they had in place and both had to deal with constant government upheaval, as stability was rare in Latin American politics at the time. The consistent governmental failures were, in part, the inspiration for the cyclical nature of the Buendías family and Macondo. The message is clear: Failure to acknowledge and learn from the past only yields repetition.

ONE FLEW OVER THE CUCKOO'S NEST

Ken Kesey

1962

In the fall of 1958, University of Oregon graduate Ken Kesey returned home to California to enroll at Stanford University's creative writing center, which he attended during the day while working as a night aide in the psychiatric ward of the Menlo Park Veterans' Hospital. At the behest of a friend who was a Stanford psychology graduate student, Kesey decided to take part in a CIA-financed study, in which he was to play the role of guinea pig as they observed the effects of psychiatric drugs. The study, called Project MKUltra, supplemented Kesey's recreational drug use, which included frequent experimentation with LSD. Believing that the drug offered the individual an unparalleled amount of access to the human mind, Kesey became a huge advocate for the de-stigmatization of the drug. Having opened his mind to new thoughts and perspectives, he also became very sympathetic toward the patients at the psychiatric ward.

That the ward in the novel resembles a prison more than it does anything else was due to the fact that, among other things, the Civil Rights Movement was targeting the way psychology was studied in the United States, encouraging deinstitutionalization while simultaneously calling into question the morality behind treating patients in psychiatric wards. French intellectual Michel Foucault led that charge, saying that widespread censorship, as a response to invisible forms of discipline, would be horrible for society.

The title of *One Flew Over the Cuckoo's Nest* was derived from a line in a nursery rhyme that reads: "Vintery, mintery, cutery, corn, / Apple seed and apple thorn, / Wire, briar, limber lock / Three geese in a flock / One flew East / One flew West / And one flew over the cuckoo's nest."

HERZOG

Saul Bellow

1964

Saul Bellow's *Herzog*, a story about a middle-aged Jewish man who experiences a midlife crisis, was autobiographical in many ways. Bellow was himself the victim of infidelity, having learned that his ex-wife had relations with his close friend during their marriage. Like his protagonist, Bellow sought comfort in the arms of another lover after the discovery. And he, like his protagonist, was in his late forties at the time all of this occurred. Their backgrounds are similar as well, as both men were sons of Jewish bootleggers who had emigrated from Russia to Canada, and both lived in Chicago for a period of their lives.

The autobiographical elements of *Herzog*, while obvious, were largely ignored when the book was published. This can mainly be attributed to the reviewers, most of whom knew Bellow personally and didn't want to shine light on his recent divorce. Some wrote that it was a report on the modern man, while others called it "a major breakthrough." Almost all warned against reading the book as an autobiography—

though they offered no real evidence as to why. Even Rosette Lamont and Jack Ludwig, real people who clearly inspired characters, treated the story as pure fiction.

GIRL WITH A PEARL EARRING

Tracy Chevalier

1999

Describing the inspiration for *Girl With a Pearl Earring*, Tracy Chavalier says, "I chose Vermeer's work because it is so beautiful and so mysterious. In his paintings, the solitary women going about their domestic tasks—pouring milk, reading letters, weighing gold, putting on a necklace—inhabit a world that we are getting a secret glimpse at. And because it feels secret— the women don't seem to know we're looking at them—it seems also that something else is going on underneath, something mysterious we can't quite grasp. The fact that so little is known about Vermeer was happenstance—happily so, as it turned out, for it meant I could make up a lot without worrying about things being 'true' or not . . . I was inspired specifically by this particular painting, though I know his other work as well. A poster of this painting has hung on the wall of my bedroom since I was nineteen and I often lie in bed and look at it and wonder about it. It's such an open painting. I'm never sure what the girl is thinking or what her expression is. Sometimes she seems sad, other times seductive. So, one morning a couple years ago I was lying in bed worrying about what I was going to write next, and I looked up at the painting and wondered what Vermeer did or said to the model to get her to look like that. And right then I made up the story."

Despite her connection to the painting, Chevalier insists her novel isn't based in a true story. "It isn't a true story. No one knows who the girl is, or in fact who any of the people in his paintings are. Very little is known about Vermeer—he left no writings, not even any drawings, just thirty-five paintings. The few known facts are based on legal documents—his baptism, his marriage, the births of his children, his will. I was careful to be true to the known facts; for instance, he married Catharina Bolnes and they had eleven surviving children. Other facts are not so clear-cut and I had to make choices: he may or may not have lived in the house of his mother-in-law (I decided he did); he converted to Catholicism at the time of his marriage but not necessarily because Catharina was Catholic (I decided he did); he may have been friends with the scientist Antony van Leeuwenhoek, who invented the microscope (I decided he was). But there was a lot I simply made up."

HARRY POTTER AND THE SORCERER'S STONE

J.K. Rowling

1997

"One weekend after flat hunting, I took the train back to London on my own and the idea for Harry Potter fell into my head," said J.K. Rowling in an interview. "A scrawny, little, black-haired, bespectacled boy became more and more of a wizard to me . . . I began to write *The Sorcerer's Stone* that very evening. Although, the first couple of pages look nothing like the finished product." Rowling would have started writing the book right then and there on the train, but she was too shy to ask for a pen. "When I look back at it [it]was the best thing for me. It gave me the full four hours on the train to think up all the ideas for the book."

Rowling's process was not easy—she experienced several major life changes during the five years she spent on the book, the first being the unexpected death of her mother. "Nine months afterwards, I desperately wanted to get away from everything and took a job in Portugal as an English teacher at a language institute. I took my manuscript with me in hopes of working on it while I was there. My feelings about Harry Potter's parents' death became more real to me, and more emotional. In my first week in Portugal, I wrote my favorite chapter in *Sorcerer's Stone*—'The Mirror of Erised.' I had hoped that I would've been done with the book by the time I was back from Portugal, but I came back with something better, my daughter, Jessica. The marriage didn't work out, but the best thing I had ever had came into my life."

Motherhood caused Rowling to value time as she never had before, as she explains: "Every time Jessica would fall asleep in her pushchair, I'd dash to the nearest café and write as much as I could. I wrote nearly every evening. Then, I had to type everything out myself. Sometimes, I hated the book, and all the while I still loved it."

WORKS CITED

Matilda

"Matilda." *Matilda - Roald Dahl*. Roalddahl. com, n.d. Web. Accessed 17 Apr. 2017.

Charlotte's Web

White, E. B. "A Book Is a Sneeze." Letter to Ursula Nordstrom. 29 Sept. 1952. *Letters of Note*. N.p., 2 Aug. 2013. Web.

Of Mice and Men

Arbeiter, Michael. "15 Things You Might Not Know About *Of Mice and Men*." *Mental Floss*. N.p., 27 Feb. 2017. Web. 17 Apr. 2017.

"Of Mice and Men: John Steinbeck Biography." Cliffsnotes.com. N.p., n.d. Web. Accessed 10 Apr. 2017.

The Girl on the Train

"Paula Hawkins Discusses The Inspiration Behind 'The Girl On The Train'." *BUILD Series NYC*. Build Series NYC, n.d. Web. 17 Apr. 2017. Video: Interview with AOL.com.

"Finding Inspiration: The Girl on the Train by Paula Hawkins." *The Magazine*. Writing.ie, n.d. Web. Accessed 17 Apr. 2017.

The Giver

"The Giver: Lois Lowry On What Inspired The Book." *Amazon*. N.p., n.d. Web. Accessed 17 Apr. 2017.

Ulaby, Neda. "Lois Lowry Says 'The Giver' Was Inspired By Her Father's Memory Loss." *NPR*. NPR, 16 Aug. 2014. Web. 17 Apr. 2017.

Ordinary People

Guest, Judith. *"Ordinary People." Judithguest. com*. 2005

Guest, Judith. "Biography." *Judithguest.com*. 2005.

Black Beauty

Norris, Michele. "How 'Black Beauty' Changed The Way We See Horses." *NPR*. NPR, 02 Nov. 2012. Web.

Brave New World

Arbeiter, Michael. "15 Things You Might Not Know About *Brave New World*." *Mental Floss*. N.p., 20 May 2015. Web. Accessed 17 Apr. 2017.

Cat's Cradle

Inglis-Arkell, Esther. "The Real-Life Scientist Who Inspired Kurt Vonnegut's Cat's Cradle." *Io9*. Gawker Media, 18 Oct. 2013. Web. Accessed 17 Apr. 2017.

Interviewed by David Hayman, David Michaelis, George Plimpton, Richard Rhodes. "Kurt Vonnegut, The Art of Fiction No. 64." *The*

Paris Review. The Paris Review, 20 Nov. 2016. Web. Accessed 17 Apr. 2017.

Charlie and the Chocolate Factory

"Repton School 'Helped Inspire Dahl' to Write Charlie." *BBC News*. BBC, 13 Sept. 2011. Web. Accessed 20 Apr. 2017.

Dahl, Roald, and Quentin Blake. *Charlie and the Chocolate Factory*. New York: Puffin, an imprint of Penguin Group (USA) Inc., 2013. Print.

Fahrenheit 451

Beley, Gene. *Ray Bradbury: Uncensored!: The unauthorized biography*. Lincoln, NE: IUniverse, 2006. *Google Books*. Web.

Memoirs of a Geisha

BookBrowse. "Arthur Golden author interview." *BookBrowse.com*. N.p., n.d. Web. Accessed 17 Apr. 2017. Published with Permission from Knopf.

Interview by Miles O'Brien. "A Talk With Arthur Golden." *CNN.com*. CNN, 23 Mar. 1999. Web transcript. Accessed 10 Apr. 2017. Transcript.

Midnight's Children

Gnagey, Laurel Thomas. "Rushdie discusses inspiration for 'Midnight's Children,' writing in general." *The University Record Online*. University of Michigan, 2003. Web. Accessed 17 Apr. 2017.

Livings, Interviewed By Jack. "Salman Rushdie,

The Art of Fiction No. 186." *The Paris Review*. The Paris Review, 14 Apr. 2017. Web. Accessed 17 Apr. 2017.

Mrs. Dalloway

Heffernan, James. "Woolf's Reading of Joyce's Ulysses, 1922-1941." *Modernism Lab Essays*. The Modernism Lab at Yale University, n.d. Web. Accessed 17 Apr. 2017.

Lanzendorfer, Joy. "10 Interesting Facts About *Mrs. Dalloway*." *Mental Floss*. Mental Floss, 27 Jan. 2015. Web. Accessed 17 Apr. 2017.

Never Let Me Go

"Interview with Kazuo Ishiguro." *Writers Write*. N.p., Oct. 2005. Web. Accessed 17 Apr. 2017.

Oh, the Places You'll Go!

Baker, Andrew. "Ten Things You May Not Have Known About Dr. Suess." *The Peel Literary Magazine*. Appalachian State University, 3 Mar. 2010. Web.

Gumbrecht, Jamie. "Dr. Seuss' 'Oh, The Places You'll Go!' turns 25." *CNN*. Cable News Network, 22 Jan. 2015. Web. Accessed 20 Apr. 2017.

Wadler, Joyce. "Mrs. Seuss Hears a Who, and Tells About It." *The New York Times*. The New York Times, 28 Nov. 2000. Web. Accessed 20 Apr. 2017.

Ragtime

Gussow, Mel. "Novelist Syncopates History in 'Ragtime.' " *The New York Times*. The New

York Times, 11 July 1975. Web. Accessed 17 Apr. 2017.

Interviewed By George Plimpton. "E. L. Doctorow, The Art of Fiction No. 94." *The Paris Review*. The Paris Review, 13 Apr. 2017. Web. Accessed 17 Apr. 2017.

Stranger in a Strange Land

Patterson, William H., Jr. "Biographies: Robert A. Heinlein." *The Heinlein Society*. N.p., n.d. Web. Accessed 20 Apr. 2017.

Vonnegut, Kurt. "Heinlein Gets the Last Word." *The New York Times*. The New York Times, 9 Dec. 1990. Web. Accessed 20 Apr. 2017.

The Great Gatsby

Chalupa, Andrea. "F. Scott Fitzgerald on Writing 'The Great Gatsby.'" *Big Think*. N.p., 09 May 2013. Web. Accessed 19 Apr. 2017.

Kellogg, Carolyn. "Last Gasp of the Gatsby House." *Los Angeles Times*. Los Angeles Times, 20 Apr. 2011. Web. Accessed 19 Apr. 2017.

Lombardi, Esther. "F. Scott Fitzgerald's Inspiration for 'The Great Gatsby'." *ThoughtCo*. N.p., 7 Apr. 2017. Web. Accessed 19 Apr. 2017.

Odegard, Dave. "The Story Behind F. Scott Fitzgerald's The Great Gatsby." *Signature Reads*. N.p., 06 Feb. 2014. Web. Accessed 19 Apr. 2017.

The Crucible

PBS, 2003. Television. *American Masters*. Public Broadcasting Service, 30 Nov. 2015. Web. Accessed 20 Apr. 2017.

The Exorcist

"A Very Special Contribution to TNC.com from Mr. Blatty Himself!" *Theninthconfiguration. com*. N.p., 3 June 2009. Web. Accessed 17 Apr. 2017.

Phillips, Camille, and Alex Heuer. "Heard Of 'The Exorcist?' This St. Louis Event Inspired It." *St. Louis Public Radio*. N.p., 30 Oct. 2013. Web. Accessed 17 Apr. 2017.

The Martian

White, Micah. "From Book to Blockbuster, The Inspiring Story of 'The Martian.' " *Biography. com*. A&E Networks Television, 05 Apr. 2016. Web. Accessed 17 Apr. 2017.

The Picture of Dorian Gray

MacCarthy, Fiona. "Fiona MacCarthy on the inspiration for Oscar Wilde's Dorian Gray." *The Guardian*. Guardian News and Media, 29 Aug. 2008. Web. Accessed 17 Apr. 2017.

The Secret Garden

Blakeslee, Vanessa. "Secret Gardens." *The Paris Review*. The Paris Review, 10 Apr. 2012. Web. Accessed 17 Apr. 2017.

Clark, Anna. "The Secret Garden's Hidden Depths." *The Guardian*. Guardian News and

Media, 05 Aug. 2011. Web. Accessed 17
Apr. 2017.

Lanzendorfer, Joy. "8 Lovely Facts About *The
Secret Garden*." *Mental Floss*. N.p., 27 Jan.
2016. Web. Accessed 17 Apr. 2017.

Stiles, Anne. "Christian Science versus the
Rest Cure in Frances Hodgson Burnett's The
Secret Garden." *MFS Modern Fiction Studies*.
The Johns Hopkins University Press, 25 June
2015. Web. Accessed 17 Apr. 2017.

Steppenwolf

Cox, Chris. "Steppenwolf by Hermann Hesse –
Review." *The Guardian*. Guardian News and
Media, 23 Feb. 2013. Web. Accessed 17 Apr.
2017.

Zeller, Bernhard. *Hermann Hesse*. Reinbek bei
Hamburg: Rowohlt, 2005. Print.

A Visit from the Goon Squad

DuChateau, Christian. "How 'The Goon Squad'
Came to Be." *CNN*. Cable News Network, 24
Apr. 2011. Web. Accessed 17 Apr. 2017.

Feldmar, Jamie. "Talking With Jennifer Egan,
Author Of A Visit From The Goon Squad."
Gothamist. N.p., 8 July 2011. Web. Accessed
17 Apr. 2017.

Alice in Wonderland

Corrigan, Maureen. "Through The Looking
Glass: Alice In Fact And Fiction." *NPR*. NPR,
26 Jan. 2010. Web. Accessed 17 Apr. 2017.

Ferro, Shaunacy. "12 Absurd Facts About Alice

in Wonderland." *Mental Floss*. N.p., 07 July
2015. Web. Accessed 17 Apr. 2017.

Lansley, Oliver. "10 Things You Didn't Know
about Alice in Wonderland." *The Guardian*.
Guardian News and Media, 17 Apr. 2015.
Web. Accessed 17 Apr. 2017.

Popova, Maria. "Meet the Girl Who Inspired
'Alice in Wonderland.'" *The Atlantic*.
Atlantic Media Company, 05 July 2012. Web.
Accessed 17 Apr. 2017.

Devlin, Keith, and Lyden, Jacki. "The Mad
Hatter's Secret Ingredient: Math." *NPR*. NPR,
13 Mar. 2010. Web. Accessed 17 Apr. 2017.

Calvin and Hobbes

"Speech by Bill Watterson: Some Thoughts on
the Real World by One Who Glimpsed it and
Fled." *Bill Watterson at Kenyon College*. N.p.,
1990. Web. Accessed 17 Apr. 2017.

Tucker, Neely. "The Tiger Strikes Again." *The
Washington Post*. WP Company, 04 Oct.
2005. Web. Accessed 17 Apr. 2017.

Giovanni's Room

Elgrably, Interviewed By Jordan. "James
Baldwin, The Art of Fiction No. 78." *The
Paris Review*. The Paris Review, 13 Apr.
2017. Web. Accessed 17 Apr. 2017.

Tóibín, Colm. "The Unsparing Confessions of
'Giovanni's Room'." *The New Yorker*. The
New Yorker, 26 Feb. 2016. Web. Accessed 17
Apr. 2017.

Gone with the Wind

Perkerson, Interview with Medora. "Margaret Mitchell: American Rebel." *PBS*. Public Broadcasting Service, 11 Dec. 2015. Web. Accessed 17 Apr. 2017.

Middlesex

"A Conversation with Jeffrey Eugenides." *Oprah.com*. N.p., n.d. Web. Accessed 17 Apr. 2017.

Misery

King, Stephen. "Misery Inspiration." *StephenKing.com*. N.p., n.d. Web. Accessed 17 Apr. 2017.

Greene, Andy. "Stephen King: The Rolling Stone Interview." *Rolling Stone*. Rolling Stone, 31 Oct. 2014. Web. Accessed 17 Apr. 2017.

Rylah, Juliet Bennett. "The Creepiest True Stories Behind Stephen King Books." *Ranker*. N.p., n.d. Web. Accessed 17 Apr. 2017.

Twenty Thousand Leagues Under the Sea

Romney, Rebecca. "Twenty Thousands Leagues Under the Sea: The Influences of Jules Verne - Rare Books Experts at Bauman Rare Books." *Bauman Rare Books Blog*. N.p., 24 Oct. 2013. Web. Accessed 21 Apr. 2017.

Rabbit, Run

Interview by Diane Osen. "Interview with John Updike." *NBF ARCHIVES: John Updike Author Study Guide, The National Book Foundation*. N.p., n.d. Web. Accessed 17 Apr. 2017.

**The Amazing Adventures of
Kavalier and Clay**

Buchwald, Interview with Laura. "Michael Chabon author interview." *BookBrowse. com*. Random House Publishing, 2001. Web. Accessed 17 Apr. 2017. Reprinted with permission from Random House Publishing.

The Awakening

"About The Awakening." *Cliffsnotes.com*. N.p., n.d. Web. Accessed 17 Apr. 2017.

The Color Purple

Akitunde, Anthonia. "Alice Walker's Makers Appearance Highlights Why She Wrote 'The Color Purple' (VIDEO)." *The Huffington Post*. TheHuffingtonPost.com, 28 Feb. 2013. Web. Accessed 17 Apr. 2017.

The Tale of Peter Rabbit

Mackey, Margaret, *Beatrix Potter's Peter Rabbit: A Children's Classic at 100*, Lanham, MD: The Scarecrow Press, Inc., 2002.

The Goldfinch

Bosman, Julie. "Writer Brings in the World While She Keeps It at Bay." *The New York Times*. The New York Times, 20 Oct. 2013. Web. Accessed 17 Apr. 2017.

Creeden, Molly. "Interview with Donna Tartt." *Goodreads*. N.p., 01 Oct. 2013. Web. Accessed 17 Apr. 2017.

Grassi, Laurie. "Chatelaine Book Club Interview with Donna Tartt, Author of The Goldfinch."

Chatelaine. N.p., 08 Nov. 2013. Web. Accessed 17 Apr. 2017.

Miller, Laura. "Donna Tartt: 'The Fun Thing about Writing a Book Is That It Really Is a Different Life'." *Salon.* N.p., n.d. Web. Accessed 17 Apr. 2017.

The House on Mango Street

Montagne, Renee. " 'House On Mango Street' Celebrates 25 Years." *NPR.* NPR, 09 Apr. 2009. Web. Accessed 17 Apr. 2017.

The Human Stain

Roth, Philip. "An Open Letter to Wikipedia." *The New Yorker.* The New Yorker, 16 July 2014. Web. Accessed 17 Apr. 2017.

The Hunger Games

Margolis, Rick. "A Killer Story: An Interview with Suzanne Collins, Author of 'The Hunger Games'." *School Library Journal.* N.p., 1 Sept. 2008. Web. Accessed 17 Apr. 2017.

The Old Man and the Sea

"About The Old Man and the Sea." *Cliffsnotes. com.* N.p., n.d. Web. Accessed 17 Apr. 2017.

Interview with Jeffrey Meyers. "Inspiration for 'Old Man and the Sea' Dies." *All Things Considered.* NPR. 14 Jan. 2002. Web. Accessed 10 Apr. 2017.

Lanzendorfer, Joy. "11 Facts About Hemingway's The Old Man And The Sea." *Mental Floss.* N.p., 27 May 2015. Web. Accessed 17 Apr. 2017.

The Sound and the Fury

"The Sound and the Fury." *SparkNotes*. SparkNotes, n.d. Web. Accessed 17 Apr. 2017.

Angels in America

Berson, Misha. "A Q&A with Tony Kushner on His 'Angels in America,' Revisiting the Intiman Theatre." *The Seattle Times*. The Seattle Times Company, 10 Aug. 2014. Web. Accessed 17 Apr. 2017.

Butler, Isaac, and Dan Kois. "How Angels in America Became the Defining Work of American Art of the Past 25 Years." *Slate Magazine*. N.p., 28 June 2016. Web. Accessed 17 Apr. 2017.

Atonement

McEwan, Ian. "An Inspiration, Yes. Did I copy from Another Author? No." *The Guardian*. Guardian News and Media, 27 Nov. 2006. Web. Accessed 17 Apr. 2017.

Zalewski, Daniel. "Ian McEwan's Art of Unease." *The New Yorker*. The New Yorker, 18 May 2016. Web. Accessed 17 Apr. 2017.

Birdsong

Faulks, Sebastian. "The war story that inspired Birdsong." *The Independent*. Independent Digital News and Media, 20 Jan. 2012. Web. Accessed 17 Apr. 2017.

Faulks, Sebastian. "How I Found The REAL Story of Birdsong in The Mud and Blood of

Flanders: A powerful and Moving Tribute to the Heroes of WWI by the Author of One of Britain's Most Cherished Literary Classics." *Daily Mail Online*. Associated Newspapers, 22 June 2014. Web. Accessed 17 Apr. 2017.

Carrie

King, Stephen. "Stephen King: How I Wrote Carrie." *The Guardian*. Guardian News and Media, 04 Apr. 2014. Web. Accessed 17 Apr. 2017.

Goodnight Moon

Cahalan, Susannah. " 'Goodnight Moon' Author Was A Bisexual Rebel Who Didn't Like Kids." *New York Post*, 07 Jan. 2017. Web. Accessed 17 Apr. 2017.

Crawford, Amy. "The Surprising Ingenuity Behind 'Goodnight Moon'." *Smithsonian. com*. Smithsonian Institution, 26 Jan. 2017. Web. Accessed 17 Apr. 2017.

Green Eggs and Ham

Kopan, Tal. "10 Facts about 'Green Eggs and Ham' " *POLITICO*. N.p., 25 Sept. 2013. Web. Accessed 17 Apr. 2017.

Holes

Sachar, Louis. "Holes Q & A." *Louissachar.com*. N.p., n.d. Web. Accessed 17 Apr. 2017.

Inherit the Wind

Blankenship, Bill. "Inherit the Controversy." *CJOnline.com*. N.p., 2 Mar. 2001. Web. Accessed 17 Apr. 2017.

Invisible Cities

Weiner, Eric. "Urban Oases: Getting Lost in 'Invisible Cities'." *NPR*. NPR, 21 Jan. 2013. Web. Accessed 17 Apr. 2017.

Jane Eyre

Lanzendorfer, Joy. "10 Moody Facts About Jane Eyre." *Mental Floss*. N.p., 21 Apr. 2015. Web. Accessed 20 Apr. 2017.

Lewis, Stephen. "Real-Life Brontë Scandal." *York Press*. N.p., 18 Nov. 2011. Web. Accessed 20 Apr. 2017.

Shorter, Clement King. *The Brontës Life and Letters; Being an Attempt to Present A Full and Final Record of the Lives of the Three Sisters, Charlotte, Emily and Anne Brontë Volume 1*. N.p.: Cambridge U Press, 2013. Print.

Wainwright, Martin. "Mystery of Jane Eyre Attic Solved." *The Guardian*. Guardian News and Media, 03 Dec. 2004. Web. Accessed 20 Apr. 2017.

Little Women

Lanzendorfer, Joy. "10 Things You May Not Know About *Little Women*." *Mental Floss*. N.p., 14 May 2014. Web. Accessed 17 Apr. 2017.

Our Lady of the Flowers

Encyclopædia Editors. "Jean Genet." *Encyclopædia Britannica*. Encyclopædia Britannica, Inc., 21 Mar. 1999. Web. Accessed 20 Apr. 2017.

Sartre, Jean-Paul. "Forward." *Our Lady of the Flowers*. By Jean Genet. N.p.: Grove Press, 1994. Print.

Stormbreaker

"An Interview with Anthony Horowitz." *Scholastic*. N.p., n.d. Web. Accessed 17 Apr. 2017.

The Day of the Jackal

Cumming, Charles. "The Day of the Jackal— The Hit We Nearly Missed." *The Guardian*. Guardian News and Media, 03 June 2011. Web. Accessed 20 Apr. 2017.

Interview by Vembu, Venkatesan. "I'm a Mercenary: I Wrote Day of the Jackal for Money: Frederick Forsyth." *DNA India*. N.p., 30 July 2010. Web. Accessed 20 Apr. 2017.

Yishau, Olukorede. "Frederick Forsyth's Biafran Story." *The Nation* (Lagos, Nigeria)

The Gift of the Magi

Fallon, Kevin. "The Gift of 'The Gift of the Magi'." *The Atlantic*. Atlantic Media Company, 10 Dec. 2010. Web. Accessed 17 Apr. 2017.

The Last Unicorn

WCWF–CW 14. "Q&A With Peter S. Beagle - The Inspiration For The Last Unicorn." *YouTube*. WCWF 14 - Green Bay, WI, 24 Sept. 2014. Web. Accessed 17 Apr. 2017.

Cold War Warriors. *YouTube*. YouTube, 28 Nov. 2010. Web. Accessed 18 Apr. 2017.

The Fellowship of the Ring

Tolley, Clive. "Old English Influences on The Lord of the Rings." PDF. Accessed 20 Apr. 2017.

The Stranger

"The Stranger." *SparkNotes*. SparkNotes, n.d. Web. Accessed 17 Apr. 2017.

The Wonderful Wizard of Oz

Baum, L. Frank; Hearn, Michael Patrick. *The Annotated Wizard of Oz*. New York: C.N. Potter, 1973. Print.

Carpenter, Angelica Shirley; Shirley, Jea. *L. Frank Baum: Royal Historian of Oz*. Minneapolis: Lerner Publishing Group, 1992. Print.

Lanzendorfer, Joy. "13 Facts About L. Frank Baum's Wonderful Wizard of Oz." *Mental Floss*. N.p., 28 July 2015. Web. Accessed 20 Apr. 2017.

Mendelsohn, Ink. "As a Piece of Fantasy, Baum's Life Was a Working Model." *The Spokesman-Review*. N.p., 24 May 1986. Web. Accessed 15 Apr. 2017.

Walden

Grammardog Guide to Walden, by Henry David Thoreau. Grammardog LLC, 2007.

Where the Wild Things Are

Warrick, Pamela. "Facing the Frightful Things: Books: These days, Maurice Sendak's Wild Creatures Are Homelessness, Aids and

Violence—Big Issues for Small Kids." *Los Angeles Times*. Los Angeles Times, 11 Oct. 1993. Web. Accessed 18 Apr. 2017.

The World According to Garp

Leve, Ariel. "The World According to John Irving." *The Times*. 18 Oct. 2009. Web. Accessed 20 Apr. 2017.

A Season in Hell

Ahearn, Edward J. *Rimbaud: Visions and Habitations*. Berkeley: University of California Press, 1983. Print.

"Arthur Rimbaud." *Poetry Foundation*. Poetry Foundation, n.d. Web. Accessed 21 Apr. 2017.

Bonnefoy, Yves. *Rimbaud*. Paris: Editions du Seuil, Ecrivains de toujours, 1961. Print.

Catch-22

Daugherty, Tracy. "The Genesis of Joseph Heller's Novel Catch 22." *Vanity Fair*. Vanity Fair, 31 Jan. 2015. Web. Accessed 18 Apr. 2017.

Plimpton, Interviewed By George. "Joseph Heller, The Art of Fiction No. 51." *The Paris Review*. N.p., Dec. 1974. Web. Accessed 18 Apr. 2017.

The Hitchhiker's Guide to the Galaxy

Gill, Peter. "Douglas Adams and the Cult of 42." *The Guardian*. Guardian News and Media, 03 Feb. 2011. Web. Accessed 18 Apr. 2017.

Ltd, Not Panicking. "A History of 'The

Hitchhiker's Guide to the Galaxy' " *H2g2—The Hitchhiker's Guide to the Galaxy: Earth Edition.* N.p., 28 Apr. 2003. Web. Accessed 18 Apr. 2017.

Portnoy's Complaint

Hofler, Robert. *Sexplosion: From Andy Warhol to* A Clockwork Orange *—How a Generation of Pop Rebels Broke All the Taboos.* New York: Itbooks, an imprint of HarperCollins Publishers, 2014. Print.

Interviewed by Lee, Hermione. "Philip Roth, The Art of Fiction No. 84." *The Paris Review.* The Paris Review, Sept. 1984. Web. Accessed 21 Apr. 2017.

The Poisonwood Bible

Kingsolver, Barbara. "Frequently Asked Questions: Some Previous Books." *Kingsolver.com.* N.p., n.d. Web. Accessed 18 Apr. 2017.

Are You There God? It's Me, Margaret

Bloom, Judy. "Are You There God? It's Me, Margaret: The Story." *Judy Blume on the Web.* Accessed N.p., n.d. Web. Accessed 18 Apr. 2017.

The Metamorphosis

Editors, Sparknotes. "Sparknotes on The Metamorphosis." *SparkNotes.com.* SparkNotes LLC, n.d. Web. Accessed 18 Apr. 2017.

Psycho

Susman, Gary. "25 Things You Never Knew About Alfred Hitchcock's 'Psycho' " *AOL Moviefone*. Moviefone, 16 June 2015. Web. Accessed 18 Apr. 2017.

Weaver, Tom. "Norman, Is That You? On the trail of the Real Norman Bates." *THE ASTOUNDING B MONSTER*. N.p., n.d. Web. Accessed 18 Apr. 2017.

The Thirty-Nine Steps

Government of Canada, Office of the Secretary to the Governor General, Information and Media Services. "Governor General: Lord Tweedsmuir of Elsfield." *Archive.gg.ca*. N.p., 30 Apr. 2009. Web. Accessed 18 Apr. 2017.

The Way We Live Now

Trollope, Anthony. *An Autobiography*. Newcastle: CSP Classic Texts, 2008. Print.

1Q84

Anderson, Sam. "The Fierce Imagination of Haruki Murakami." *The New York Times*. The New York Times, 22 Oct. 2011. Web. Accessed 18 Apr. 2017.

Flood, Alison. "Murakami reveals Orwell and Aum as Twin Inspirations for New Novel." *The Guardian*. Guardian News and Media, 26 June 2009. Web. Accessed 18 Apr. 2017.

The Secret Agent

Conrad, Joseph. *The Secret Agent: A Simple*

Tale. Ware, Hertfordshire: Wordsworth Editions, 2000. Print. "Author's Note."

Shulevitz, Judith. "Chasing After Conrad's Secret Agent." *Slate Magazine.* N.p., 26 Sept. 2001. Web. Accessed 18 Apr. 2017.

Ender's Game

Card, Orson Scott. "OSC Help Desk - Frequently Asked Questions." *Hatrack River.* N.p., n.d. Web. Accessed 18 Apr. 2017.

Room

Donoghue, Emma. "Emma Donoghue on How She Wrote Room." *The Guardian.* Guardian News and Media, 21 Mar. 2014. Web. Accessed 18 Apr. 2017.

Fight Club

Jemielity, Sam. "Chuck Palahniuk: The Playboy. conversation" Archived October 16, 2006, at the Wayback Machine. Accessed 10 Apr 2017.

The Road

Interviewed by Oprah Winfrey. *Oprah.com.* N.p., n.d. Web. Accessed 18 Apr. 2017.

A Grief Observed

Hooper, Walter. C.S. Lewis: A Companion and Guide. San Francisco: HarperCollins, 1996. Page 196. Print.

Life of Pi

"Conversation: Life of Pi." Interview by Ray Suarez. *PBS News Hour.* PBS. 11 Nov. 2002. Television.

Something Wicked This Way Comes

Bradbury, Ray. "In His Words: Entry 2." *RayBradbury.com*. N.p., Dec. 2001. Web. Accessed 19 Apr. 2017.

The Worm Ouroboros

Flood, Alison. "World of Fantasy: The Worm Ouroboros." *The Guardian*. Guardian News and Media, 02 Oct. 2009. Web. Accessed 21 Apr. 2017.

Starship Troopers

Gifford, James. "The Nature of Federal Service in Robert A. Heinlein's Starship Troopers." PDF. Accessed 19 Apr 2017.

Patterson, William H., Jr., and Robert James, PhD. "Biographies of Robert and Virginia Heinlein." *Heinlein Society*. N.p., n.d. Web. Accessed 19 Apr. 2017.

Patterson, William H. *Robert A. Heinlein In Dialogue With His Century; the Man Who Learned Better 1948-1988*. N.p.: Tor, 2016. Print.

Native Son

Marsak, Nathan. "Life and Death Of and In the Astoria." *On Bunker Hill*. N.p., 24 Feb. 2016. Web. Accessed 19 Apr. 2017.

Taylor, David A. "Literary Cubs, Canceling Out Each Other's Reticence." *The American Scholar*. N.p., 1 Mar. 2009. Web. Accessed 18 Apr. 2017.

Of Human Bondage

Archer, Stanley. "Artists and Paintings in Maugham's Of Human Bondage." *English Literature in Transition, 1880-1920*. Vol. 14, No. 3. 1971, pp. 181-189. Project MUSE.

Ruth Franklin, "The Great and the Good." *The New Yorker*. 31 May 2010. Web. Accessed 18 Apr 2017.

The Outsiders

Biedenharn, Isabella. " 'The Outsiders' Author on 50th Anniversary: 'I Could Never Be That Un-Self-Conscious Again' " *EW.com*. Time Inc, 17 Aug. 2016. Web. Accessed 18 Apr. 2017.

Michaud, Jon. "S. E. Hinton and the Y.A. Debate." *The New Yorker*. The New Yorker, 14 Oct. 2014. Web. Accessed 18 Apr. 2017.

Smith, Dinitia. "An Outsider, Out of the Shadows." *The New York Times*. The New York Times, 07 Sept. 2005. Web. Accessed 18 Apr. 2017.

Micalaux. *YouTube*. YouTube, 14 Nov. 2010. Web. Accessed 18 Apr. 2017.

Cloudy with a Chance of Meatballs

PS 124 Community Website. N.p., 12 Apr. 2010. Web. Accessed 18 Apr. 2017.

The Jungle

Van Wienen, Mark W. (2012). "American Socialist Triptych: The Literary-Political Work of Charlotte Perkins Gilman, Upton

Sinclair, and W.E.B. Du Bois." N.p. *Book Review Digest Plus (H.W. Wilson).* University of Michigan Press, 2012.

Sinclair, Upton. "Note." *The Jungle.* Dover Thrift, 1906. pp. Viii–x.

Sophie's Choice

Mathé, Sylvie. "The 'Grey Zone' in William Styron's Sophie's Choice." *Études Anglaises* 57 (2004): 453–66. Web. Accessed 15 Apr. 2017.

Camus, Albert. "The Human Crisis." McMillin Academic Theatre, Columbia University, New York, NY. 28 Mar. 1946.

An American Tragedy

Brandon, Craig. "Murder in the Adirondacks." *Craig Brandon.* N.p., June 2006. Web. Accessed 18 Apr. 2017.

Appointment in Samarra

Baker, Lyman. "The Appointment in Samarra." *K-State.edu.* Kansas State University, n.d. Web. Accessed 18 Apr. 2017.

At Swim-Two-Birds

Clune, Anne, and Tess Hurson. *Conjuring Complexities: Essays on Flann O'Brien.* Belfast: Institute of Irish Studies, the Queen's U of Belfast, 1997. Print.

O'Brien, Flann, and John Wyse Jackson. *Myles Before Myles: A Selection of the Earlier Writings of Brian O'Nolan.* London: Grafton, 1988. Print.

American Psycho

Grow, Kory. "'American Psycho' at 25: Bret
Easton Ellis Looks Back." *Rolling Stone.*
Rolling Stone, 31 Mar. 2016. Web. Accessed
18 Apr. 2017.

The Blind Assassin

Atwood, Margaret. "Margaret Atwood on The
Blind Assassin—Guardian Book Club." *The
Guardian.* Guardian News and Media, 09
Aug. 2013. Web. Accessed 18 Apr. 2017.

The Moviegoer

Abádi-Nagy, Interviewed By Zoltán. "Walker
Percy, The Art of Fiction No. 97." *The Paris
Review.* The Paris Review, 14 Apr. 2017.
Web. Accessed 18 Apr. 2017.

Heart of Darkness

Ankomah, Baffour. "The Butcher of Congo."
New African. October 1999. Print.

Bloom, Harold. *Joseph Conrad's Heart of
Darkness.* New York: Infobase Pub., 2008.
Print.

Conrad, Joseph, Laurence Davies, and Frederick
Robert Karl. *The Collected Letters of Joseph
Conrad.* Cambridge: Cambridge U Press,
1983. Print.

Dune

Herbert, Frank, Brian Herbert, Kevin J.
Anderson, and Brian Herbert. *The Road to
Dune.* New York: Tor, 2005. Print.

Cloud Atlas

Interviewed By Adam Begley. "David Mitchell, The Art of Fiction No. 204." *The Paris Review*. The Paris Review, 14 Apr. 2017. Web. Accessed 18 Apr. 2017.

Gulliver's Travels

Probyn, Clive. Swift, Jonathan (1667–1745), Oxford Dictionary of National Biography. Oxford: Oxford University Press, 2004. Print.

Wide Sargasso Sea

Read, Bridget. "Charlotte Brontë May Have Started the Fire, But Jean Rhys Burned Down the House." *Literary Hub*. N.p., 03 May 2016. Web. Accessed 19 Apr. 2017.

The Sheltering Sky

Bowles, Paul. *Without Stopping: An Auto-biography*. New York: Putnam, 1972. Print.

McInerney, Jay. "Paul Bowles in Exile." *Vanity Fair* Sept. 1985: N.p. Print.

Seidner, David. "Paul Bowles." *BOMB Magazine*. N.p., Sept. 1982. Web. Accessed 19 Apr. 2017.

The Big Sleep

Chandler, Raymond, Tom Hiney, and Frank MacShane. *The Raymond Chandler Papers: Selected Letters and Nonfiction, 1909–1959*. New York: Grove Press, 2002. Print.

MacShane, Frank. *The Life of Raymond Chandler*. New York: E.P. Dutton, 1976. Print.

To the Lighthouse

Davies, Stevie. *Virginia Woolf To the Lighthouse*. Great Britain: Penguin Books, 1989. Print.

Merkin, Daphne. "To The Lighthouse And Beyond." *The New York Times*. The New York Times, 12 Sept. 2004. Web. Accessed 21 Apr. 2017.

Panken, Shirley. *Virginia Woolf and the "Lust of Creation": A Psychoanalytic Exploration*. Albany: State U of New York Press, 1987. Print.

The Cat in the Hat

Morgan, Judith, and Neil Morgan. *Dr. Seuss & Mr. Geisel: A Biography*. New York: Da Capo Press, 1996. Print.

Bio Staff. "The Story Behind Dr. Seuss' 'Cat in the Hat' " *Biography.com*. A&E Networks Television, 09 Mar. 2017. Web. Accessed 18 Apr. 2017.

The Very Hungry Caterpillar

Bird, Elizabeth. "Top 100 Picture Books #2: The Very Hungry Caterpillar by Eric Carle." *School Library Journal*. Fuse 8, 28 June 2012. Web. Accessed 19 Apr. 2017.

Khan, Urmee. "Google Celebrates Eric Carle's Very Hungry Caterpillar." *The Telegraph*. Telegraph Media Group, 20 Mar. 2009. Web. Accessed 19 Apr. 2017.

Because of Winn Dixie
"Kate DiCamillo Interview Transcript."
  Scholastic. N.p., 27 Jan. 2005. Web. Accessed
  18 Apr. 2017.
The Hunt for Red October
Guttridge, Leonard F. *Mutiny: A History of
  Naval Insurrection*. New York: Berkley,
  2002. Print.
Smith, Sean, dir. "True Story: The Hunt for Red
  October." *True Story*. The History Channel.
  26 Nov. 2009. Television.
The Maltese Falcon
Hammett, Dashiell. "Introduction to The
  Maltese Falcon." *The Maltese Falcon*.
  N.p.: The Modern Library, 1934. N.p.
  ThrillingDetective.com. Web. Accessed 10
  Apr. 2017.
The Adventures of Huckleberry Finn
Churchwell, Sarah. "Mark Twain: Not An
  American But The American." *The Guardian*.
  Guardian News and Media, 29 Oct. 2010.
  Web. Accessed 18 Apr. 2017.
Twain, Mark, Leslie Diane Myrick, Harriet
  Elinor Smith, Sharon K. Goetz, Michael B.
  Frank, Benjamin Griffin, and Victor Fischer.
  Autobiography of Mark Twain. Berkeley,
  Calif: U of California Press, 2010. Print.
The Call of the Wild
Doctorow, E. L.; London, Jack. "Introduction."
  The Call of the Wild, White Fang & To Build

a Fire. N.p.: Modern Library, 2000. N.p. Print.

Courbier-Tavenier, Jacqueline. "*The Call of the Wild* and *The Jungle*: Jack London and Upton Sinclair's Animal and Human Jungles." In Pizer, Donald. *Cambridge Companion to American Realism and Naturalism: Howells to London*. New York: Cambridge University Press, 1999. Print.

Labor, Earle; Reesman, Jeanne Campbell. *Jack London*. Twayne's United States authors series. New York: Twayne Publishers, 1994. Print.

Dyer, Daniel. "Answering the Call of the Wild." *The English Journal*. National Council of Teachers of English. April 1988. Accessed 10 Apr. 2017.

The Pigman

"Paul Zindel Interview on His Book The Pigman." *PaulZindel.com*. N.p., n.d. Web. Accessed 17 Apr. 2017.

"Paul Zindel Interviewed by Scholastic Students." *PaulZindel.com*. N.p., n.d. Web. Accessed 17 Apr. 2017.

A Confederacy of Dunces

Nevils, René Pol., and Deborah George. Hardy. *Ignatius Rising: The Life of John Kennedy Toole*. Baton Rouge: Louisiana State U Press, 2005. Print.

Percy, Walker, and John Kennedy Toole.

"Forward." *A Confederacy of Dunces*. Baton Rouge: LSU Press, 1980. Vii–iii. Print.

Leaves of Grass

Loving, Jerome. *Walt Whitman: The Song of Himself*. University of California Press, 1999. Print.

Reynolds, David S. *Walt Whitman's America: A Cultural Biography*. New York: Vintage Books, 1995. Print.

To Kill a Mockingbird

Baddeley, Anna. "To Kill a Mockingbird: 10 Things You Didn't Know about the Novel." *The Telegraph*. Telegraph Media Group, 04 Feb. 2015. Web. Accessed 19 Apr. 2017.

Lanzendorfer, Joy. "11 Facts About *To Kill A Mockingbird*." *Mental Floss*. N.p., 08 Apr. 2015. Web. Accessed 19 Apr. 2017.

The Narrative of Arthur Gordon Pym of Nantucket

Hoffman, Daniel. *Poe Poe Poe Poe Poe Poe Poe*. Baton Rouge: Louisiana State University Press, 1972. Print.

Kennedy, J. Gerald. "Trust No Man: Poe, Douglass, and the Culture of Slavery," *Romancing the Shadow: Poe and Race*, J. Gerald Kennedy and Liliane Weissberg, editors. New York: Oxford University Press, 2001. Print.

Peeples, Scott. *Edgar Allan Poe Revisited*. New York: Twayne Publishers, 1998. Print.

Silverman, Kenneth. *Edgar A. Poe: Mournful and Never-ending Remembrance*. New York: HarperPerennial, 1991. Print.

Sova, Dawn B. *Edgar Allan Poe: A to Z*. New York: Checkmark Books, 2001. Print.

The Age of Innocence

Wharton, Edith. *A Backward Glance: An Autobiography*. New York: The Curtis Publishing Co., 1993. Print.

The Phantom Tollbooth

Juster, Norton. "My Accidental Masterpiece: The Phantom Tollbooth." *All Things Considered*. NPR. 25 Oct. 2011. *NPR.org*. Web. Accessed 16 Apr. 2017.

Fear and Loathing in Las Vegas

Thompson, Hunter S. "Jacket Copy." *Fear and Loathing in Las Vegas: A Savage Journey to the Heart of the American Dream*. New York: Random House, 1972. Print.

The Bonfire of the Vanities

McFadden, Robert D. "Tom Wolfe's Model Justice Dies at 88." *The New York Times*. 24 October 2010. Accessed 10 Apr. 2017.

Animal Farm

Orwell, George. "Preface to the Ukrainian Edition of Animal Farm." March 1947. Print.

The Alchemist

Pool, Hannah Azieb. "Question Time: Author Paulo Coelho." *The Guardian*. Guardian News and Media, 18 Mar. 2009. Web. Accessed 19 Apr. 2017.

"Q&A with Paulo Coelho Discussion." *Goodreads*. N.p., 22 Feb. 2008. Web. Accessed 19 Apr. 2017.

The Lord of the Flies

Kundu, Rama. *New Perspectives on British Authors: From William Shakespeare to Graham Greene*. Sarup & Sons, 2006. Print.

Reiff, Raychel Haugrud. *William Golding: Lord of the Flies*. Marshall Cavendish, 2020. Print.

Singh, Minnie. "The Government of Boys: Golding's *Lord of the Flies* and Ballantyne's *Coral Island*." Children's Literature, 1997. Print.

A Prayer for Owen Meany

Jeon, Hoon Pyo, and Eugena Jung. "Award Winning Novelist Talks Effects of War." *Yale Daily News* . N.p., 9 Apr. 2002. Web. Accessed 19 Apr. 2017.

A Handful of Dust

Hastings, Selina. *Evelyn Waugh: A Biography*. London: Sinclair-Stevenson, 1994. Print.

Waugh, Evelyn. *Ninety-Two Days*. London: Duckworth, 1934. Print.

Waugh, Evelyn. "Fan-Fare: An Answer to the Ladies All Over the U.S.A." *Life (International: Chicago)*, 8 April 1946. Print.

Breakfast at Tiffany's

Clarke, Gerald. *Capote: A Biography.* Carroll & Graf Publishers, 2005. Print.

Saxon, Wolfgang. "Carol Matthau, a Frank and Tart Memoirist, Dies at 78". *New York Times*, 24 July 2003. Web. Accessed 15 Apr. 2017.

"Maeve Golightly?" *Publishersweekly.com.* 25 Oct. 2004. Web. Accessed 10 Apr. 2017.

"Doris Lilly; Author, Columnist." *Los Angeles Times*. 11 Oct. 1991. Web. Accessed 10 Apr. 2017.

Sagolla, Lisa Jo. *The Girl Who Fell Down: A Biography of Joan McCracken.* Boston: Northeastern University Press. 2003. Print.

"Hello I'm Holly." *The Times*. London. 7 Feb. 2004. Web. Accessed 10 Apr. 2017.

Infinite Jest

Max, D. T. "Beyond 'Infinite Jest' " *The New Yorker*. The New Yorker, 19 Feb. 2016. Web. Accessed 19 Apr. 2017.

"David Foster Wallace." Interview by Laura Miller. *Salon*. N.p., 9 Mar. 1996. Web. Accessed 19 Apr. 2017.

The Sot-Weed Factor

Clavier, Berndt. *John Barth and Postmodernism: Spatiality, Travel, Montage.* Peter Lang, 2007. Print.

Elias, Amy J. *Sublime Desire: History and Post-1960s Fiction.* Baltimore: Johns Hopkins U Press, 2001. Print.

Water for Elephants

Rosenfeld, Jordan E. "The WD Interview: Sara Gruen." *WritersDigest.com*. N.p., 07 July 2011. Web. Accessed 19 Apr. 2017.

Lucky Jim

Barber, Interviewed By Michael. "Kingsley Amis, The Art of Fiction No. 59." *The Paris Review*. The Paris Review, 1975. Web. Accessed 19 Apr. 2017.

The Red Badge of Courage

Davis, Linda H. *Badge of Courage: The Life of Stephan Crane*. New York: Mifflin, 1998. Print.

Linson, Corwin K. *My Stephen Crane*. Syracuse: Syracuse University Press, 1958. Print.

Johanningsmeier, Charles. "The 1894 Syndicated Newspaper Appearances of The Red Badge of Courage." *American Literary Realism*. Vol. 40, No. 3, pp. 226–247. 2008. Print.

Wertheim, Stanley. *A Stephen Crane Encyclopedia*. Westport, CT: Greenwood Press, 1997. Print.

The Odyssey

Mayor, Adrienne. *The First Fossil Hunters: Paleontology in Greek and Roman Times*. Princeton University Press, 2000. Print.

The Long Goodbye

Iyer, Pico. "The Knight of Sunset Boulevard." *New York Review of Books*. pp. 31–33. 6 Dec. 2007. Web. Accessed 19 Apr. 2017.

Spender, Natasha. "Chapter 11: His Own Long Goodbye." In Gross, Miriam. *The World of Raymond Chandler*. New York: A & W Publishers, 1978. Print.

A Clockwork Orange

Dexter, Gary. *Why Not Catch-21?: The Stories Behind the Titles*. Frances Lincoln Ltd., 2008. Print.

"An Examination of Kubrick's A Clockwork Orange." *Camera Three: Creative Arts Television*, 4 August 2010. Video. Accessed 16 Apr. 2017.

Interview by Samira Ahmed. "A Clockwork Orange—Interview with Will Self." Nightwaves, *BBC*. 3 Jul. 2012. Accessed 16 Apr. 2017.

The Recognitions

Interviewed by Z. Abádi-Nagy. "William Gaddis, The Art of Fiction No. 101." *The Paris Review*. The Paris Review, 1987. Web. Accessed 19 Apr. 2017.

Moore, Steven. "Sheri Martinelli: A Modernist Muse." *Gargoyle* Jun. & Jul. 1998. Print.

Mary Poppins

Arkell, Harriet. "The real Mary Poppins? PL Travers' Story about Her 'Aunt Sass' Who 'Unconsciously' Inspired the Famous Nanny to Be Published." *Daily Mail Online*. Associated Newspapers, 24 June 2014. Web. Accessed 19 Apr. 2017.

McDonald, Shae. "PL Travers Biographer Valerie Lawson Says the Real Mary Poppins Lived in Woollahra." Wentworth Courier. Sydney: The Daily Telegraph [dailytelegraph. com.au]. 18 December 2013. Web. Accessed 19 Apr. 2017.

"P L Travers." *Desert Island Discs*. BBC Radio 4. 21 May 1977.

Naked Lunch

Burroughs, William S. Grauerholtz, James; Miles, Barry, eds. *Naked Lunch* (the restored text ed.). Grove Press, 2001. Print.

Interviewed By Conrad Knickerbocker. "William S. Burroughs, The Art of Fiction No. 36." *The Paris Review*. The Paris Review, 1965. Web. Accessed 19 Apr. 2017.

Woodard, Rob. "Naked Lunch is Still Fresh." *The Guardian*. Guardian News and Media, 16 Apr. 2009. Web. Accessed 19 Apr. 2017.

Trainspotting

Welsh, Irvine. "Trainspotting: Motivation." *The Guardian*. Guardian News and Media, 13 June 2008. Web. Accessed 19 Apr. 2017.

Death of a Salesman

Interviewed by Olga Carlisle and Rose Styron. "Arthur Miller, The Art of Theater No. 2." *The Paris Review*. N.p., 1966. Web. Accessed 19 Apr. 2017.

All Quiet on the Western Front

"Erich Maria Remarque Biography."

Encyclopedia of World Biography. N.p., n.d. Web. Accessed 21 Apr. 2017.

Great Expectations

Forster, John. *The Life of Charles Dickens*, London: J. M. Dent & Sons, edited by J. W. T. Ley, 1928. Print.

Schlicke, Paul. *Oxford Reader's Companion to Dickens*, New York: Oxford University Press, 1999. Print.

The Curious Incident of the Dog in the Night-Time

Haddon, Mark. "Mark Haddon on His Best Seller, The Curious Incident of the Dog in the Night-Time." *The Observer*. Guardian News and Media, 11 Apr. 2004. Web. Accessed 19 Apr. 2017.

Frankenstein

Shelley, Mary Wollstonecraft, and Karen Karbiener. *Frankenstein*. New York: Barnes & Noble, 2003. Print.

Sunstein, Emily W. *Mary Shelley: Romance and Reality*. 1989. Baltimore: Johns Hopkins University Press, 1991. Print.

Invisible Man

Seidlitz, Anne. "Ralph Ellison: An American Journey." *PBS*. Public Broadcasting Service, 26 Jan. 2010. Web. Accessed 19 Apr. 2017.

IT

King, Stephen. "IT Inspiration." *StephenKing. com*. N.p., n.d. Web. Accessed 19 Apr. 2017.

Middlemarch

Ashton, Rosemary. *George Eliot*. Oxford: Oxford University Press, 1983. Print.

Swinden, Patrick, ed. *George Eliot: Middlemarch: A Casebook*. London: Macmillan, 1972. Print.

Beaty, Jerome. *Middlemarch from Notebook to Novel: A Study of George Eliot's Creative Method*. Urbana: University of Illinois Press,1960. Print.

Their Eyes Were Watching God

Bloom, Harold. *Bloom's Guides - Zora Neale Hurston's Their Eyes Were Watching God*. New York: Infobase Publishing, 2009. Print.

King, Lovalerie. *The Cambridge Introduction to Zora Neale Hurston*. Cambridge, UK: Cambridge U Press, 2013. Print.

The Eatonville Speaker, 1889. Cited in Lester, Neal. *Understanding Their Eyes Were Watching God*. London: The Greenwood Press, 1999. Print.

The Naked and the Dead

Interviewed By Steven Marcus. "Norman Mailer, The Art of Fiction No. 32." *The Paris Review*. N.p., 1964. Web. Accessed 19 Apr. 2017. Print.

The Catcher in the Rye

Salzman, Jack. *New Essays on* The Catcher in the Rye. Cambridge University Press, 1991.

The Da Vinci Code
Goodnow, Cecelia. "Brown Drew Inspiration from Local Author's Books for 'Da Vinci Code.'" *Seattlepi.com*. N.p., 17 May 2006. Web. Accessed 19 Apr. 2017.

Bel Canto
"A Conversation with Ann Patchett." *BookBrowse.com*. N.p., n.d. Web. Accessed 19 Apr. 2017. Reprinted with permission from the publisher, Perennial Books
Interview by Gwen Ifill. "Conversation: Ann Patchett." *PBS News Hour*. PBS, 2 July 2002. Web. Accessed 19 Apr. 2017.

Resurrection
Simmons, Ernest J. "11. Resurrection." *Introduction To Tolstoy's Writings*. Chicago, IL: University of Chicago Press. Print.

The Prime of Miss Jean Brodie
"In the Footsteps of Muriel Spark." *The History Zone*. BBC Radio Scotland, 18 August 2009. Web. Accessed 18 Apr. 2017.

Money
Interviewed By Francesca Riviere. "Martin Amis, The Art of Fiction No. 151." *The Paris Review*. N.p., 1998. Web. Accessed 19 Apr. 2017.
"Martin Amis: You Ask The Questions," *The Independent*. 15 Jan. 2007. Web. Accessed 20 Apr. 2017.
Stout, Mira. "Martin Amis: Down London's

Mean Streets." *New York Times*, 4 Feb. 1990. Web. Accessed 20 Apr. 2017.

Austerlitz

Crary, Alice. *Inside Ethics: On the Demands of Moral Thought*. Cambridge, Massachusetts and London, England: Harvard U Press, 2016. Print.

Tinker Tailor Soldier Spy

Anthony, Andrew. "Observer Profile: John le Carré: A Man of Great Intelligence". *The Observer*. London, 1 Nov. 2009. Accessed 20 Apr. 2017.

The Tropic of Cancer

Interviewed By George Wickes. "Henry Miller, The Art of Fiction No. 28." *The Paris Review*. N.p., 1962. Web. Accessed 19 Apr. 2017.

The Tin Drum

Gaffney, Interviewed by Elizabeth. "Günter Grass, The Art of Fiction No. 124." *The Paris Review*. N.p., 1991. Web. Accessed 19 Apr. 2017.

Jaggi, Maya. "A Life in Writing: Günter Grass." *The Guardian*. Guardian News and Media, 01 Nov. 2010. Web. Accessed 19 Apr. 2017.

The Diary of a Nobody

Grossmith, George. "A Society Clown Chapter II: Early Recollections." *The Gilbert and Sullivan Archive*. N.p., 27 Sept. 2007. Web. Accessed 21 Apr. 2017.

Grossmith, George, and Weedon Grossmith.

"Introduction." *Diary of a Nobody*. N.p.:
Wordsworth Editions, 1999. Print.

Joseph, Tony. "Grossmith, George". *Oxford
Dictionary of National Biography.* Web.
Accessed 10 Apr. 2017.

The Girl with the Dragon Tattoo

Baski, Kurdo. "How a Brutal Rape and a
Lifelong Burden of Guilt Fuelled Girl with the
Dragon Tattoo Writer Stieg Larsson." *Daily
Mail Online*. Associated Newspapers, 02 Aug.
2010. Web. Accessed 19 Apr. 2017.

Riddle of the Sands

Boyle, Andrew. *The Riddle of Erskine Childers*.
London: Hutchinson, 1997. Print.

Buchan, Alastair; McGreary, Jeremy. "The Book
and the Boat." Cruising World. Middletown,
Rhode Island: World Publications, January
2006. Print.

The Strange Case of Dr. Jekyll and Mr. Hyde

Balfour, Graham. *The Life of Robert Louis
Stevenson*. New York: Charles Scribner's
Sons, 1912. Print.

Campbell, James. "The Beast Within: Interpeting
Jekyll and Hyde." *The Guardian*. Guardian
News and Media, 12 Dec. 2008. Web.
Accessed 19 Apr. 2017.

Hodges, Jeremy. "Lamplit Vicious Fairy Land."
Robert Louis Stevenson Organization. N.p.,
n.d. Web. Accessed 19 Apr. 2017.

Sinclair, Jill. "Review: The Unknown Gertrude

Jekyll Edited by Martin Wood." *The Guardian*. Guardian News and Media, 16 June 2006. Web. Accessed 19 Apr. 2017.

All the President's Men

Snider, Eric D. "13 Investigative Facts About All the President's Men." *Mental Floss*. N.p., 08 Apr. 2016. Web. Accessed 21 Apr. 2017.

Looking for Mr. Goodbar

Willbern, David. *The American Popular Novel After World War II: A Study of 25 Best Sellers, 1947–2000*. Jefferson, NC: McFarland, 2013. Print.

Interview with a Vampire

"Anne Rice." *Encyclopedia of World Biography*. 2004. Web. Accessed 12 Apr. 2017.

Husband, Stuart. "Anne Rice: Interview with the Vampire Writer." *The Telegraph*. Telegraph Media Group, 02 Nov. 2008. Web. Accessed 19 Apr. 2017.

Ramsland, Katherine. *Prism of the Night: A Biography of Anne Rice*. New York: Penguin Group, 1991. Print.

Gorky Park

Wroe, Nicholas. "Profile: Martin Cruz Smith." *The Guardian*. Guardian News and Media, 25 Mar. 2005. Web. Accessed 21 Apr. 2017.

A Wrinkle in Time

Chase, Carole F. "A Chronology of Madeleine L'Engle's Life and Books." *Suncatcher: A*

Study of Madeleine L'Engle And Her Writing.
Farrar, Straus & Giroux, 1972. Print.

CK. "2004 National Humanities Medalist
Madeleine L'Engle." *National Endowment for
the Humanities.* N.p., n.d. Web. Accessed 19
Apr. 2017.

L'Engle, Madeleine. *A Circle of Quiet.* New
York: Farrar, Straus & Giroux, 1972. Print.

The Bell Jar

Dunkle, Iris Jamahl. "Sylvia Plath's The Bell
Jar: Understanding Cultural and Historical
Context in an Iconic Text." In Janet McCann,
Critical Insights: The Bell Jar. Pasadena, CA:
Salem Press, 2011. Print.

Flowers for Algernon

"Daniel Keyes: 40 Years of Algernon." *Locus
Magazine.* June 1997. Web. Accessed 20 Apr.
2017.

Hill, Cheryl (2004). "A History of Daniel Keyes'
Flowers for Algernon." PDF. Accessed 20
Apr. 2017.

Langer, Emily. "Daniel Keyes, Author of the
Classic Book 'Flowers for Algernon,' Dies
at 86." *The Washington Post*, 18 Jun. 2014.
Web. Accessed 20 Apr. 2017.

Where the Red Fern Grows

Rawls, Wilson. *Dreams Can Come True.*
Reading Tree Productions, 1993. Audiobook.

Valley of the Dolls

Collins, Amy Fine. "Once Was Never Enough."

Vanity Fair, Jan. 2000. Web. Accessed 20 Apr. 2017.

Kasindorf, Martin. "Jackie Susann Picks Up the Marbles." *The New York Times*, 12 Aug. 1973. Web. Accessed 20 Apr. 2017.

Seaman, Barbara. *Lovely Me: The Life of Jacqueline Susann. 2nd ed.* New York: Seven Stories Press, 1996. Print.

The Things They Carried

"Looking Back at the Vietnam War with Author, Veteran Tim O'Brien." Interview by Jeffrey Brown. *PBS News Hour*. PBS. 28 Apr. 2010. Television.

A Streetcar Named Desire

Editors, Sparknotes. "A Streetcar Named Desire." *SparkNotes.com*. SparkNotes LLC, n.d. Web. Accessed 19 Apr. 2017.

Hiroshima

Michaub, Jon. "Eighty-Five from the Archive: John Hersey." *The New Yorker*. 8 Jun. 2010. Web. Accessed 18 Apr. 2017.

DeGroot, Gerard J. *The Bomb: A Life.* Massachusetts: Harvard University Press, 2005. Print.

Curious George

Brooks, Katherine. "Meet The Extraordinary Husband-Wife Duo Behind 'Curious George.' " *The Huffington Post*. TheHuffingtonPost.com, 15 Aug. 2016. Web. Accessed 19 Apr. 2017.

The Sun Also Rises

Balassi, William. "Hemingway's Greatest Iceberg: The Composition of *The Sun Also Rises*." In Barbour, James and Quirk, Tom (eds), *Writing the American Classics*. Chapel Hill: North Carolina UP, 1990. Print.

Meyers, Jeffrey. *Hemingway: A Biography*. New York: Macmillan, 1985. Print.

Nagel, James. "Brett and the Other Women in *The Sun Also Rises*." In Donaldson, Scott (ed), *The Cambridge Companion to Ernest Hemingway*. New York: Cambridge UP, 1996. Print.

The Castle

Ormsby, Eric. "Franz Kafka & the Trip to Spindelmühle." *The New Criterion*. N.p., Nov. 1998. Web. Accessed 21 Apr. 2017.

All the Light We Cannot See

Horowitz, Joy. "Interview with Anthony Doerr." *Goodreads*. N.p., 05 Dec. 2014. Web. Accessed 19 Apr. 2017.

Wonder

"How One Unkind Moment Gave Way To 'Wonder.'" Interview by Michele Norris. *All Things Considered*. NPR. 12 Sept. 2013. Radio.

The Help

Suddath, Claire. "Kathryn Stockett, Author of The Help." *Time*. Time Inc., 11 Nov. 2009. Web. Accessed 19 Apr. 2017.

Extremely Loud and Incredibly Close
Shenk, Joshua Wolf. "Jonathan Safran Foer: Living to Tell the Tale." *Mother Jones,* May 2005. Web. Accessed 19 Apr. 2017.
Watership Down
Farrier, John. "10 Facts You Might Not Know about Watership Down." *Neatorama.* N.p., 18 May 2012. Web. Accessed 01 May 2017.
Let the Right One In
Moriarty. "The Northlander Sits Down With The Writer of LET THE RIGHT ONE IN." *Aint It Cool News*. N.p., 21 Dec. 2012. Web. Accessed 19 Apr. 2017.
The Executioner's Song
Interviewed By Andrew O'Hagan. "Norman Mailer, The Art of Fiction No. 193." *The Paris Review*. N.p., 2007. Web. Accessed 19 Apr. 2017.
The Prince and the Pauper
Cope, Jim and Cope, Wendy. *A Teacher's Guide to the Signet Classic Edition of Mark Twain's The Prince and the Pauper.* New York: Penguin, 1996. Print.
A Thousand Splendid Suns
"A Conversation with Khaled Hosseini." *KhaledHosseini.com*. N.p., n.d. Web. Accessed 19 Apr. 2017.
The Grapes of Wrath
"Biographies: Sanora Babb." *PBS*. Public

Broadcasting Service, n.d. Web. Accessed 19
Apr. 2017.

DeMott, Robert. *Robert DeMott's Introduction
to The Grapes of Wrath.* Viking Penguin, a
Division of Penguin Books, 1992. Print.

1984

Orwell, George. "George Orwell's Letter on
Why He Wrote '1984.' " *The Daily Beast.* The
Daily Beast Company, 12 Aug. 2013. Web.
Accessed 21 Apr. 2017.

Dog Soldiers

Interviewed By William C. Woods. "Robert Stone,
The Art of Fiction No. 90." *The Paris Review.*
N.p., 1985. Web. Accessed 19 Apr. 2017.

Lolita

Nabokov, Vladimir. *Lolita* (2nd Vintage
International ed.). New York: Random House,
1997. Print.

Appel, Alfred, Jr. *The Annotated Lolita* (revised
ed.). New York: Vintage Books, 1991. Print.

Strong Motion

Burn, Interviewed By Stephen J. "Jonathan
Franzen, The Art of Fiction No. 207." *The
Paris Review.* N.p., 2010. Web. Accessed 19
Apr. 2017.

Sarah's Key

Company, The Weinstein. "Interview with
SARAH'S KEY Author Tatiana de Rosnay."
The Weinstein Company. N.p., 22 July 2011.
Web. Accessed 19 Apr. 2017.

The Bridge over the River Kwai

Kirkup, James. "Obituary: Pierre Boulle." *The Independent*. Independent Digital News and Media, 01 Feb. 1994. Web. Accessed 21 Apr. 2017.

"CWGC - Cemetery Details." *Cwgc.org*. Web. Accessed 1 Apr. 2017.

On the Road

Interviewed By Ted Berrigan. "Jack Kerouac, The Art of Fiction No. 41." *The Paris Review*. N.p., 1968. Web. Accessed 19 Apr. 2017.

100 Years of Solitude

Elie, Paul. "The Secret History of One Hundred Years of Solitude." *Vanity Fair*. Vanity Fair, 08 Dec. 2015. Web. Accessed 19 Apr. 2017.

One Flew over the Cuckoo's Nest

"America's Civil Rights Timeline." *International Civil Rights Center & Museum*. 2015.

Huffman, Bennett. "Ken Kesey (1935–2001)." *The Literary Encyclopedia*, 17 May 2002. Web. Accessed 19 Apr. 2017.

"Life in a Loony Bin." *Time*. February 16, 1962. Web. Accessed 20 Apr. 2017.

Stroman, Duane. *The Disability Rights Movement: From Deinstitutionalization to Self-Determination*. University Press of America, 2003. Print.

Herzog

Menand, Louis. "Saul Bellow's Revenge." *The*

New Yorker. The New Yorker, 03 May 2015. Web. Accessed 19 Apr. 2017.

Girl with a Pearl Earring

BookBrowse. "Tracy Chevalier Author Interview." *BookBrowse.com*. N.p., n.d. Web. Accessed 19 Apr. 2017. Reprinted with permission from the publisher, Penguin Putnam Publishing.

Harry Potter and the Sorcerer's Stone

Davis, Angela. "JK Rowling On Getting Published." *URBANETTE*. N.p., 27 Apr. 2016. Web. Accessed 19 Apr. 2017.

ABOUT THE AUTHOR

JAKE GROGAN is originally from Ellenville, New York, and currently resides in Queens. He has a BA from Fordham University, where he studied journalism. The story behind his favorite book, *Watership Down*, inspired his taking on *Origins of a Story*.

Books are produced in the United States using U.S.-based materials

Books are printed using a revolutionary new process called THINKtech™ that lowers energy usage by 70% and increases overall quality

Books are durable and flexible because of Smyth-sewing

Paper is sourced using environmentally responsible foresting methods and the paper is acid-free

Center Point Large Print

600 Brooks Road / PO Box 1
Thorndike, ME 04986-0001 USA

(207) 568-3717

US & Canada:
1 800 929-9108
www.centerpointlargeprint.com